Life Beyond Death

Life Beyond Death

Selected lectures by
Rudolf Steiner

RUDOLF STEINER PRESS

Compiled and edited by Frank Teichmann

Rudolf Steiner Press
Hillside House, The Square
Forest Row, RH18 5ES

Published by Rudolf Steiner Press 1995
Reprinted 2003

Originally published in German under the title *Das Leben nach dem Tod*
by Verlag Freies Geistesleben, Stuttgart, in 1987

A catalogue record for this book is available from the British Library

ISBN 1 85584 017 0

Cover by Andrew Morgan
Typeset by Imprint Publicity Service, Crawley Down, Sussex
Printed and bound in Great Britain by Cromwell Press Limited,
Trowbridge, Wiltshire

Contents

Introduction

by Frank Teichmann

DEATH PRESENTS the human being with a mysterious phenomenon. It can strike all of a sudden into the midst of our daily life, altering everything we are used to, and yet also, in spite of all sadness and mourning, permeating us in the first few days with a blessing and strength. Even if the dying person has prepared us for this moment of death by, say, a long illness, it is still such an incisive event that our hearts and minds are always moved by its mystery. The moment of death alters the whole life-context of those who are left behind. The one who has died can no longer be spoken to, he no longer responds to the thoughts we send him. The world of the dead appears hidden, inaccessible and silent; we can see no way of bridging this gulf. It is only with the passing of time that this soul-experience transforms itself into a deeper questioning – or into a forgetfulness covered over by the busy preoccupations of our life.

Everyone encounters such experiences in their life. But they grow more real as a person becomes older. This is apparent, for example, in the pictures of dead friends and relations which an older person often exihibits – people with whose life and destiny he was closely connected.

One's experience of death is intensified if one is present when someone is dying. One can often observe that the characteristics a person had during life recede and alter when he is faced with the significance of crossing over the threshold. The unexpected transformations which can occur at such a time are among the most moving one may experience here on earth.

In the light of this, questions about the continued life and destiny of the dead become all the more pressing. It is not only on occasional visits to the grave-side that memories can resurface; sometimes the image of a person who has died is conjured up in the semi-consciousness of our dreams. This is hardly ever in the form of memories of specific events and occurrences; on the contrary, we may often see the dead person in a quite unaccustomed environment, often as a young person and in a context which we would not normally associate with him. One also seems to continue one's connection with the dead person in waking life, perhaps through memories which enter one's soul now and then during the day, or through a thought which one might send out towards him or her.

But one may well also ask: 'Does he still live in some form and continue his own existence? What does he experience now? Does he still have consciousness of any kind? Is he able to think of those who are left behind here?' These are questions which human beings have always asked themselves through the ages; and have always asked with particular urgency during wars and catastrophes when apparently point-less deaths brought the world of the dead very close to common experience. After the events of the last war, in whose dreadful battles thousands of people at a time crossed the threshold of death, Max Frisch expressed the urgency of this question in his play *Nun singen sie wieder* (Now they sing again). In it he drew attention with great clarity and awareness to the legions of the dead and their significance. But hardly anyone took notice of this, either in the play at that time or in the years which followed those disastrous events.

Science, which has made giant strides by confining its re-search to observation of the world of senses, cannot help us in this domain. It does not take the sense-free world, in which the dead live, into account. Even the threshold experiences of people who have successfully been resuscitated and brought back to life, cannot tell us much more than that the person has certainly continued conscious existence, although in an-other form. Rudolf Steiner attempted, even in his early writings, to extend the scientific method of observation into soul-spiritual realms. The method of research which he developed ultimately enabled him to accompany the essence of the human being on its after-death journey in a conscious and discriminating way.

In earlier times, life after death was accepted as self evident. One often remained closely connected with those who had died and followed the progress of their continuing existence. Likewise, the dead accompanied the earthly life of those they were close to and, if necessary, sometimes even took part in it. Old legends recount that some valiant heroes, even after their death, rode at the front of earthly armies, helping them on to victory.

Gradually the widespread and common powers of clair-voyance of very ancient times diminished and faded; but there were still sages in many parts of the world who had knowledge of the spiritual worlds through their initiation into the Mysteries. Under the cultural influence of these Mysteries, temples and institutions were founded whose teachings spoke of the reality of the after-death world. Burial sites, rituals and memorial festivals for the dead were introduced; knowledge of the after life was formed and presented in pictures and images.

In Egypt the pharaoh was the representative of this knowledge. He was initiated into the sense-free worlds and had knowledge of them while still alive. He knew of the sun-god's journey through the 'underworld' and of the spirits which inhabit it. His kingdom was founded upon this knowledge. Only one who could perceive the realms in which the dead live could be king on earth. For it was through this perception and wisdom that he could speak to the living and guide their destiny. So he could say, at the end of the Book of the Underworld (*Amduat*), in which images of this realm were portrayed:

> Whoever knows these mysterious images is
> a spirit well-provided for.
> Continually he leaves and enters the underworld,
> continually he speaks to the living.

There he could meet the souls of those who had died and share in their after-death experiences. The knowledge of this existence flowed into the conceptions and images which the Egyptian people had of life after death. These were represented in their burial places and have survived to this day. We can conclude from them that the Egyptian possessed a detailed and differentiated view of the essence of the human being according to which he incarnated into various 'members' of his being and inhabited them during earthly life. After death, he separated from them in several stages: first of all he detached himself from his body, which was embalmed; then from his 'Ka', a constituent of his being in which the formative life-forces were experienced; and finally also from his 'Ba', a kind of personification of his soul which had first of all to be judged and purified before it could enter, transformed, into the realm of the sun god.

One can observe, however, that a marked change in conceptions about the life after death occurred already during the Egyptian cultural epoch. At the beginning of the third millennium BC, there still existed an unshaken conviction that souls lived on after death; gradually, though, doubt entered in. Towards the end of the second millennium, a song could even end with the refrain:

> Live for the day
> and do not grow weary.
> For no one takes with him
> the things that he cherished,
> and no one returns
> when once he has perished.

As in Egypt, so it was elsewhere in the other countries of the ancient Orient. Questions arose everywhere about the continued life and destiny of the dead, but could no longer be answered with the same certainty as previously. Gilgamesh, at the death of his friend Enkidu, felt the deep urgency of this question and was spurred on by it to undertake the far journey to Utnapishtim. Although he did not succeed in the trial he met there, he was given the magic herb with which he could renew his life. Through his carelessness, though, a snake ate the herb, shed its skin and became young again. At the end of the Gilgamesh epic the hero still retains a close connection with his dead friend, who rises up for moments at a time from the realm of the dead and speaks to him, revealing to him secrets of the underworld.

The mystery of death becomes a really pressing problem in the Greek cultural epoch. For the first time in his long evolution, the human being now learns to fully inhabit the world of the senses. He feels himself at home in his body and can only imagine life without it as the bleak existence of disembodied shadows. 'Rather a beggar in the upper world than a king in the realm of shades' is a phrase which aptly expresses this feeling. The Greek still knows that there is an afterlife, but the nature of it is as shadowy for him as the phantoms of the dead. Only the Mysteries still brighten this shadowy teaching and allow at least a few rays of light from the greater knowledge of the past to shine into the pallid world of the dead. There is a saying by Sophocles about the Mysteries of Eleusis, which conveys his trust and belief in them: 'Those mortals are thrice blessed who have known this initiation and go to Hades; they alone find life there, while for all others there is only suffering.' Plato and Socrates still pass on to their pupils what they have learned from the initiates. But they do not simply hand down to them the ancient images and wisdom; they also try to examine and understand these with the power of thinking. Socrates, in his farewell speech to his pupils before drinking the cup of poison, not only refers to reincarnation but also tries to explain it and make it understandable. According to him, whoever dedicates himself to philosophy will find access to inner mysteries, for the world of thought reaches into supersensible regions: 'All those who engage themselves, in the right way, with philosophy, are also evidently occupied – although others do not notice this – with nothing other really than dying and death.' (Phaedon, 64a) This fact was of the greatest significance for the Greeks. They were convinced that by means of a trained and disciplined thinking they could rise up into supersensible regions, in which truth could be found and where the dead also lived.

In Christianity also there was a conviction that the human being lives on after death, although the idea of reincarnation – in spite of being hinted at in the Gospels – faded for the time being into the background. The Christian churches contin- ued the old traditions in modified form; they remembered the dead regularly in prayer, inaugurated acts of worship and the reading of masses for their succour, and established festivals wholly devoted to them.

At the same time, though, a way of thinking which had begun with the Greeks continued to evolve. Various Christian schools of thought paid particular attention to thinking, enhancing and disciplining it until it could become an organ of perception for higher worlds. This practice, which now proceeded in a quieter, more concealed way, led to new images and conceptions. What was thus discerned by a thinker was experienced as something holy, which should not be profaned. Overall, though, it has to be recognized that the differentiated ancient oriental perception of life after death did not yet find renewal.

Through the ages, people's conception of this realm became static and constricted; it only received new life in the time of Goethe, when the idea of evolution arose. Suddenly, the great poets and thinkers could only make sense of history if they saw the human being taking part in its great transfor- mations through repeated incarnations, in the course of which he could gradually perfect himself. Novalis, for exam- ple, remarked in his scientific notebooks (1798–9, No. 5): 'Whoever does not achieve perfection here, achieves it per- haps in the hereafter – or must otherwise embark on a new earthly life. Might there not well be also death on the other

side, whose result is to be born here on earth?' Seen in this
light, mankind's spiritual evolution could continually
progress. Ever new levels could be attained, without any final
limit. Why, such thinkers wondered, should the dogma of one
life only, current up until then in occidental lands, continue
to be valid? Must our spiritual evolution really be terminated
after a few years? Once and for all? What about those who die
young? No, if the idea of evolution can really also be applied
to the spiritual realm, then not only must there be life after
death but also a reincarnation of the spirit.

The thoughts of Rudolf Steiner become pertinent at this
point. By the term 'Theosophy' he understands the highest
level of evolved thinking. And such thinking results in the
concept of reincarnation. One of the earliest essays in the
periodical *Luzifer*, which he founded, had the title: 'Reincarnation and Karma from the point of view of conceptions
necessary to science' (1903). The fundamental idea is, at this
point, still only sketched out and hinted at; but as a
consequence of the continual training of his thinking it led
ultimately to a concrete, precise and accessible content.

Rudolf Steiner first provides a basis which can be built
upon in his book *Theosophy* (1904). Here he develops concepts which can facilitate an understanding for life after
death. He takes his starting point from Goethe, but redefines
the concepts of *body, soul and spirit*. In particular he makes a
distinction between the soul and spirit, and characterizes the
properties and attributes of each one. These concepts, it is
true, existed since the late Greek and early Christian period;
in the course of time, however, their particular differentiated
meanings became unclear and eventually undiscernible. Today people normally only believe that the human being
possesses a body and perhaps also a soul; they no longer know
anything of the threefold constitution of body, soul and spirit.
In contrast, say, to an Origenes or an Augustine, who were
both convinced of the existence of the human soul and spirit,
it is usual in contemporary science to refer everything back to

the physical body and senses. People believe that a concept of spirit is unnecessary, but do not notice that this involves overlooking themselves, suspending their own statements – nothing one might say would have any worth if it was simply secreted from the brain's cells, as is suggested by standard scientific views.

Those who comprehend this believe themselves mostly to be unconstrained by such a view, as long as they recognize a 'soul' to which can be attributed all the faculties which constitute a person. They forget, however, that this conception also only represents the last stage of an evolution during which human beings gradually lost sight of the significance of the spirit. In the universities nowadays one can study psychology, but no longer pneumatology, the field of knowledge concerned with the human spirit! Rudolf Steiner introduces clarity here. By means of his characterization of the concepts of body, soul and spirit, a path is opened up whereby these 'members' of the human being can also be traced and followed after death.

In the chapter 'The Essential Nature of the Human Being' in *Theosophy*, the separate attributes and interactions of the body, soul and spirit are delineated. Especially important for our theme is, in this context, the division of the various soul faculties. The *sentient soul* is the first level, in which the soul reacts to the impressions of the world which our senses convey to it. For example one may see something moving which has a particular shape and form and is of a yellow-brown colour, and recognize a lion. Everything we encounter is immediately recognized and named by the sentient soul. This reply to the stimulation of the sense world connects with our feelings, desires and also instincts. Every kind of impression which we encounter stirs the sentient soul.

The next level is attained through the activity of thinking. We no longer only experience, we also evaluate our experiences. If they proved pleasant, we strive to repeat them. To this end we make rational plans to enable our wishes to find fulfilment.

Thinking is used initially wherever it proves to be of use. It serves the sentient soul. But it is not long before it becomes independent and generates its own systems, taking pleasure in self-created contexts. Rudolf Steiner called this activity the *intellectual soul*. At this stage of development the thinker is still convinced of the evident truth of his thoughts. He cannot detach himself from his thoughts, cannot observe and test his own thought-processes. Not until he reaches the level of the *consciousness soul* does the human being strive for an 'objective' thinking, which is in accord and harmony with the world, and is wholly true. It is no longer important to him merely to have thoughts and think things out, but for his thinking to reflect the truth. This becomes an aim worth striving for, because he thereby unites himself with something eternal. For what is really true shares in the nature of eternity. 'By letting what is intrinsically true and good come to life within us, we rise above the mere sentient soul. The eternal spirit shines into the sentient soul, kindling in it a light that will never go out. To the extent that our soul lives in this light, it takes part in something eternal, which it links to its own existence. What the soul carries within itself as truth and goodness is immortal.' With these words Rudolf Steiner points to the core of the soul, which cannot perish even at death. It remains precisely because it is formed of eternal 'substance'.

The second chapter of *Theosophy*, 'Destiny and the Reincarnation of the Spirit' contains – as an addition to the chapter heading – the phrase: 'Only the human spirit reincarnates; and the eternal truths which he makes his own, remain united with him.' Rudolf Steiner then proceeds to draw attention to the fact that a single truth has virtually no significance on its own. It is only one element in a living whole; one single element also in the whole living context of a human being's biography. A truth receives meaning from the context of which it is a part. And this context changes and transforms itself. It transforms itself in different ways, according to the specific aptitudes which a human being 'brings with him' into the world. Mozart, for example, was musically gifted from a very young age and also skilled in manual dexterity, so that his remarkable musical abilities were evident in early childhood. Somebody else, perhaps, can learn languages with extraordinary ease. Take Champollion, for example, the man who deciphered the Egyptian hieroglyphs. As a child he was thrilled by the reward offered to him for getting good reports: he was allowed to learn yet another language. When the aptitude someone brings with him is present as a capacity which would otherwise require effort and application, one may ask: where has this gifted person been able to practise his skill? Unless one believes that the spirit – which expresses itself specifically and individually in capacities which can only be attained by individual effort – simply falls from heaven, then there is only one other possibility; that a particular capacity must have been developed in a previous life. Besides the bodily heredity from one's ancestors, there is also an 'inheritance' of the spirit which comes only from oneself.

Although such a train of thought leads only to an outline of the idea of reincarnation, it still, nevertheless, provides a foundation for understanding life after death. Upon this foundation Rudolf Steiner constructed a lofty edifice. His increasingly precise observations reveal, step by step, the experiences of the human soul and spirit after death and the continued connections and collaboration with relatives and friends. Rudolf Steiner communicated these findings to the initially small groups of members of the Anthroposophical Society.

Since such ideas were completely new, even for those listeners who were in some way prepared, he tried first of all to establish a basis for them by means of extensive expositions in lecture cycles. These were taken down in shorthand and copied for the members. Rudolf Steiner, though, was not able to read through and correct them, and they were not initially intended for publication. However, as soon as they were available for the members, Rudolf Steiner took it for granted that his listeners were familiar with them, and continually enlarged upon them with new insights and points of view. Together they now form the most comprehensive description of life after death. Those who listened to these lectures for the first time, experienced them as courageous communications which went far beyond anything they had heard before. A reader of today would need to imagine the situation at that time if he wished even to begin to evaluate their style.

Most of the lectures gathered in this volume were also spoken to people who had lost friends and relatives in the First World War and who therefore had a consuming interest in such knowledge. It was possible to say things within these intimate circles which might perhaps not have been possible in larger groups, or which would at least have had to be said differently.

Rudolf Steiner's audience had a basic familiarity with the fundamental works of anthroposophy, such as *Theosophy* and *Occult Science*; these had already appeared and provided an initial framework for an understanding of life after death. This framework was expanded by the lecture cycles referred to. The reader of this volume, in contrast, is presented only with a selection of lectures, not the entire cycle. However, each lecture has its particular place within the whole. This volume was compiled for those who wish to gain an initial insight into the event of death, the after-death journey of the human being and his connections with those who are left behind. Those who would like to pursue the subject in greater depth should refer to the bibliography at the end of this book. Much of what is only touched on here is elaborated in the volumes of Rudolf Steiner's collected works.

This selection begins with a public lecture which Rudolf Steiner held in the Architects' House in Berlin. Although the audience was familiar with the fundamental teachings of anthroposophy, Rudolf Steiner warns his listeners not to take what he has to say in too superficial a manner, nor judge it too quickly; for these results of his research only became accessible to him after long and disciplined training. They deserve, he says, an attitude of awe and respect, as does everything issuing from the realms of truth.

In the next six lectures the main events and stages of life after death are characterized, in each case from a different aspect: the death of the physical body with the fading away of the etheric body; the soul-spiritual re-experiencing of the life which is past; and the purely spiritual existence in planetary spheres together with purely spiritual beings. The various descriptions are a good example of how the same thing can appear different when seen from different angles.

During the First World War, Rudolf Steiner observed and traced the after-death progress of many who died. For most of them death came violently and too early. Only a few of them were prepared for it. In this difficult situation Rudolf Steiner was particularly concerned to show ways in which a connection between the dead person and relatives could be established. The suggestions and advice which he gave in this respect are among the most intimate sources for a future civilization in which the Mysteries will again have a place. Since such a connection is so important for a healthy future, the lectures in the second half of this volume were chosen with this aspect in mind. Rudolf Steiner repeatedly describes how we can 'speak' with a dead person, how we must listen for the very delicate 'replies', in what manner we should think of our communication with the dead. We can be continually surprised to discover how very differently we must learn to think and feel if such a connection is to be sought. The common experience of meeting the dead in our dreams has usually nothing to do with their real being. They are, though, present in what seem to be our own decisions and initiatives – in fact in the very domain where we do not expect their influence. If we could learn to take notice of very subtle phenomena and could learn, once again, to communicate with the dead, then, according to Rudolf Steiner, our culture would be immeasurably blessed.

This is really how Rudolf Steiner viewed the cultural task of anthroposophy. It should help to re-establish the connection and communication between human and supersensible beings. We could begin to do this by turning to our own dead, as happened in earlier times, and forming a connection with them. They can, by our selfless striving, be moved to take an active, wholesome part in helping the world to thrive and flourish. An enormous amount depends on this. That is the deeper reason for Rudolf Steiner's repeated emphasis on the phenomena which can be observed in this respect and on the possibility we have of actively engaging them. This selection of lectures is intended to help open the first doors to such an involvement.

I. Life between Death and Rebirth

Berlin, 19 March 1914

TODAY'S THEME is without doubt a most hazardous and difficult one. Nevertheless, it is one which I would like to broach, concerning as it does a very special object of spiritual-scientific research.[1] I believe that my very respected listeners – some of whom have been present at these lectures over many years – will find this object of spiritual-scientific research acceptable, since I have often endeavoured to present here, in a general way, the possible proofs and justifications for such research. Today, though, we must distance ourselves a little from these proofs and justifications. For the findings of spiritual-scientific research, about the life of the human being between death and rebirth, will be presented here in a descriptive form. In spite of the fact that today's theme is a conceptually difficult one for contemporary consciousness (and must still be wholly rejected by such a consciousness, which regards the results of this research as unproven), I would nevertheless like to make the following introductory remark: I am fully aware that I speak in an age which has advanced sixty years since Julius Robert Mayer made the great discovery of the metamorphosis of natural forces; and more than half a century since the great discoveries of Darwin; in an age which has experienced great successes in science such as, for example, spectro-analysis and astro-physics and, in more recent times, experimental biology. Although I recognize and am fully aware of these scientific achievements, I still wish to address the theme of today's lecture, in spite of the fact that this must seem contradictory to those who believe that spiritual-scientific research and spiritual-scientific conviction should be rejected if one is to proceed in a truly scientific way. I would also like to make one further introductory remark: if I was not quite clear that what is to be presented about the life between death and rebirth adheres to the most rigorous spiritual-scientific method and can be upheld on equal terms with the results of science, then I would regard it as thoughtless, even frivolous to speak of spiritual-scientific results before this assembly. I am fully aware of my responsibility, precisely in regard to this theme, to speak in a scientific way. Yet the whole manner in which one must approach the truth and truthfulness of spiritual-scientific research involves an open, receptive mood and gesture of soul, which is today hardly a common one. I would like first of all, very briefly, to examine the mood of soul needed by the spiritual researcher and also, to a certain extent, by anyone who would recognize the truth of the results of spiritual-scientific research.

A quite different attitude towards truth and truthfulness from the one prevalent nowadays is needed. Whoever wishes to achieve spiritual-scientific results with the methods which have been elaborated in these lectures must above all have an attitude of awe and unbounded reverence towards truth and knowledge. In our time one so easily accepts an attitude towards the truth which is based on making decisions about everything arising in human life; decisions of the kind which presuppose that I am in a position to judge life and reality simply with the attitude and mood of soul in which I find myself, which are present in me. The spiritual researcher – and whoever wishes to receive the results of his research – needs a quite different attitude of soul. He needs one which says to itself: to receive the truth and share in it my soul needs to be prepared, needs to immerse itself in an attitude and mood which goes beyond ordinary life. And when one becomes involved in spiritual science – please do not misunderstand this term as having to do with any such thing as asceticism – then the ordinary attitude of soul of daily life is felt to be quite useless for genuinely experiencing truth and knowledge. Knowledge is then perceived as something which hovers above one, which can only be approached by going beyond one's ordinary self, by exerting all the strength at one's disposal in order to prepare to receive the truth in a worthy fashion.

Through spiritual science, the inappropriateness of judging truth on the basis of the ordinary attitudes of soul of daily life is experienced; one tries, rather, to wait until the soul has made a little more progress, has gathered its strength and prepared a fitting vessel for receiving truth. And one may often say: I prefer to wait patiently, let the truth hover over me, for I may not yet pass over its threshold; if I should do so now, I might spoil my experience of this truth, for which I am not yet ready. Awe and unbounded reverence towards truth, truthfulness and knowledge must be inherent in spiritual-scientific research. As one progresses on this path it becomes ever clearer that the soul must grow beyond itself, must be less and less concerned with making final judgements on the basis of ordinary attitudes of daily life and must take ever more care in preparing the forces through which it can make itself worthy to receive the truth. In short, whoever seeks the truth through spiritual science must take more and more care to prepare his soul, to develop capacities for receiving truth; any desire he might have to approach this truth with ordinary, critical faculties, will dwindle and disappear.

When the human being passes through the Gate of Death, he becomes part of a world which is otherwise only accessible to the kind of spiritual research of which I have long spoken and written. Such spiritual research can achieve knowledge and understanding that is only possible for self-aware soul faculties, unbound from the physical. We have often spoken of the methods by which the human soul comes to gain knowledge; not only by using its body and senses to come into contact with the outer world, but also by stepping out of the body, which is then separate from the soul, just as an outer object is usually separate from it – then, in this separation from the body, it can experience itself as part of a spiritual environment. I have often described how the soul of the spiritual researcher reaches this point. By so doing, it enters the same world which the human being passes into through the Gate of Death. And now I wish to describe, without any further preparation, what the spiritual researcher can discover, by means of methods which have often been elaborated here, about the life of the human being between death and rebirth.

The first thing which the human soul experiences after shedding the physical body, in a natural way, at death – just as the spiritual researcher can free himself from the body at certain moments during his life – is a change in his relationship to what we normally call thinking. I have often said that the human soul bears within itself the forces of thinking, feeling and willing. This division of the forces of the human soul is really only correct for the life of the soul within the body between birth and death. Besides the general difficulty of today's theme, I will also have to struggle with the difficulty of finding suitable expressions for the quite other world which the human being passes through between death and a new birth. Normal expressions of speech are formed in accordance with the life of senses which we experience through our physical body. I will only be able to do justice to this region of experience, so far removed from what we are used to, by making use of words in an approximate way. It must be remembered that we will be speaking of a region of experience for which words are, in fact, wholly inadequate.

After the human being has passed through the Gate of Death, he experiences his thought-life, his thinking, in a different way. In our life between birth and death we experience thoughts within our soul, we think. And these thoughts, between birth and death, are no more than images of an outer reality. When the human being has laid aside his physical body, then thought becomes an outer reality. This is the first experience in the spiritual world for someone who has died; he perceives his thoughts to be, as it were, set free from himself. They are outside and beyond his soul, just as, in the life between birth and death, sensory objects are outside and beyond us. His thoughts migrate, as it were, into an outer world of soul; they free themselves from immediate soul experience in a similar way to thoughts which become memories in ordinary life. The only difference is that we experience memories as sinking down into the unconscious, from where they can be recalled at an appropriate moment – we still have the feeling that they are within us, although they are removed from our immediate awareness. Thoughts, after death, also loosen themselves from us, but in such a way that the whole thought-world which the human being has gathered to himself between birth and death becomes an objective world. They do not separate from us by sinking down into an unformed darkness; they become independent and form a thought-world outside us. In this world is contained, as thought, everything in the way of life experiences which accrued to us in our last life, all the wealth of experience gained simply by having lived. This is loosened and released into a kind of tableau of life-experiences which surrounds the soul after death. These thoughts, though, are not fleeting, for as they separate from the soul and take on independent life they grow more solid, vital and full of motion, and form a world of beings. This world, in which we then live, is the world composed of our migrating thoughts, which assume independent existence.

This world is often described as a kind of memory-tableau of the life which is past. It is, indeed, a memory-tableau, but one which has emancipated itself and of which we can say: 'That has come from myself, yet it stands there, objectively, in the outer world; it is alive!'

This experience of the soul within a world of thought which has become objective lasts different lengths of time according to each individual, but in all cases it is a matter of days. After some days – I have drawn attention in *Occult Science* to the connection of this with human life – the human being who has passed through the Gate of Death, experiences this whole world, which has become his world, distancing itself from him, as though diminishing in a spiritual perspective, as though it was going far, far away from him in spiritual regions. It is a matter of days until this point is reached, at which the thought world recedes and becomes ever thinner and thinner, ever mistier and mistier, ever more veiled in obscurity as it moves away into far distances. I have mentioned in *Occult Science* that spiritual-scientific research reveals that this first condition after death lasts longer for those who, before death, were more easily able to do without sleep without losing their strength. The memory tableau lasts roughly as long as one is able, in life, to do without sleep. One can discover this fact by means of spiritual-scientific research. Whoever tires easily – but it is above all a question of how much strength a human being has – whoever really cannot do without sleep even when it might be necessary, will find that this memory-tableau recedes sooner than for the person who can make an effort to rally his strength and do without sleep for longer. There is no need to make strenuous efforts in this direction; it is just a question of what each human being is able to do.

This is also connected with a new kind of consciousness which appears. Our ordinary waking consciousness arises between birth and death as we encounter objects of the outer world. This is not so during sleep, when our ordinary consciousness is set aside; but we develop our everyday consciousness by encountering and coming up against the outer world through our senses. Just as consciousness, in ordinary life, is stimulated by contact with the outer world, so after death our consciousness unfolds as a result of the human being becoming aware of his connection with the receding thought-world which I have described. Consciousness after death is further stimulated by the soul feeling: 'Your thoughts are disappearing into the distance and you must seek them.' This is how I might characterize the experience of the soul, which thereby develops the strength necessary to awaken a spiritual consciousness after death: 'You must seek your thoughts, which have receded into the distance!' This consciousness of the thoughts which have gone on ahead of us forms a part of our self-awareness after death. We will see shortly what further role this self-awareness has to play.

What we can call the worlds of willing and feeling change after death in a different way. The distinction between feeling life and will-life that exists from birth to death is no longer at all relevant after death. There is present in the soul after death something like a willing or desiring feeling-life, or a will-life that is wholly imbued with feeling. The expressions with which we describe feeling and willing cannot really be applied to the time after death. Feeling is then more similar to one's experience of willing; and willing is far more imbued with feeling than is so between birth and death. Whereas our thoughts become a world outside the soul after death, our willed feeling and feeling-imbued will bind themselves much more closely and intimately with our soul. The soul, besides developing self-awareness in the way I have described, now begins to experience itself through an empowering and strengthening of its life of willed feeling and feeling-imbued will. This creates an inner life which is immeasurably more intense than the inner life of the soul when it lives within the body. After his thoughts have receded, the human being inhabits his inner world for a long time, for decades even, experiencing it as his principal world. His inner world becomes so mighty that he must – and here I have to use an expression which is not really correct for the life after death – direct his attention towards the willed feeling and feeling-imbued will which streams up within him. For years this felt willing and willed feeling looks back upon its past earthly life. The human soul feels, after death, something like a longing, like a turning back towards what was offered by its previous life. For every life can be seen to have offered far more possibilities of experience than the human being in fact took advantage of. When the human being passes through the Gate of Death, he has the longing and the will to relive everything of which he – I cannot say knows, but – feels: 'You should have experienced this.' All the indistinct emotions, all the possible experiences which life could have given us, but failed to give, all this unites with what the soul experiences in connection with the life that is past. In particular, the soul has intense inner experiences of what it feels it should have done. What the soul owes to other people, the harm it has done to others, all this appears as an intense feeling of deficient love, of which we are not at all aware in the life between birth and death.

Years go by after death during which the soul is occupied in gradually separating, unbinding itself from the context of its last life. During this time we are not, however, sundered from the experiences of our previous life. We remain connected to the people whom we have left, whom we have loved. But our connection with them is sustained by the feelings and affinities which we developed towards them in life; we are connected to them also in a roundabout way as a result of what life offered and failed to offer us. It is necessary to express these things in metaphorical terms. It is quite possible to remain in connection, after death, with people who one was close to during life, but only through an emotional affinity which one had with them then. An intense connection is formed as a result of such affinity. After death one lives together with the living; but also with those who have already died with whom one had a connection during life. This is how one must imagine the life after death, which continues in this way for years. It is a life in which the soul chiefly lives through everything which it wills and desires and longs for in connection with its felt and willed memories of the life that is past.

If we attempt to research spiritually into the length of time that this period lasts, we find that the early years of childhood have no influence on these initial years after death. Life between birth and the point which, later, we can remember back to – that is, the point at which we learn to experience ourselves inwardly with self-awareness – has no significance for these years after death. Similarly, the period of life after our middle twenties has little significance for the length of time that we remain in the soul-condition after death that I have described. The average period, then, that the soul lives through in this way, is roughly equal to the years between the third, fourth or fifth year of life and the middle twenties – the twenty-fourth or twenty-fifth year. For approximately that length of time, the soul is aware of itself by means of knowing: 'Your thought-world has gone on before you with your life-experiences into the distance. You have a connection, you are related to this thought-experience and you must find it again, for it is by means of it that you became what you are in your earthly life. But now it has disappeared into the distance.' We stand before this world of life-experiences that have transformed themselves into thoughts, as before an outer world which we know to be there. And the other world, which we live through after death, after the thought-world has receded, is experienced in the strengthened inner life of will and feeling.

Then the time comes when we emancipate ourself from what is merely a strengthened inner life. Then it seems that gradually beings arise from the spiritual environment, which belong to the spiritual world in the same way that beings of the physical world – minerals, plants, animals and the physical nature of human beings – belong to our sensory, physical world. In other words, we grow beyond ourself into a spiritual world. But we grow into the spiritual environment in a way that gives us a quite different feeling for it from the feeling we have in our body towards the world of sense-phenomena. I would need to describe this different kind of feeling at great length in order to properly characterize it; but instead I will describe only one important thing about it.

We see the objects of the outer world through our eyes when light falls upon them from a source of light; we are aware of them because they are illumined by such a source. When we leave behind the condition of feeling back towards our last earthly life and begin to grow into an objective condition of the spiritual world, then we have this experience: 'In your last life you let ripen in you something like inner light, inner strength of soul; this gives you now, increasingly, the possibility of looking upon and perceiving the outer world of spiritual beings and processes, and of living among them.' Whereas we can experience the period previously described as a time of separation and emancipation of the soul from the connection with its past life, we now experience that in the inmost depth of the feeling-will and willed-feeling an inner light has ripened in the inner world – an inner world achieved over many years – just as, within the blossom, a seed is ripened. By means of this inner light, which we radiate, like strength, the processes and beings of the outer spiritual world become visible to us. Then we know that if we had not developed this inner light, everything in the spiritual world would have remained dark, would not have been perceived. The strength required to overcome our connection with the previous life is like an inner power of light. At this point a power of soul awakens for which there is really no expression in the ordinary world, for it does not exist in the world of senses, except for the researcher who penetrates the spiritual world. In order to express what the human being experiences as a strength emanating from himself and illuminating the spiritual environment, I would say: it is like a creative activity of will, permeated by intense feeling. We feel ourself to be a creative part of the universe, through which the spiritual world streams. And we have the feeling: 'By knowing yourself to be a creative part of the universe you can now feel and knowingly experience the spiritual world.' Thus we experience what can be called 'soulhood' after death, as we grow out into what approaches us with more and more fullness and clarity.

Today I am describing this world between death and a new birth more from the inner experience of it. In my books *Theosophy* and *Occult Science* I have described it more from an outer spiritual-scientific perspective. Since I do not in the least like repeating myself I am today taking a different approach. But if you know how many angles there are on any field or subject of the sense-world, you will also know that what I have described with other words in the above-mentioned books is essentially identical.

The soul experiences itself as living into the world of spiritual beings and processes. And it must be expressly said that included within these spiritual beings and processes into which the soul grows through its own power of illumination

are those human souls with whom we formed a connection
during life; but only those, not others with whom we did not
form a connection. Until now we experienced, over years, our
inner life through willed-longing and felt-willing; but now we
begin, increasingly, to experience the objective outer spiritual
world, to work within it just as we work within the sense-world
according to our particular tasks and disposition. However,
what we experience inwardly as power of illumination develops only gradually, and to use a phrase familiar to the spiritual
researcher, in a rhythmic, cyclical way. It develops in such a
way that we feel: 'The power of illumination has awoken in
you; by means of it you are able to experience certain other
beings and processes of the spiritual world; but now it is
fading again to some extent, growing dim.' To use a comparison from the ordinary sense-world, it is similar to what we feel
towards evening, when the outer sun goes down; we feel, in
the life between death and rebirth, that the inner power of
light fades away again and again. But when it has faded,
another condition arises in which the soul again experiences
its inwardness and feels itself now to be really full of strength;
it experiences inwardly, if I may use such an expression, what
it has brought back with it from the condition in which it
developed a power of illumination. So the condition in which
we are given over to all the spiritual beings and processes
alternates with one in which the inner light again grows dim
and finally is extinguished altogether; in which, though, our
felt-willing and willed-feeling reawaken, yet do so in a way
which retains a memory of everything which we experienced
in the spiritual world, which came to us from outside ourselves. Thus we have alternating states, comparable to living,
first of all, wholly in our surroundings, then taking these
surroundings into our inner life so that they rise up in us as
inner experience, as though what we experienced outwardly
became enfolded within us in the interior of our soul. There
is an alternation between these two conditions. Another way
of describing this is to say: we first experience ourself opened

wide in companionship with the whole spiritual world; then
this condition alters to one of inner loneliness, one in which
the soul grows self-aware, in which the whole experienced
spiritual cosmos is contained within us. At the same time,
though, we know: 'You are living within yourself now; what
you now experience is what your soul has retained – you are
no longer in connection with anything outside yourself.'
These conditions in the spiritual world between death and a
new birth alternate with a regularity similar to sleeping and
waking in ordinary life: the condition of soul which expands
into an outer soul world and the one in which the soul knows
and savours itself, in which we feel: 'Now you are alone in
yourself, shut off from all outer beings and processes. Now
you experience yourself within yourself.' These two conditions need to alternate, for the inner power of illumination can
only be sustained when the human being is time and time
again thrown back upon himself. These processes are described in more detail in my book, *The Threshold of the
Spiritual World*. The soul grows, lives into ever-richer worlds
of spirit for whose perception it requires ever-greater inner
powers of illumination. This continues for a long time. Then
we begin to have the feeling that as we grow into these
worlds of spirit a certain boundary is encountered. This is
connected with the capacities which we developed in life. One
soul will create for itself a narrower horizon, another soul will
create a wider one, over a smaller or larger spiritual world.

But then a time comes when we feel the inner power of
illumination diminishing. That happens when we approach
the midpoint between death and the next birth. Then we feel:
'Now the inner light is growing weaker and weaker; now you
can illumine less and less of what is around you.' Everything
grows dimmer and dimmer and the periods of inner experience, which grow more and more intense, assume increasing
importance; then everything that we have already inwardly
experienced moves and flows, rises and falls. Inner experience
grows richer and richer, while perception grows darker and

dimmer, until the midpoint of the time between death and rebirth is reached. Then we experience what I described in my Mystery Drama, *The Soul's Awakening*, as 'spiritual midnight'. We experience a time during which we are filled with the spiritual world, when we awaken, yet awaken into 'night', when we experience ourself as closed and contained within the spiritual world. It is a most intense feeling of being within oneself at the midpoint between death and rebirth. This experience of being within oneself creates a condition of soul which cannot be borne for long. It is an awareness of knowing which is unbearable, which one does not want, because it is only knowing. We feel within ourself: 'You carry a world within you which you only experience by knowing, a world from whose reality you are shut off: you have lost the power of illuminating it.' Night comes in the spiritual world. Yet in this condition we have experiences which in our body, on earth, are passive soul experiences, but which now become active. As we become more and more deeply immersed in the twilight and then the night of the spiritual world, the longing for an outer world becomes ever stronger. And whereas longings and wishes in earthly life are something which have to find fulfilment from without, the longing which we experience in the spiritual midnight is a power which develops in a similar way to electric or magnetic power on earth. The longing in the soul begets a new power, a power which can again conjure an outer world before the soul. The soul has immersed itself more and more deeply in a spiritual inner world and has grown ever larger, more and more huge and mighty. Yet within it there lives a longing to have, once again, an outer world surrounding it. This longing is an active force which creates for itself an outer world, but of a most unusual kind.

The first thing which we experience when we have reached the midpoint between death and rebirth is that an outer world arises before us; yet it is, after all, not one. When we awaken out of loneliness, we encounter images which rise up out of our previous earthly life. Our past outer world surrounds us once more, to which our longing, as an active force, has led us. We encounter for a while, and judge, our past earthly experiences in the form of an outer world. Previously we stood within them and lived through them; now we encounter and confront them. And now the further longing arises to make good in a new earthly life what is perceived by the newly awoken consciousness as lack, inadequacy and insufficiency of previous earthly lives. Now the soul feels what it needs to do in regard to the thoughts which receded and fled away from it. It receives the sure knowledge which awakens in the second half of the life between death and a new birth: 'Your thought-experiences have flown ahead of you; you can only rediscover them by travelling once more through an earthly life.' These experiences of encountering our previous earthly life and the realization that we can only find the thoughts which have flown ahead of us by calling them back through a new earthly life, are what create an instinctive urge towards rebirth. This urge cannot be judged in terms of the previous life. At this period, the soul finds it natural to reunite with the thoughts which have departed from it, which it can only do by passing once more through earthly life; this is also the only way for it to make good what it encountered as lack and inadequacy in the images of its previous life.

And now one new experience after another arises out of the dim darkness of the spiritual world. One thing which arises is our connection with those people closest to us. We were engaged in this connection before the mid-point period; but then we worked with them in the spiritual world and were united in spirit with them. Now those souls reappear with whom we have unfinished business from our previous life; those to whom we were related by blood, as well as those we were close to in life. As they appear we are able to judge what is still incomplete in us, what we still owe them, what we need to do to balance out our insufficiencies with regard to them. We feel ourselves united with these souls who appear, because we lived together with them in past lives. We experience a desire to live closely together again with those souls with whom we had a close connection in the past. As this period continues, souls begin to appear with whom we had some kind of lesser connection: with whom, for example, we shared a religious belief or a nationality; with whom, in some way or other, we formed a whole group. From the way in which these souls appear, our soul can see how it should form its new incarnation in order to seek the right effect and result of previous lives in community with these souls. Finally, out of the dim darkness of the spiritual world, there appear connections either with souls or with other spiritual essences which can be called 'ideal'. After we have encountered and confronted our previous life, after the human beings we were close to and the communities of which we were a part have reappeared, then we encounter, finally, and in a vivid way, the people who shone out for us in life as ideal figures, even if we were not personally close to them. What we refer to in life as our personal ideals, as our spiritual orientation, is encountered last of all.

These experiences furnish the soul with the strength to unite once more with earthly life. But in the second half of the life between death and a new birth things still proceed in a rhythmic and cyclical way. We must still distinguish between periods when the soul lives in an outer world, in which it perceives its previous friends, relations, ideals and so forth in an outward, objective way; and periods when it is removed from them and experiences them only inwardly. These periods again alternate with the same necessity as sleeping and waking in ordinary life. The strength which develops in the soul in the presence of everything which I have characterized gives it the capacity to create for itself a formative image – initially a soul-spiritual one – of a new earthly life. We do not immediately perceive the life-experiences which transformed themselves into thoughts and receded from us when we enter the second half of the life between death and rebirth. But the soul experiences this period as a time of intensified creative willing and feeling; and the result of this intensification is that a formative image of a new earthly life crystallizes out of the surrounding spiritual substance. For there is, in the spiritual world, a different relationship between perception and feeling-experience to the one which exists in the physical world: in the physical world we perceive the outer world, which is then present, but passively so, in our thoughts. When, on the other hand, we experience the spiritual world in the way I have described, when we perceive the inheritance of our past life – those who were close to us, our previous friends, our ideals – then we develop a force which permeates us, lives and weaves within us, empowers us. This empowering drives us on towards a new earthly life. Please forgive the unusualness of some of the expressions I am having to make use of; I am describing conditions which, from the point of view of ordinary life, are, after all, unusual.

The human being who illumines the spiritual world around him discovers forces in himself, at first only dimly sensed, which draw him towards his vanished life-experiences. The formative image of a new life becomes clearer and more defined and the human being feels himself, as a result of the forces which accumulate in him, to be driven down towards physical earthly life. He feels himself drawn towards the parents who can give him a bodily frame most in keeping with the formative image of his approaching life on earth which he has created in the spiritual world. Three elements are united at the human being's rebirth: the male, the female and the spiritual. Long before the human being enters a new earthly life at birth, the forces he has developed draw him to particular parents. Yet many different possible conditions play into this process. What we chiefly need to concern ourselves with is that the human being looks back and takes account of his previous lives. Because of this, he quite naturally develops an inner longing for a new life on earth. It can happen, however, that the human being feels: 'You must be embodied upon the earth; but you are not able to incarnate into a new earthly body in a way that would allow you to catch up with and grasp the life-experiences which flew on ahead of you.'

Let us look at such a case, which is certainly one familiar to spiritual research. When we live on the earth, we by no means experience everything which it would be possible to experience. This can be observed without the help of spiritual science. Much escapes our attention in earthly life and still more reaches us but does not become conscious. We have to admit, if we look into these matters, that there are many experiences we could have which we do not have. The experiences approach us though. If we see ourselves as pupils of life, we have to say: 'All this approaches us.' This is true also of the life between death and rebirth. And when we come to the second half of this life after death, we may have the conviction: 'You cannot now, with everything you have developed and experienced, fully unite yourself with a new earthly life.' Then it becomes necessary to unite oneself sooner with a new earth life than would have been occasioned by the vanished thought-world. And then one must tell oneself: 'Only in a subsequent earthly life, perhaps only after two or three further earthly lives, will you have reached the point of experiencing the thought-world which has now flown ahead of you.' This results in the human being failing to have such an intense longing for earthly life, failing to take hold of it as fully as he otherwise would. It is possible for the human being to fail to unite intensely enough with earthly life. He develops the strength to reincarnate but not the strength which would allow him to experience everything that was to be experienced. In such circumstances he does not have sufficient pleasure in earthly life in the depths of his soul. From this fact comes everything which causes a human being to fail to take earthly life seriously or fully enough. And in this respect the spiritual researcher discovers something which can often weigh heavily on his soul.

As spiritual researcher one meets everything in life with

interest and sympathy. Let us assume that, as spiritual researcher, one looks into the life of a criminal who has turned
against human society in an extreme way. Even when not
denying such a person's culpability, it is still possible to have
the deepest sympathy for him and wish to interpret his actions
by looking into the circumstances of his life. When trying to
explain his actions, one discovers that he has come to crime
and wrong-doing through an inability to take hold of life
in its full significance for reasons I have already indicated. I
am convinced, having investigated such things, even to the
extent of studying criminals' slang, that underlying such
phenomena is a failure to take life seriously; life is not valued
but despised. Such a failure to take life seriously need not be
fully conscious. Waking consciousness often knows little of
what lies in the depths of the soul. The criminal often develops
a strong feeling of self; he desires life. Yet in the depths
of his soul, unplumbed by his consciousness, lives a hatred
for life. The reason why he does not take life fully seriously is
that he did not manage to reach the point which his thought-
world arrived at. In investigating the lives of criminals one
will find a mood of hatred towards life which even expresses
itself in their jargon and slang. The attentive observer can
discover through these things the answer to great mysteries
and enigmas of life. Such souls can be seen as having been
born spiritually premature. Because they came too soon, they
did not have the strength to take a serious hold on life or
develop towards life a feeling of responsibility in the fullest
sense of the word. Someone who has at least come near the
point of time which his thoughts, transformed into objective
beings, flew ahead to, can unite most inwardly with earthly
life, with the forces which can only be developed upon earth.
Such forces are: conscience, love of the earth and responsibility, by means of which personal morality is formed and
developed. If true personal morality is to grow within the soul
one must have the will to unite fully with earthly life. This is
something which spiritual science can illuminate for us: our

feelings towards life and human beings are thereby enriched, for we then understand them better and can find our bearings within life more easily.

The spiritual researcher can also throw light on what may occur with someone whose life ends prematurely, whether through illness or accident. Essentially, the effect on the life between death and rebirth of entering earlier than usual into the spiritual world is that forces are created for the soul which would otherwise not be available for it. It may sound strange and paradoxical, but we can perhaps only attain the forces we lack from a previous life – which might be available to us under other conditions – if our life ends earlier than normal. But spiritual science will never consider that anyone is justified in taking their own life, which is an artificial way of hastening the proper moment of death.

When investigating in this way the life between death and rebirth, one can see that quite other forces are at work than those active between birth and death, and yet they are forces which seem to follow on quite naturally from our outward, bodily life.

I should never have been able to arrive at the results of research which I have dared to present to you today merely by means of philosophical thoughts and exertions of the mind. Only a path of spiritual research – which has so often been described here – can reveal such things. But once these conclusions have been reached, one can ask whether they agree and correspond with earthly life between birth and death; which, indeed, they would seem fully to do. And if one should ask why the human being does not remember his previous lives, the following answer can be given: the spiritual researcher observes that the human being descending to earthly life must initially make use of the forces of such memory for the inner sculpting and forming of his physical, sensory body. The human being himself must sculpt, form and maintain this body. The forces which he makes use of to transform the body, so that the dawn of early childhood can change into the full waking light of consciousness in subsequent earthly life, are those which he could otherwise transform to remember his previous lives. They flow into his body and make him strong for life between birth and death. It is only when the spiritual researcher unbinds his soul from the physical body and frees the forces which he otherwise uses to see, to hear, to move his limbs, using them instead for pure soul perception, that his gaze broadens to take in a wholly spiritual horizon and he can experience the things I have described.

Within the human being there resides the eternal, immortal kernel of the soul. But in the life between birth and death it is engaged and engrossed in the energies and processes of the sensory, physical body. However, we find ourselves currently in a period of transition, during which the human being will establish a new relationship to his body, a strengthened inner life of the body. Spiritual science feels that it has the task of communicating what it perceives, for as the soul progresses from life to life it becomes more and more inward and will, in the fast-approaching future, consider these things to be essential knowledge, without which it cannot truly live. At the same time, a natural clairvoyant faculty will reappear and allow such things to be understood.

Spiritual research, therefore, pursues a different path to the one taken by a merely conceptual philosophy. It does not approach the question of immortality by trying to provide intellectual proofs, but by seeking the paths which lead to the essence of the soul itself. And once one has found the soul and knows how it inwardly experiences itself, there is no need to think up external philosophical proofs of the immortality of the soul. One realizes then that what passes beyond death and enters into a life between death and rebirth, and into ever-renewed earthly lives, is already within us during the life between birth and death. When we recognize it in ourselves then we also, simultaneously, recognize our immortality. We recognize it as surely as we recognize that the seed of a plant has the power to develop and bring forth a new plant. But we also know that the plant-seed can be used for human nourishment, whereas no such external function can be perceived in the case of the soul; it cannot be put to any other use. What lives in the soul is the aspiration towards future earthly lives, and consequently the aspiration to immortality. Therefore one can speak of the immortality of every soul.

As I have already mentioned at the beginning of today's lecture, such things are quite opposed to the views of contemporary consciousness. How could this contemporary consciousness easily relate to what has been described in this and other lectures? Although, on the one hand, such a consciousness feels a great longing to know something about the soul, on the other hand it is intent on narrowing its focus in order to gain knowledge. Spiritual science is often accused of being illogical and superstitious. But it can bear such an accusation. For when the 'logic' which believes itself opposed to spiritual science is examined, it becomes clear why spiritual science is taking so long to enter people's hearts and minds. I can point to a book [by Artur Brausewetter, *Gedanken über den Tod*, 1913] which expresses thoughts about death in which there is a strange passage, which I only cite here to show you what I mean: 'Immortality cannot be proven. Even Plato, and the platonist Mendelssohn, were not able to give grounds for the immortality and indivisibility of the soul; for even if one wishes to concede the indivisibility of the soul, it is still, after all, an object of inner assertion, which is unproven and unprovable.'[2] One does not need to read any further, for whoever is capable of writing that Plato and Mendelssohn could not deduce the immortality of the soul from its indestructibility might just as well write that we cannot deduce the immortality of the rose from its redness. For, unless we are unthinking, we cannot say that the soul is not immortal because it cannot be proved to be so. Such things are written nowadays and can be found in a work that will be read by many, because such books please our contemporaries, who fail to take notice of the logical inconsistencies.

They fail to notice inconsistencies which are used to attack and oppose spiritual science. If they accuse spiritual science of being illogical, they should first of all examine their own logic. I have often spoken about all the other objections made to spiritual science and therefore will not discuss them again now, but rather end this lecture with a conclusion and sentiment which I have expressed in previous lectures.

In espousing the results of spiritual science, we always feel ourselves to be in accord with the most enlightened spirits of human earthly evolution. They might not, it is true, have known of spiritual science, for only in our time could it take the form in which it now exists; nevertheless, they had a sense and presentiment of the direction in which spiritual science moves. And when someone of monistic or similar persuasion speaks of the unprovability of the soul's immortality, one can, as spiritual researcher, point to one of the great spirits with whom one feels in accord and harmony. Spiritual science shows us that essence in ourselves which develops between birth and death and then, freed from the body, must pass through all the stages and conditions I have described. We cannot gain knowledge about the human soul residing in the human body between birth and death if we do not know of its capacities between death and rebirth. If some system or other of religious belief does not agree with spiritual science because the latter creates a broader conception of God, then one can only reply: 'How feeble you are, with your concept of God and your religious feeling!' An entrenched position of that kind is like someone saying to Columbus: 'Don't discover America, for why should you bother to discover an undiscovered land? The sun shines so beautifully in our country; how is one to know whether it will shine so beautifully elsewhere?' Anyone with sense would, of course, say: 'It will shine beautifully everywhere.' The spiritual scientist perceives what significance his conception of God has for him. He experiences its greatness, like a shining spiritual sun! And he knows that any concept of God, any religious feeling, any belief must be feeble that states: 'The God whom we worship in our religious life cannot rule in the worlds of the spiritual researcher.' But if religious feeling is vigorous enough, it will receive from the spiritual researcher's conception of God the illumination of spiritual worlds; the concept of God will be as little harmed by spiritual science as it was by Copernicus and Galileo.

Spiritual science knows that the soul residing in the body is already preparing itself for the life between death and rebirth. Life between birth and death receives sense and significance when we observe existence between death and the next birth. Then we feel ourselves in harmony with the most illumined spirits, one of whom expressed his presentiment of what we have today considered. Goethe once said: 'I agree with Lorenzo de Medici that those people are already dead to this life who do not hope for another.'[3] Spiritual science feels itself in complete accord with this, for it knows: the soul must take into itself what it can receive from the life beyond life in the body. Just as the seed of the plant receives its meaning from the new plant-life it is preparing, so we are preparing in our soul not what we already have within us, but what we can have expectation of. Yes, spiritual science leads us to the fundamental feeling which illumines and permeates our whole life, and which Goethe expressed so well in the words I have cited. Spiritual science tells us, proves to us and justifies our feeling that those people are dead to bodily life who do not hope for life in the spirit and for what the spiritual nature of the soul means for the whole world!

II. Metamorphosis of the Memory in the Life after Death

Dornach, 10 February 1924[4]

A STUDY of man's faculty of memory can give us valuable insight into the whole of human life and its cosmic connections. So today we will study this faculty of memory as such, in the various phases of its manifestation in human life, beginning with its manifestation in the ordinary consciousness that man has between birth and death.

What man experiences in concrete, everyday life, in thinking, feeling and willing, in unfolding his physical forces, too – all this he transforms into memories which he recalls from time to time.

But if you compare the shadowy character of these memory-pictures, whether spontaneous or deliberately sought, with the robust experiences to which they refer, you will say that they exist as mere thoughts or mental presentations; you are led to call memories just 'pictures'. Nevertheless, it is these pictures that we retain in our ego from our experiences in the outer world; in a sense, we bear them with us as the treasure won from experience. If a part of these memories should be lost – as in certain pathological cases of which I have already spoken – our ego itself suffers injury. We feel that our innermost being, our ego, has been damaged if it must forfeit this or that from its treasury of memories, for it is this treasury that makes our life a complete whole. One could also point to the very serious conditions that sometimes result in cases of apoplectic stroke when certain portions of the patient's past life are obliterated from his memory.

Moreover, when we survey from a given moment our life since our most recent birth, we must feel our memories as a connected whole if we are to regard ourselves rightly as human souls.

These few features indicate the role of the faculty of memory in physical, earthly life. But its role is far greater still. What would the external world with all its impressions constantly renewed, with all it gives us, however vividly – what would it be to us if we could not link new impressions to the memories of past ones! Last, but not least, we may say that, after all, all learning consists in linking new impressions to the content borne in memory. A great part of educational method depends on finding the most rational way of linking the new things we have to teach the children to what we can draw from their store of memories.

In short, whenever we have to bring the external world to the soul, to evoke the soul's own life that it may feel and experience inwardly its own existence, we appeal to memory in the last resort. So we must say that, on earth, memory constitutes the most important and most comprehensive part of man's inner life.

Let us now study memory from yet another point of view. It is quite easy to see that the sum of memories we bear within us is really a fragment. We have forgotten so much in the course of life; but there are moments, frequently abnormal, when what has been long forgotten comes before us again. These are especially such moments in which a person comes near to death and many things emerge that have long been far from his conscious memory. Old people, when dying, suddenly remember things that had long disappeared from their conscious memory. Moreover, if we study dreams really intimately – and they, too, link on to memory – we find things arising which have quite certainly been experienced, but they passed us by unnoticed. Nevertheless, they are in our soul life, and arise in sleep when the hindrances of the physical and etheric organism are not acting and the astral body and ego are alone. We do not usually notice these things and so fail to observe that conscious memory is but a fragment of all we receive; in the course of life we take in much in the same form, only it is received into the subconscious directly where it is inwardly elaborated.

Now, as long as we are living on earth, we continue to regard the memories that arise from the depths of our soul in the form of thoughts as the essential part of memory. Thoughts of past experience come and go. We search for them. We regard that as the essence of memory.

However, when we go through the Gate of Death our life on earth is followed by a few days in which pictures of the life just ended come before us in a gigantic perspective. These pictures are suddenly there: the events of years long past and of the last few days are there simultaneously. As the spatial exists side by side and only possesses spatial perspective, so the temporal events of our earthly life are now seen side by side and possess 'time-perspective'. This tableau appears suddenly, but, during the short time it is there, it becomes more and more shadowy, weaker and weaker. Whereas in earthly life we look into ourselves and feel that we have our memory-pictures 'rolled up' within us, *these* pictures now become greater and greater. We feel as if they were being received by the universe. What is at first comprised within the memory tableau as in a narrow space, becomes greater and greater, more and more shadowy, until we find it has expanded to a universe, becoming so faint that we can scarcely decipher what we first saw plainly. We can still divine it; then it vanishes in the far spaces and is no longer there.

That is the second form taken by memory – in a sense, its second metamorphosis – in the first few days after death. It is the phase which we can describe as the flight of our memories out into the cosmos. And all that, like memory, we have bound so closely to our life between birth and death, expands and becomes more and more shadowy, to be finally lost in the wide spaces of the cosmos.

It is really as if we saw what we have actually been calling our ego during earthly life disappear into the wide spaces of the cosmos. This experience lasts a few days and, when these have passed, we feel that we ourselves are being expanded too. Between birth and death we feel ourselves within our memories; and now we actually feel ourselves within these rapidly retreating memories and being received into the wide spaces of the universe.

After we have suffered this supersensible stupor, or faintness, which takes from us the sum-total of our memories and our inner consciousness of earthly life, we live in the third phase of memory. This third phase of memory teaches us that what we had called ourself during earthly life – in virtue of our memories – has spread itself through the wide spaces of the universe, thereby proving its insubstantiality for us. If we were only what can be preserved in our memories between birth and death, we would be nothing at all a few days after death.

But we now enter a totally different element. We have realized that we cannot retain our memories, for the world takes them from us after death. But there is something objective behind all the memories we have harboured during earthly life. The spiritual counterpart is engraved into the world; and it is this counterpart of our memories that we now enter. Between birth and death we have experienced this or that with this or that person or plant or mountain spring, with all we have approached during life. There is no single experience whose spiritual counterpart is not engraved into the spiritual world in which we are ever present, even while on earth. Every handshake we have exchanged has its spiritual counterpart; it is there, inscribed into the spiritual world. Only while we are surveying our life in the first days after death do we have these pictures of our life before us. These conceal, to a certain extent, what we have inscribed into the world through our deeds, thoughts and feelings.

The moment we pass through the Gate of Death to this other 'life', we are at once filled with the content of our life-tableau, i.e. with pictures which extend, in perspective, back to birth and even beyond. But all this vanishes into the wide cosmic spaces and we now see the spiritual counter-images of all the deeds we have done since birth. All the spiritual counter-images we have experienced (unconsciously, in sleep) become visible, and in such a way that we are immediately impelled to retrace our steps and go through all these experiences once more. In ordinary life, when we go from Dornach to Basle we know we can also go from Basle to Dornach, for we have in the physical world an appropriate conception of space. But in ordinary consciousness we do not know, when we go from birth to death, that we can also go from death to birth. As in the physical world one can go from Dornach to Basle and return from Basle to Dornach, so we go from birth to death during earthly life and, after death, can return from death to birth.

This is what we do in the spiritual world when we experience backwards the spiritual counter-images of all we have undergone during earthly life. Suppose you have had an experience with something in the external realm of Nature – let us say, with a tree. You have observed the tree or, as a woodman, cut it down. Now all this has its spiritual counterpart; above all, whether you have merely observed the tree, or cut it down, or done something else to it, has its significance for the whole universe. What you can experience with the physical tree you experience in physical, earthly life; now, as you go backwards from death to birth, it is the spiritual counterpart of this experience that you live through.

If, however, our experience was with another human being – if, for example, we have caused him pain – there is already a spiritual counterpart in the physical world; only, it is not our experience: it is the pain experienced by the other person. Perhaps the fact that we were the cause of his pain gave us a certain feeling of satisfaction; we may have been moved by a feeling of revenge or the like. Now, on going backwards through our life, we do not undergo *our* experience, but *his*. We experience what he experienced through our deed. That, too, is a part of the spiritual counterpart and is inscribed into the spiritual world. In short, man lives through his experiences once more, but in a spiritual way, going backwards from death to birth.

As I said yesterday, it is a part of this experience to feel that beings whom, for the present, we may call 'superhuman', are participating in it. Pressing onwards through these spiritual counterparts of our experiences, we feel as if these spiritual beings were showering down their sympathies and antipathies upon our deeds and thoughts, as we experience them backwards. Thereby we feel what each deed done by us on earth, each thought, feeling, or impulse of will, is worth for purely spiritual existence. In bitter pain we experience the harmfulness of some deed we have done. In burning thirst we experience the passions we have harboured in our soul; and this continues until we have sufficiently realized the worthlessness, for the spiritual world, of harbouring passions and have outgrown these states which depend on our physical, earthly personality.

At this point of our studies we can see where the boundary between the psychical and the physical really is. You see, we can easily regard things like thirst or hunger as physical. But I ask you to imagine that the same physical changes that are in your organism when you are thirsty were in a body not ensouled. The same changes could be there, but the soulless body would not suffer thirst. As a chemist you might investigate the changes in your body when you are thirsty. But if, by some means, you could produce these same changes, in the same substances and in the same complex of forces, in a body without a soul, it would not suffer thirst. Thirst is not something in the body; it lives in the soul – in the astral – through changes in the physical body. It is the same with hunger. And if someone, in his soul, takes great pleasure in something that can only be satisfied by physical measures in physical life, it is as if he were experiencing thirst in physical life; the psychical part of him feels thirst, burning thirst, for those things which he was accustomed to satisfy by physical means. For one cannot carry out physical functions when the physical body has been laid aside. Man must first accustom himself to live in his psycho-spiritual being without his physical body; and a great part of the backward journey I have described is concerned with this. At first he experiences continually burning thirst for what can only be gratified through a physical body. Just as the child must accustom himself to use his organs – must learn to speak, for example – so man between death and a new birth must accustom himself to do without his physical body as the foundation of his psychical experiences. He must grow into the spiritual world.

There are descriptions of this experience which lasts one-third of the time of physical life that depict it as a veritable hell. For example, if you read descriptions like those given in the literature of the Theosophical Society where, following orien-tal custom, this life is called Kamaloka, they will certainly make your flesh creep. Well, these experiences are not like that. They can appear so if you compare them directly with earthly life, for they are something to which we are so utterly unaccustomed. We must suddenly adapt ourselves to the spiritual counter-images and counter-values of our earthly experience. What we felt on earth as pleasure is there priva-tion, bitter privation, and, strictly speaking, only our unsatisfying, painful or sorrowful experiences on earth are satisfying there. In many respects that is somewhat horrible when compared with earthly life; but we simply cannot compare it with earthly life directly, for it is not experienced here but in the life after death where we do not judge with earthly conceptions.

So when, for example, you experience after death the pain of another man through having caused him pain on earth, you say to yourself at once: 'If I did not feel this pain, I would remain an imperfect human soul, for the pain I have caused in the universe would continually take something from me. I only become a whole human being by experiencing this compensation.'

It may cost us a struggle to see that pain experienced after death in return for pain caused to another is really a blessing.

It will depend on the inner constitution of our soul whether we find this difficult or not; but there is a certain state of soul in which this painful compensation for many things done on earth is even experienced as bliss. It is the state of soul that results from acquiring on earth some knowledge of the supersensible life. We feel that, through this painful compensation, we are perfecting our human being, while, without it, we should fall short of full human stature. If you have caused another pain, you are of less value than before; so, if you judge reasonably, you will say: 'In face of the universe I am a worse human soul after causing pain to another than before. You will feel it a blessing that you are able, after death, to compensate for this pain by experiencing it yourself.'

That, my dear friends, is the third phase of memory. At first what we have within us as memory is condensed to pictures, which last some days after death; then it is scattered through the universe, your whole inner life in the form of thoughts returning thereto. But while we lose the memories locked up within us during earthly life – while these seek the cosmic spaces – the world, from out of all we have spiritually engraved upon it, gives us back to ourselves in objective form.

There is scarcely a stronger proof of man's intimate connection with the world than this; that after death, in regard to our inner life, we have first to lose ourselves, in order to be given back to ourselves from out of the universe. And we experience this, even in the face of painful events, as something that belongs to our human being as a whole. We do, indeed, feel that the world takes to itself the inner life we possessed here, and gives back to us again what we have engraved upon it. It is just the part we did not notice, the part we passed by but inscribed upon spiritual existence with clear strokes, that gives us our own self again. Then, as we retrace our life backwards through birth and beyond, we reach out into the wide spaces of spiritual existence.

It is only now, after having undergone all this, that we enter the spiritual world and are really able to live there. Our faculty of memory now undergoes its fourth metamorphosis. We feel that everywhere behind the ordinary memory of earthly life something has been living in us, though we were not aware of it. It has engraved itself into the world and now we, ourselves, become it. We have received our earthly life in its spiritual significance; we now become this significance. After travelling back through birth to the spiritual world we find ourselves confronting it in a very peculiar way. In a sense, we ourselves in our spiritual counterpart – in our true spiritual worth – now confront the world. We have passed through the above experiences, have experienced the pain caused to another, have experienced the spiritual value corresponding to an experience with a tree, let us say; we have experienced all this, but it was not self-experience. We might compare this with the embryonic stage of human life; for then – and even throughout the first years of life – all we experience does not yet reach the level of self-consciousness, which only awakens gradually.

Thus, when we enter the spiritual world, all we have experienced backwards gradually becomes ourself, our spiritual self-consciousness. We *are* now what we have experienced; we *are* our own spiritual worth corresponding thereto. With this existence, that really represents the other side of our earthly existence, we enter the world that contains nothing of the ordinary kingdoms of external Nature – mineral, plant and animal kingdoms – for these belong to the earth. But in that world there immediately come before us, first, the souls of those who have died before us and to whom we stood in some kind of relationship, and then the individualities of higher spiritual beings.

We live as spirit among human and non-human spirits, and this environment of spiritual individualities is now our world. The relationship of these spiritual individualities, human or non-human, to ourselves now constitutes our experience. As on earth we have our experience with the beings of the external kingdoms of Nature, so now, with spiritual beings of different ranks. And it is especially important that we have felt their sympathies and antipathies like spiritual rain – to use a metaphor – permeating these experiences during the retrospective part of the life between death and birth that I have described to you schematically. We now stand face to face with these beings of whom we previously perceived only their sympathies and antipathies while we were living through the spiritual counterpart of our earthly life: we live among these beings now that we have reached the spiritual world. We gradually feel as if inwardly permeated with force, with impulses proceeding from the spiritual beings around us. All that we have previously experienced now becomes more and more real to us, in a spiritual way. We gradually feel as if, to a certain extent, we are standing in the light or shadow of these beings in whom we are beginning to live. Before, through living through the spiritual worth corresponding to some earthly experience, we felt this or that about it, found it valuable or harmful to the cosmos. We now feel: there is something I have done on earth, in thought or deed; it has its corresponding spiritual worth, and this is engraved into the spiritual cosmos. The beings whom I now encounter can either do something with it, or not; it either lies in the direction of their evolution or of the evolution for which they are striving, or it does not. We feel ourselves placed before the beings of the spiritual world and realize that we have acted in accordance with their intentions or against them, have either added to, or subtracted from, what they willed for the evolution of the world.

Above all, it is no mere ideal judgement of ourselves that we feel, but a real evaluation; and this evaluation is itself the reality of our existence when we enter the spiritual world after death.

When you have done something wrong as a person in the physical world, you condemn it yourself if you have sufficient conscience and reason; or it is condemned by the law, or by the judge, or by other people who despise you for it. But you do not grow thin on this account – at least, not very thin, unless you are quite specially constituted. On entering the world of spiritual beings, however, we do not merely meet the ideal judgement that we are of little worth in respect of any fault or disgraceful deed we have committed; we feel the gaze of these beings resting upon us as if it would annihilate our very being. In respect of all we have done that is valuable, the gaze of these beings falls upon us as if we first attained thereby our full reality as psycho-spiritual beings. Our reality depends upon our value. Should we have hindered the evolution that was intended in the spiritual world, it is as if darkness were robbing us of our very existence. If we have done something in accordance with the evolution of the spiritual world, and its effects continue, it is as if light were calling us to fresh spiritual life. We experience all I have described and enter the realm of spiritual beings. This enhances our consciousness in the spiritual world and keeps us awake. Through all the demands made upon us there, we realize that we have won something in the universe in regard to our own reality.

Suppose we have done something that hinders the evolution of the world and can only arouse the antipathy of the spiritual beings whose realm we now enter. The after-effect takes its course as I have described and we feel our conscious-ness darken; stupefaction ensues, sometimes complete extinction of consciousness. We must now wake up again. On doing so, we feel in regard to our spiritual existence as if someone were cutting into our flesh in the physical world; but this experience in the spiritual is much more real, though it is real enough in the physical world. In short, what we are in the spiritual world proves to be the result of what we ourselves have initiated. You see from this that man has sufficient inducement to return again to earthly life.

Why to return? Well, through what he has engraved into the spiritual world man has himself experienced all he has done for good or ill in earthly life; and it is only by returning to earth that he can actually compensate for what, after all, he has only learnt to know through earthly experience. In fact, when he reads his value for the world in the countenances of these spiritual beings – to put it metaphorically – he is sufficiently impelled to return, when able, to the physical world, in order to live his life in a different way from before. Many incapacities for this he will still retain, and only after many lives on earth will full compensation really be possible.

If we look into ourselves during earthly life, we find, at first, memories. It is of these that, to begin with, we build our soul-life when we shut out the external world; and it is upon these alone that the creative imagination of the artist draws. That is the first form of memory. Behind it are the mighty 'pictures' which become perceptible immediately after we have passed through the Gate of Death. These are taken from us: they expand to the wide spaces of the universe. When we survey our memory-pictures we can say that there lives behind them something that at once proceeds towards the cosmic spaces when our body is taken from us. Through our body we hold together what is really seeking to become 'ideal' in the universe. But while we go through life and retain memories of our experiences, we leave behind in the world something that lies still further behind in the sequence of events than our memories. We leave it behind us in the course of time and must experience it again as we retrace our steps. This lies behind our memory as a third 'structure'. First, we have the tapestry of memory; behind it, the mighty cosmic pictures we have 'rolled up' within us; behind this, again, lives what we have written into the world. Not until we have lived through this are we really ourselves, standing naked in spirit before the spiritual universe which clothes us in its garments when we enter it.

We must, indeed, look at our memories if we want to get gradually beyond the transient life of man. Our earthly memories are transient and become dispersed through the universe. But our Self lives behind them: the Self that is given us again from out of the spiritual world that we may find our way from time to eternity.

III. Life between Death and a New Incarnation

Christiania (Oslo), 17 May 1923

IMMEDIATELY AFTER passing through the portal of death, the human being first experiences the withdrawing of his ideational world. The ideas, the powers of thought, become objects, become something like active forces spreading out into the universe. Thus man feels at first the withdrawal from him of all the experiences he has *consciously* undergone during his earth-life between birth and death. But whereas earth-life, as experienced through thinking, withdraws from the human being and goes out into the vast cosmos (a process that occurs a few days after death[5]), man's inner depths send forth a consciousness of all that he has undergone *unconsciously* during earth-life while asleep. This stage takes shape in such a way that he goes backward and recapitulates his earth-life in a period of one third of its actual duration.

During this time, the human being is intensely wrapped up in his own self. It might be said that he is still intensely connected with his own earthly affairs. He is thoroughly interwoven with what he passed through, while asleep, during the successive nights of his earthly life.

You will realize that the human being, while continuously occupied with his nightly experiences, must necessarily be led back to his self. Just consider the dreams, the only element in man's earth-life that surges up from the sleeping state. These dreams are the least part of his experiences while asleep. Everything else, however, remains unconscious. Only the dreams surge up into consciousness. Yet it could be said that the dreams, be they ever so interesting, ever so manifold, ever so rich in many-hued colours, represent something that restricts the human being completely to his own self. If a number of persons sleep in the same room, each of them has, nevertheless, his own dream world. And, when they tell their dreams to one another, these persons will speak of things that seem to have happened in entirely different worlds. For in sleep, each person is alone within himself. And only by inserting our will into our organism do we occupy the same world situated in the same space as is occupied by others. If we were always asleep, each of us would live in a world of his own.

But this world of our own which we pass through every night between falling asleep and awaking is the world we pass through in reverse, after death, during a period encompassing one third of our life-span.

If people possessed nothing but this world, they would be occupied for two or three decades after death (if they die at an old age) exclusively with themselves. This, however, is not the case. What we experience as our own affairs nevertheless connects us with the whole world. For the world through which each of us passes by himself is interwoven with relations to all those human beings with whom we were associated in life.

This interweaving of relations is caused by the fact that, when looking down from the soul world on the earthly experiences of those persons with whom we were associated in some way, we experience together with them what occurs on earth. Hence anyone willing to try may perceive, if he acquaints himself with spiritual-scientific methods,[6] how the dead, immediately after their transition, are helped to participate intensively in earthly events by those of their former companions who are still alive. And so we find that the dead, in the measure in which they shared this or that interest with others, underwent common destinies with others, remain connected with all these earthly interests; are still interested in earthly events. And, being no longer hindered by the physical body, they judge earthly events much more lucidly and sagaciously than people who are still alive. By attaining a conscious relation to the dead, we are enabled to gain, by means of their judgement, an extraordinary lucidity concerning earthly events.

Furthermore, something else must be considered. We can see that certain things existing within earthly relations will be preserved in the spiritual world. Thus an eternal element is intermingled, as it were, with our terrestrial experiences.

Descriptions of the spiritual world often sound almost absurd. Nonetheless, since I am addressing myself presumably to anthroposophists of long standing, I may venture to speak frankly of these matters. In looking for a way to communicate with the dead, it is even possible to use earthly words: ask questions and receive answers. And now a peculiar fact is to be noticed: the ability lost first by the dead is that of using nouns; whereas verbs are retained by them for a long time. Their favourite forms of expression, however, are exclamatory words; all that is connected with emotion and heart. An Oh!, an Ah!, as expressions of amazement, of surprise, and so forth, are often used by the dead in *their* language. We must, as it were, first learn the language of the dead.

These things are not at all as the spiritists imagine. These people believe that they can communicate with the dead, by means of a medium, in ordinary earthly language. The character of these communications immediately indicates that we are concerned here with subconscious states of living persons, and not with actual, direct utterances of the dead transmitted through a medium. For the dead outgrow ordinary human language by degrees. After the passing of several years, we can communicate with the dead only by acquiring their language – which can best be done by suggesting, through simple symbolic drawings, what we want to express. Then the answers will be given by means of similar symbolic forms necessarily received by us in shadowy outlines.

All this is described by me for the purpose of indicating that the dead, although dwelling in an element akin to sleep, yet have a vast range of interests and sweep the whole world with their glance. And we ourselves can greatly assist them. This may be done by thinking of the dead as vividly as possible; especially by sending thoughts to them which bring to life, in the most striking way, what we experienced in their company. Abstract concepts are not understood by the dead. Hence I must send out such thoughts as the following: here is the road between Christiania and a nearby place. Here we two walked together. The other person, who is now dead, walked at my side. I can still hear him speaking. I hear the sound of his voice. I try to recall how he moved his arms, how he moved his head. By visualizing, as vividly as possible, what we experienced together with the dead; by sending out our thoughts to the dead whom we conjure up before our soul in a familiar image, we can make these thoughts, as it were, soar or stream towards the dead. Thus we provide the dead with something like a window through which they can look at the world. Not only the thought sent by us to the dead comes forth within them, but a whole world. They can gaze at our world as if through a window.

Conversely, the dead can experience their present spiritual environment only to the degree in which they formerly reflected, as much as earthly people are capable of doing, on the spiritual world.

You know how many people are saying nowadays: why should I worry about life after death? We might as well wait. Once we are dead, we shall see what is going to happen. This thought, however, is completely misleading. People who have not reflected, while still alive, on the spiritual world, who have lived in a purely materialistic way, will see absolutely nothing after death.

Here I have outlined to you how the dead are living during the period in which – commensurate with their experiences in the sleeping state – they pass through their life in reverse. The human being who has now discarded his physical and etheric body feels himself to be at this time in the realm of spiritual moon forces. We must realize that all the world organisms – moon, sun and stars – inasmuch as they are visible to physical eyes, actually represent only physical formations of a spiritual element.

Just as the single human being, who is sitting here on a chair, consists not only of flesh and blood (which can be regarded as matter), but also of soul and spirit, so the whole universe, the whole cosmos, is indwelled by soul and spirit. And not only one unified spiritual entity dwells therein, but many, innumerably many spiritual entities dwell therein. Thus numerous spiritual entities are connected with the moon, which is seen only externally as a silver disc by our physical eye. We are in the realm of these entities while retracing our earth-life, as has been described, until we arrive again at the starting point. Thus it might be said: until then we dwell in the realm of the moon.

While we are in the midst of this going backward, our whole life becomes intermingled with certain things, which are brought to an approximate conclusion after we have left the moon realm.

Immediately after the etheric body has been discarded by us in the wake of death, a moral judgement on our worth as human beings emerges from the nightly experiences. Then we cannot do otherwise than judge, in a moral sense, the events through which we pass in reverse. And it is very strange how things develop from this point.

Here on earth we carry a body made of bones, muscles, arteries and so forth. Then, after death, we acquire a spiritual body, formed out of our moral qualities. A good person acquires a moral body radiating with beauty; a depraved person a moral body radiating with evil. This is formed while we are living backward. Our spirit-body, however, is only partly formed out of that which is now joined to us. Whereas one part of the spirit-body received by us in the spiritual world is formed out of our moral qualities, the other part is simply put on us as a garment woven from the substances of the spiritual world.

Now, after finishing our reverse course and arriving again

at the starting-point, we must find the transition to which I alluded in my *Theosophy* as the transition from the soul world into the spirit realm. This is connected with the necessity of leaving the moon-sphere and entering the sun-sphere of the cosmos. We become gradually acquainted with the all-encompassing entities dwelling, in the form of spirit and soul, within the sun-sphere. This we must enter. In the next few days I shall discuss to what degree the Christ plays a leading role in helping the human being to make this transition from the moon-sphere to the sun-sphere. (This role is different *after* the Mystery of Golgotha from the role He played before the Mystery of Golgotha.) Today we shall describe the passage through this world in a more objective way. What ensues at this point is the necessity of depositing in the moon-sphere all that was woven for us, as it were, out of our moral qualities. This represents something like a small package, which we must deposit in the moon-sphere in order that we may enter, as *purely spiritual* beings, into the pure sun-sphere. Then we see the sun in its real aspect: not from the side turned towards earth but from the *reverse* side, where it is completely filled with spiritual entities; where we can fully see that it is a spiritual realm.

It is here that we give as nourishment to the universe everything that does not belong to our moral qualities, but which has been granted to us by the gods in the form of earthly experiences. We give to the universe whatever it can use for maintaining the world's course. These things are actually true. If I compared the universe to a machine – you know that I do this merely in a pictorial sense, for I am certainly not inclined to designate the universe a machine – then everything brought by us into the sun-sphere after depositing our small package in the moon-sphere would be something like fuel, apportioned by us to the cosmos as fuel is apportioned to a machine.

Thus we enter the realm of the spiritual world. For it does

not matter whether we call our new abode the sun-sphere, in its spiritual aspect, or the spiritual world.

Here we dwell as a spirit among spirits, just as we dwelt on earth as a physical person among the entities of the various natural kingdoms. Now we dwell among those entities which I described and named in my *Occult Science;* and we also dwell among those souls which have died *before* us, or are still awaiting their *coming* earth-life. For we are dwelling as a spirit among spirits.

These spiritual entities may belong to the higher Hierarchies or be incorporeal human beings dwelling in the spiritual world. And now the question arises: what is our next stage?

Here on earth we stand at a certain point of the physical universe. Looking around in every direction we see what lies *outside* the human being. That which lies *inside* him we are utterly unable to see.

Now you will say: what you tell us is foolish. It may be granted that ordinary people cannot see man's inside; but the learned anatomists, who cut up dead people in hospitals, are certainly familiar with it. They are not familiar with it in the least! For what can be learned about a person in this way is only something external. After all, if we regard a human being merely from the outside, it does not matter whether we investigate his outer skin or his insides. What lies inside the human skin is not that which anatomists discover in an external way, but what lies inside the human skin are whole worlds. In the human lung, for instance, in every human organ, whole universes are compressed to miniature forms.

We see marvellous sights when admiring a beautiful landscape; marvellous sights when admiring at night the starry sky in all its splendour. Yet if viewing a human lung, a human liver, not with the anatomist's physical eye but with the eye of the spirit, we see whole *worlds* compressed into a small space. Apart from the splendour and glory of all the rivers and mountains on the surface of the earth, a still more exalted splendour adorns what lies inside man's skin, even in its merely physical aspect. It is

irrelevant that all this is of smaller scale than the seemingly vast
world of space. If you survey what lies in a single pulmonary
vesicle, it will appear as more grandiose than the whole range of
the mighty Alps. For what lies inside man is the whole spiritual
cosmos in condensed form. In man's inner organism we have an
image of the entire cosmos.

We can visualize these things also in a somewhat different
way. Imagine that you are thirty years old and, looking into
yourself with a glance of the soul, remember something which
you experienced between your tenth and twentieth years.
Here the outer event has been transformed into an inner soul-
image. In a single moment, you may survey widely spread
experiences undergone by you in the course of years. A world
has been woven into an ideational image. Only think of what
you experience when brief memory-images of widely spread
events passed through by you come forth in your soul-life.
Here you have the soul-essence of what you experienced on
earth. Now, if viewing your brain, the inside of your eye – the
inside of the eye alone represents a whole world – your lung,
your other organs in the same way as your memory-images,
then these organs are not images of events passed through by
you but images – even if appearing in material form – of the
whole spiritual cosmos.

Let us suppose that man could solve the riddle of what is
contained in his brain, in the inside of his eye, in the inside of
his lung, just as he can solve the riddle of the memories
contained in his soul-life. Then the whole spiritual cosmos
would be opened up to him, just as a series of events
undergone in life are opened up to man by a single memory-
image. As human beings, we incorporate the whole memory
of the world. If you consider these things in the right way, you
will understand the following: the human being, who has
undergone after death all the states described by me previously, now becomes manifest to the vision of man himself.
The human being is a spirit among spirits; yet what he sees
now as his world is the marvel of the human organism itself

in the form of the universe, the whole cosmos. Just as mountains, rivers, stars and clouds form our surroundings here on earth, so, when dwelling as spirit among spirits, we find our surroundings, our world, in man's wonderful organism. We look around in the spiritual world; we look – if I may express myself pictorially – to the right and to the left. As here we found rocks, river, mountains on all sides, so there above we find the human being, MAN, on all sides. Man is the world. And we are working for this world which is fundamentally man. Just as, on earth, we build machines, keep books, sew clothes, make shoes or write books, thus weaving together what is called the content of civilization, of culture, so above, together with the spirits of the higher Hierarchies and incorporeal human beings, we weave the woof and weft of mankind. We weave mankind out of the cosmos. Here on earth we appear as finished products. There we lay down the spiritual germ of earthly man.

This is the great mystery: that man's heavenly occupation consists in weaving, in co-operation with the spirits of the higher Hierarchies, the great spiritual germ of the future terrestrial human being. Inside the spiritual cosmos, all of us are weaving, in magnificent spiritual grandeur, the woof and weft of our own earthly existence, which will be attained by us after descending again into earthly life. Our work, performed in co-operation with the gods, is the fashioning of the earthly human being.

When we speak of germs here on earth, we think of something small which becomes big. If we speak, however, of the germ of the physical human being as it exists in the spiritual world – for the physical germ maturing in the mother's body is only an image of the spiritual germ – we must think of it as immense, enormous. It is a universe, and all other human beings are interlinked with this universe. It might be said: all human beings are in the same 'place' yet numerically differentiated. And then the spiritual germ diminishes more and more. What we undergo in the time between death and a new birth is the experience of fashioning a spiritual germ, as large as the universe, of our coming earthly existence. Then this spiritual germ begins to shrink. More and more its essence becomes convoluted. Finally it produces its own image in the mother's body.

Materialistic physiology has entirely wrong conceptions of these things. It assumes that man, whose marvellous form I have tried to sketch for you, came forth from a merely physical human germ. This science considers the ovum to be a highly complicated matter; and physiological chemists investigate the fact that molecules or atoms, becoming more and more complicated, produce the germ, the most complicated phenomenon of all.

All this, however, is not true. In reality, the ovum consists of chaotic matter. Matter, when transformed into a germ, is dissolved; it becomes completely pulverized. The nature of the physical germ, and the human germ particularly, is characterized by being composed of completely pulverized matter, which wants nothing for itself.

Because this matter is completely pulverized and wants nothing for itself, it enables the *spiritual germ,* which has been prepared for a long time, to enter into it. And this pulverization of the physical germ is brought about by conception. Physical matter is completely destroyed in order that the spiritual germ may be sunk into it and make the physical matter into an image of the spiritual germ woven out of the cosmos.

It is doubtless justified to sing the praises of all that human beings are doing for civilization, for culture, on earth. Far from condemning this singing of praises, I declare myself, once and for all, in favour of it when it is done in a reasonable way. But a much more encompassing, a much more exalted, a much more magnificent work than all earthly cultural activity is performed by heavenly civilization, as it might be called, between death and a new birth: the spiritual preparation, the spiritual weaving, of the human body. For nothing more exalted exists in the world order than the weaving of the human being out of the world's ingredients. With the help of the gods, the human being is woven during the important period between death and a new birth.

If yesterday I had to say that, in a certain sense, all the experience and knowledge acquired by us on earth provide nourishment for the cosmos, it must be said again today: after offering to the cosmos, as nourishment or fuel, all the earthly experiences that could be of use to it, we receive, from the fullness of the cosmos, all the substances out of which we are able to weave again the new human being into whom we shall enter at a later time.

The human being, now devoting himself wholly to a spiritual world, lives as a spirit. His entire weaving and being is spiritual work, spiritual essence. This stage lasts for a long time. For it must be repeated again and again: to weave something like the human being is a mighty and grandiose task. Not without justification did the ancient Mysteries call the human physical body a temple. The greater the insight we gain into the science of initiation, into what takes place between death and a new birth, the deeper do we feel the significance of this word. Our life between death and a new birth is of such a nature that we, as spiritual beings, become directly aware of other spiritual beings. This condition lasts for some time. Then a new stage sets in.

What took place previously was of such a nature that the single spiritual beings could really be viewed as individualities. The spiritual beings with whom one worked were met face to face, as it were. At a later stage, however, these spiritual entities – to express it pictorially, because such things can be suggested only in images – become less and less distinct, finally being merged into an aggregation of spirits. This can be expressed in the following way: a certain period between death and a new birth is spent in immediate proximity to spiritual beings. Then comes a time when one experiences only the revelation of these spiritual beings, when they become manifest to us as a whole. I want to use a very trivial metaphor. On seeing what seems to be a tiny grey cloud in the distance, you would be sure that this was just a tiny grey cloud. But, by coming closer, you would recognize it to be a swarm of flies. Now you can see each single fly. In the case of the spiritual beings, the opposite takes place. First you behold the divine-spiritual beings, with whom you are working, as single individualities. Then, after living with them more intensively, you behold their general spiritual atmosphere, just as you beheld the swarm of flies in the shape of a cloud. Here, where the single individualities disappear more and more, you live – I might say – in pantheistic fashion in the midst of a general spiritual world.

Although we live now in a general spiritual world, we feel arising out of our inner depth a stronger sense of self-consciousness than we experienced before. Formerly your self was constituted in such a way that you seemed to be at one with the spiritual world, which you experienced by means of its individualities. Now you perceive the spiritual world only as a general spiritual atmosphere. Your own self-conscious-ness, however, is perceived in greater degree. It awakens with heightened intensity. And thus, slowly and gradually, the desire to return to earth again arises in the human being. This desire must be described in the following way:

During the entire period which I have described and which lasts for centuries, the human being – except in the first stage when he was still connected with the earth and returned to his starting point – is fundamentally interested in nothing but the spiritual world. He weaves, in the large scale that I have described, the fabric of mankind.

At the moment when the individualities of the spiritual world are merged together, as it were, and man perceives the spiritual world in a general way, there arises in him a renewed interest in earth-life. This interest for earth-life appears in a certain specialized manner, in a certain concrete manner. The human beings begin to be interested in definite persons living below on earth, and again in their children, and again in their children's children. Whereas the human beings were formerly interested only in heavenly events, they now become, after beholding the spiritual world as a revelation, strangely interested in certain successive generations. These are the generations leading to our own parents, who will bear us on our return to earth. Yet we are interested, a long time before, in our parents' ancestors. We follow the line of generations until reaching our parents. Not only do we follow each generation as it passes through time, but – once the spiritual world has been manifested to us as a revelation – we also foresee, as if prophetically, the whole span of generations. Across the succession of great-great-great-grandfathers, great-great-grandfathers, great-grand-fathers, grandfathers, and so forth, we can foresee the path on which we shall descend again to earth. Having first grown into the cosmos, we grow later into real, concrete human history. And thus comes the moment when we gradually (in regard to our consciousness) leave the sun-sphere.

Of course, we still remain within the sun-sphere; but the distinct, clear, conscious relation to it becomes dim and we are drawn back into the moon-sphere. And here, in the moon-sphere, we find the 'small package' deposited by us (I can describe it only by means of this image); we find again what represents the worth of our moral qualities. And this package must be retrieved.

It will be seen in the course of the next days what a significant part is played in this connection by the Christ-impulse. We must embody within us this package of destiny. But while embodying within us the package of destiny and entering the moon-sphere, while gaining a stronger and stronger feeling of self-consciousness and transforming ourselves inwardly more and more into soul-beings, we gradually lose the tissue woven by us of our physical body. The spiritual germ woven by ourselves is lost at the moment when the physical germ, which we shall have to assume on earth, is engendered through the act of conception.

The spiritual germ of the physical body has already descended to earth, whereas we still dwell in the spiritual world. And now a vehement feeling of bereavement sets in. We have lost the spiritual germ of the physical body. This has already arrived below and united itself with the last of those successive generations which we have watched. We ourselves, however, are still above. The feeling of bereavement becomes violent. And now this feeling of bereavement draws out of the universe the needful ingredients of the world-ether. Having sent the spiritual germ of the physical body down to earth and remained behind as a soul (ego and astral body), we draw etheric substance out of the world-ether and form our own etheric body. And to this etheric body, formed by ourselves, is joined – approximately three weeks after the fecundation has taken place on earth – the physical germ which formed itself out of the spiritual germ, as I have previously described.

It was said that we form our etheric body before uniting ourselves with our own physical germ, and into this etheric body is woven the small package containing our moral worth. We weave this package into our ego, our astral body, and also into our etheric body. Thus it is joined to the physical body. In this way we bring our karma down to earth. First it was left behind in the moon sphere; for, had we taken it with us into the sun-sphere, we would have formed a diseased, a disfigured physical body.

The human physical body acquires individuality only through the circumstance of its being permeated by the etheric body. Otherwise, all physical bodies would be exactly alike; for human beings, while dwelling in the spiritual world, weave identical spiritual germs for their physical body. We become individualities only by means of our karma, by means of the small package interwoven by us with our etheric body which shapes, constitutes and pervades our physical body already during the embryonic stage.

Of course, I shall have to enlarge during the next days on

this sketch concerning the human being's transition between death and a new birth. Yet you will have realized what a wealth of experiences is undergone by us: the great experience of how we are first merged into the cosmos and then, out of the cosmos, again are shaped in order to attain a new human earth-life.

Fundamentally, we pass through three stages. First, we dwell as spirit-soul among spirit-souls. This is a *genuine experiencing* of the spiritual world. Secondly, we are given a *revelation* of the spiritual world. The individualities of the single spiritual entities become blurred as it were. The spiritual world is revealed to us as a whole. Now we approach again the moon-sphere. Within ourselves the feeling of self-consciousness awakens; this is a preparation for earthly self-consciousness. Whereas we did not desire earth-life while being conscious of our spiritual self within the spiritual world, we now begin, during the period of revelation, to desire earth-life and develop a vigorous self-consciousness directed towards the earth.

In the third stage we enter the moon-sphere and, having yielded our spiritual germ to the physical world, draw together out of all the heavenly worlds the etheric substance needed for our own etheric body. Three successive stages: *a genuine life within the spiritual world; a life amid the revelations of the spiritual world, in which we feel ourselves already as an egoistic self; a life devoted to the drawing together of the world ether.*

The counterparts of these stages are produced after the human being has moved again into his physical body. These counterparts are of a most surprising nature. We see the child. We see it before us in its physical body. The child develops. This development of the child is the most wonderful thing to behold in the physical world. We see how it first crawls, and then assumes a state of balance with regard to the world. We observe how the child learns to walk. Immeasurably great things are connected with this learning to walk. It represents an entrance of the child's whole being into the state of equilibrium of the world. It represents a genuine orientation of the whole cosmos towards the world's three spatial dimensions. And the child's wonderful achievement consists in the fact that it finds the correct human state of equilibrium within the world.

These things are a modest, terrestrial counterpart of all that the human being, while dwelling as a spirit among spirits, underwent in the course of long centuries. We feel great reverence for the world if we look at it in such wise that we observe a child: how it first kicks its limbs awkwardly in every direction, then gradually learns to control itself. This is the after-effect of the movements which we executed, during centuries, as a spiritual being among spiritual beings. It is really wonderful to discover in the child's single movements, in its search for a state of equilibrium, the terrestrial after-effects of those heavenly movements executed, in a purely spiritual sense, as spirit among spirits.

Every child – unless some abnormal condition changes the sequence – should first learn to walk (attain a state of equilibrium) and then learn to speak.

Now again the child, by an imitative process, adjusts itself through the use of language to its environment. But in every sound, every word formation shaping itself in the child, we find a modest, terrestrial echo of the experience undergone by us when our knowledge of the spiritual world becomes revelation; when this knowledge is compressed, as it were, into a uniform haze. Then the World Logos is formed out of the world's single being, which we experienced previously in an individualized way. And when the child utters one word after the other, this is the audible terrestrial counterpart of a marvellous world tableau experienced by us during the time of revelation before we return again to the moon-sphere.

And when the child, having learned to walk and speak, gradually develops its thoughts – for learning to think should be the third step in a normal human development – this is a counterpart of the work performed by man while forming his own etheric body out of the world ether gathered from every part of the universe.

Thus, in looking at the child as it enters the world, we see in the three modest faculties needed to gain a dynamic static relationship to the world – learning to maintain equilibrium (what we call learning to walk), learning to speak, learning to think – the compressed, modest, terrestrial counterparts of that which, spread out into grandiose cosmic dimensions, represents the stages passed through by us between death and a new birth.

Only by gaining a knowledge of the spiritual life between death and a new birth, do we gain a knowledge of the mystery coming forth from man's innermost depth when the child, having been born in a uniform state, becomes increasingly differentiated. Hence, by pointing to every single being as a revelation of the divine, we learn to understand the world as a revelation of the divine.

IV. Our Experiences during the Night and the Life after Death

Christiania (Oslo), 18 May 1923

YESTERDAY WE had to speak of the path pursued by man between death and a new birth; and the whole gist of my remarks will have shown you that every night during sleep we must return to the starting-point of our earth-life.

We can indeed gain insight into these significant matters if we realize that on sinking into slumber we do not stand still at the date reached in the course of our earthly existence (as was already explained in the previous lectures), but that we actually go back to our starting-point. Every time, during sleep, we are carried back to our childhood, and even to the state before our childhood, before our arrival on earth. Hence, while we are asleep, our ego and our astral body return to the spiritual world, to the world of our origin which we left in order to become earth people.

At this point of our discourse, it becomes necessary to let pass before our soul in greater detail what the human being undergoes while asleep; undergoes unconsciously, but, none-theless, most vividly.

The duration of our sleep does not really matter. Although it is difficult for our ordinary consciousness to conceive of the fact that time and space conditions are utterly different in the spiritual world, we must learn to form conceptions of such a kind.

I have already said that the human being, when suddenly awakened after he has fallen asleep and hence lost conscious-ness, experiences during that brief moment whatever he would have experienced had his sleep continued for a long time. In measuring the length of our sleep according to its physical duration, we take into account only our physical body and our etheric body. Utterly different time-conditions prevail for that which is undergone by our ego and astral body. Hence the things that I shall presently explain to you are valid for either a long or a short sleep.

When the human personality enters the realm of sleep with his soul, the first state experienced by him – all this takes place in the unconscious, yet with great vividness – engenders a feeling in him of dwelling, as it were, in a general world ether. (In speaking of feeling, I mean an unconscious feeling. It is impossible to express these matters otherwise than by terms used in ordinary conscious life.) The person feels himself, as it were, disseminated into the whole cosmos. We cease to have the definite perceptions that formerly connected us with all the things surrounding us in our earthly existence. At first, we take part in the general weaving and surging of the cosmos, and this is accompanied by the feeling that our souls have their being in a bottomless element. Hence the soul, while existing in this bottomless element, has an ardent desire for divine support. Thus we experience every evening, when falling asleep, the religious need of having the whole world permeated by an all-encompassing divine-spiritual element. This is our real experience when falling asleep.

Our whole constitution as human beings enables us to transfer this desire for the divine into our waking life. Day in and day out, we are indebted to our nightly experiences for renewing our religious needs.

Thus only a contemplation of our entire being enables us to gain insight into the various life-experiences undergone by us. Fundamentally, we live very thoughtlessly if we take into account only the conscious life passed between morning and evening; for many night experiences are interwoven with this. The human being does not always realize whence he derives his living religious need. He derives it from the general experiences undergone by him every night just after having fallen asleep – and also, although perhaps less intensively, during an afternoon nap.

Then, in our sleep, another stage sets in – all this, as was said before, being passed through unconsciously, but nonetheless vividly. Now it does not seem to the sleeper that his soul is, as it were, disseminated into the general cosmos, but it seems as if the single parts of his entity were divided. Were our experiences to become conscious, we would feel as though we were being disjointed. And, from the bottom of our soul, an unconscious fear rises up. Every night, while asleep, we experience the fear of being divided up into the whole universe.

Now you might say: what does all this matter, as long as we know nothing about it? Well, it matters a great deal. I should like to explain, by means of a comparison, how much it matters.

Suppose that we become frightened in ordinary daily life. We turn pale. The emotion of fear is consciously felt by the soul. A definite change in our organism makes us turn pale. The blood streams back into the body's interior. This is an objective process. We can describe the emotion of fear in connection with an objective process taking place, in daily conscious life, within the physical body. What we experience in our soul is, as it were, a mirrored image reflecting this streaming away of the blood from the body's surface to its inner parts. Thus an objective process corresponds, in the waking state, to the emotion of fear. When we are asleep, a similar objective process, wholly independent of our consciousness, occurs in our astral body.

Anyone able to form imaginative and inspired conceptions will experience this objective process in the astral body as an emotion of fear. The *objective* element in fear, however, is actually experienced by man every night, because he feels himself being divided into parts inside his soul. And how is he being divided? Every night he is divided among the universe of stars. One part of his soul substance is striving towards Mercury, another part towards Jupiter, and so forth. Yet this process can only be correctly characterized by saying: during ordinary sleep we do not *actually* penetrate the worlds of stars, as is the case on the path between death and a new birth. What we really undergo every night is not an actual division among the stars, but only among the *counterparts* of the stars which we carry within us during our entire earth life. While asleep, we are divided among the *counterparts* of Mercury, Venus, moon, sun, and so forth. Thus we are concerned here not with the original stars themselves but with their counterparts in us.

This emotion of fear, experienced by us relatively soon after falling asleep, can be removed only from that human being who feels a genuine kinship to the Christ. At this point, we become aware how much the human being needs this kinship with the Christ. In speaking of this kinship, it is necessary to envisage man's evolution on earth. Mankind's evolution on earth can be comprehended only by someone having real insight into the significant turning point brought to human evolution by the Mystery of Golgotha. It is a fact that the human beings before the Mystery of Golgotha were different with regard to soul and spirit from the human beings after the Mystery of Golgotha had occurred on earth. This must be taken into account if man's soul is to be viewed in its true light.

When the human beings who lived before the Mystery of Golgotha – and these human beings were actually we ourselves in a former life – fell asleep and experienced the fear of which I have just spoken, then the counterpart of the Christ in the world of stars existed for the human beings of that time as much as did the counterparts of the other heavenly bodies. And as the Christ approached the sleeping human being, He came as a helper to dissipate fear, to destroy fear. People of earlier ages, still gifted with instinctive clairvoyance, remembered after awaking, in a dream-like consciousness, that the Christ had been with them in their sleep. Only they did not call Him the Christ. They called Him the Sun-spirit. Yet these people, who lived before the Mystery of Golgotha, avowed from their innermost depth that the great Sun-spirit was also the great guide and helper of the human being, who approached him every night in sleep and relieved him of the fear of being disseminated into the universe. The Christ appeared as a spirit strengthening mankind and consolidating its inner life.

Who binds together man's forces during his life? asked the followers of ancient religions. It is the great Sun-spirit, who firmly binds together man's single elements and combines them into one personality. And this avowal was uttered by the followers of ancient religions, because their consciousness was pervaded by the memory that the Christ approached man every night.

We do not need to be amazed at these things. In those ancient times, when the human being was still capable of instinctive clairvoyance, he could look back at significant moments of his life into the period passed through by him before his soul and spirit descended to earth and was clothed in a physical body. Thus it seemed quite natural to the human being that he could look upward into a pre-earthly existence.

But is it not a fact that – as we explained before – every period of sleep carries us back into pre-earthly existence, into an existence preceding the stage before we became a truly conscious child? This question must be answered in the affirmative. And just as human beings knew that they had been together, in their pre-earthly existence, with the exalted Sun-spirit who had given them the strength to pass through death as immortal beings, so they also consciously remembered after every sleep that the exalted Sun-spirit had stood at their side, helping them to become real human beings, integrated personalities.

The human soul, while acquainting itself with the world of planets, passes through this stage during sleep. It is as if the soul were first dispersed among the counterparts of the planets, and then united and held together by the Christ.

Consider that this whole soul-experience during sleep has changed, with regard to the human being, since the Mystery of Golgotha. For the Mystery of Golgotha has originated the unfolding of a vigorous human ego-consciousness. This ego-consciousness, pervading human culture only gradually after the Mystery of Golgotha, became especially apparent after the first third of the fifteenth century. And the same vigorous ego-consciousness, which enables the human being to place himself as a free, fully self-conscious being into the sense world, this same consciousness – as though trying to maintain equilibrium – also darkens his retrospect into pre-earthly existence, darkens his conscious memory of the helping Christ, who stood at his side during sleep.

It is remarkable that, since the Mystery of Golgotha, human evolution has taken the following course: on the one hand, man acquired a vigorous ego-consciousness in his waking state; on the other hand, utter darkness gradually overlaid that which had formerly radiated out of sleep-consciousness. Therefore human beings are obliged, since the Mystery of Golgotha, to establish a conscious relationship to Christ Jesus while they are awake. They must acquire, in a conscious way, a comprehension of what the Mystery of Golgotha really signifies: that, by means of the Mystery of Golgotha, the exalted Sun-spirit, Christ, descended to earth, became a human being in the body of Jesus of Nazareth, passed through earth-life and death, and, after death, still taught His disciples who were permitted to behold Him in His etheric body after death.

Those personalities who acquire, in the time following the Mystery of Golgotha, a waking consciousness of their kinship with the Christ, and gain a living conception of what took place through the Mystery of Golgotha: to these the possibility will be given of being helped by the Christ impulse, as it is carried from their waking state into their sleep.

This shows us how differently human sleep was constituted before and after the Mystery of Golgotha. Before the Mystery of Golgotha, the Christ invariably appeared as Helper while the human being slept. Man could remember even after awaking that the Christ had been with him during his sleep. After the Mystery of Golgotha, however, he would be utterly bereft of the Christ's help, if he were not to establish a conscious relation with the Christ during the day while awake and carry its echo, its after-effect, into his sleep. Only in this way can the Christ help him to maintain his personality while asleep.

What the human being had received unconsciously from the wide heavenly reaches before the Mystery of Golgotha, the help of the Christ, the human soul must now acquire gradually by establishing a conscious relation with the Mystery of Golgotha. This inner soul-responsibility has been laid upon the human being since the Mystery of Golgotha. Thus we are unable to study the nature of human sleep unless we are able to envisage the immense transformation undergone by human sleep since the Mystery of Golgotha.

When we enter the realm of sleep, our whole world becomes different from that experienced in the waking state. How do we live as physical people while awake? We are confined, through our physical body, by natural laws. The laws working outside in nature are also working within us. That which we recognize as moral responsibilities and impulses, as moral world order, stands like an abstract world amidst the laws of nature. And because present-day natural science takes into account only the waking world, it is completely ignorant of the moral world.

Thus natural science tells us – although hypothetically, yet in conformity with its principles – that the Kant-Laplace primeval fog marked the starting-point of world evolution; and that this world evolution will be terminated through a state of heat which will kill all living things and bury them, as it were, in a huge cosmic cemetery. (These conceptions have been modified, but still prevail among natural scientists.) Natural science, in describing the evolution of the cosmos, begins and ends with a physical state. Here the moral world order appears as a stranger. The human being, however, would not be aware of his dignity, would not even experience himself as a human being, unless he experienced himself as a moral being. But what moral impulses could be found in the

Kant-Laplace primeval fog? Here were nothing but physical laws. Will there be moral impulses when the earth shall perish from heat? Then, also, nothing but physical laws will prevail. Thus speaks natural science. And out of the natural process germinate all living things, and out of living things the human soul-element. The human being forms certain conceptions: one should act in a certain way or one should not act in that way. He experiences a moral world order. But this cannot be nurtured by natural law. To the waking human being, the moral world order appears like a merely abstract world amid the rigid, massive world of natural laws.

It is entirely different when imaginative, inspirative, and intuitive consciousness passes through that which the human being, between falling asleep and awaking, experiences in his ego and astral body. Here the moral world order appears real, whereas the natural order below appears like something abstract, something dreamlike. Although it is difficult to conceive of these things, they are nonetheless true. The whole world has been turned upside down. To the sleeper acquiring clairvoyance in his sleep, the moral world order would seem something real, something secure, and the physical world order of natural laws would seem to sink below, not rise above, the moral world order. And if the sleeper possessed consciousness, he would not place the Kant-Laplace theory at the starting-point of world evolution, and the death through heat at its end. At the starting-point, he would recognize the world of spiritual Hierarchies – all the spirit and soul beings who lead man into existence. At the end of world evolution, he would again recognize the spirit and soul beings who extend to man who has passed through the course of evolution a welcome to enter their community. And below, as an illusion, the abstract physical world order would have its welling and streaming existence. If you were gifted with clairvoyance in the very midst between falling asleep and awaking you would view all the natural laws of which you have learned during the day as a mirage of dreams, dreamed by the earth. It would be the moral world order which would give you a firm ground, and this moral world order could be experienced by us if we worked our way – after having received the help of the Christ – into the peace of the fixed stars in the firmament, seen by us again, during nightly sleep, in the form of their counterparts. Soaring upward to the fixed stars, to their counterparts, we look down into the physical realm of natural law.

This is the wholly divergent form of the experiences undergone by the human being between falling asleep and awaking, leading his soul every night into the image of the cosmos. And just as the human being is led at a certain moment between death and a new birth, as I explained yesterday, by the moon forces into earthly existence and is beset by a sort of longing for earthly existence, so is he beset by the longing, after experiencing heavenly existence in his sleep, to immerse himself again into his physical body and etheric body.

While we get accustomed to earth-life after our birth, we live in a sort of sleep and dream state. If we, disregarding our dreams, look back in the morning, after being awake for an hour, to the moment of awaking, our consciousness is halted abruptly and we see behind us the darkness of slumber. It is similar when we look back into our childhood. In our fourth or the fifth year, sometimes earlier, sometimes later, our consciousness comes to a stop. Beyond the last stage that we can still remember lies something which is as deeply immersed in the darkness of the sleep and dream life of early childhood as is the life of the human soul immersed every night in the darkness of sleep. Yet the child is not wholly asleep, but is wrapped in a sort of waking dream. During this waking dream occur the three important phases of human life which I indicated yesterday. As they occur in the sequence characterized by me, we can see in them echoes and after-effects of the life between death and a new birth. First the child learns, out of a life wrapped in dream and sleep, what we call simply *learning how to walk.*

Something all-encompassing happens when a child learns how to walk, something which appears as a grandiose and overwhelming process to anyone able to perceive how the subtlest parts of the human body are changed at this time. The child, by adapting himself to the relationships of gravity, learns how to attain equilibrium. The child no longer falls down. By unfolding inner forces, he conforms to spatial directions.

What if we had to do all this *consciously:* overcome the lack of equilibrium that pulled us to the ground, adapt our organism to a firm state of equilibrium with regard to the three spatial directions, and even maintain this state of equilibrium by swinging our legs like pendulums as we learn how to walk? The child, in performing such a grandiose mechanical task, performs it as an echo of what he experienced while dwelling among spirits between death and a new birth. Here we encounter something so comprehensive, so marvellous, that the most eminent engineer, with all his earthly scientific equipment, could not calculate how the child's human forces adapt themselves to the world's spatial connections. What we, as a child, attain unconsciously is the most miraculous unfolding of mathematical-mechanical, physical forces. We call it simply learning how to walk. Yet in this learning how to walk lies an element of utmost grandeur.

Simultaneously, the correct use of arms and hands is attained. And by placing himself, as physical being, within the three spatial directions, the human being receives the foundation for all that is called *learning how to talk.*

The only thing known to physiology about the connection between man's dynamics of walking and standing and the faculty of speech is the fact that the speech-centre of right-handed persons lies in the left portion of the brain. The gestures of the right hand, vigorously executed by means of man's will-power, are led, by some mysterious process, into the interior of the brain whence the faculty of speech is brought to the human being.

More, however, exists than this connection between the right hand and the third convolution at the left, the so-called Broca cerebral convolution. The whole mobility of arms and fingers; the human being's whole ability to move and maintain equilibrium reaches up into the brain, becomes part of the brain, and thence reaches down into the larynx. Language develops out of walking, out of the grasping of objects, out of gestures flowing from the organs of movement.

Anyone viewing these things correctly will know that a child with the tendency to walk on his toes speaks differently from a child walking on his heels, employs different shadings of sound. The organism of speaking develops from the organism of walking and moving. And speech is again a counterpart of that which I described yesterday as the outpouring of revelation upon the human being passing through the stage between death and a new birth. The child, when learning how to speak, does not grasp the words with his thoughts, but alone with his emotions. He lives in the language as if it were an emotional element; and a child of normal development learns conceptual thinking only *after* acquiring the faculty of speech. A child's thoughts actually develop out of the words. Just as walking and the grasping of objects, the gestures of legs and hands, reach up into the speech organism, so all that lives in the speech organism and is gained through adaptation to the language of the surrounding world reaches up into the thought-organs. In the third stage, the child learns how *to think*.

While encompassed by this dream and sleep state, the child passes through three stages: walking, speaking and thinking. These are the three terrestrial counterparts of that which we experienced between death and a new birth: living contact with the spiritual world, revelation of the spiritual world, and the gathering of the world ether in order to form our etheric body.

The child's development during these three stages can be correctly estimated only by someone observing the adult human being during his sleep. Here we can observe how we, when sleep puts a stop to our thoughts – for our thoughts are silenced by sleep – let our thought-forces be nurtured, between falling asleep and awaking, by those beings known to us as Angels, as Angeloi. These beings, approaching us during sleep, nurture our thought-forces while we cannot do so ourselves.

During sleep, the human being also ceases to talk. Only in abnormal cases, which could be explained, does he talk in his sleep. At present, however, we may disregard these things. The normal human being ceases to talk after going to sleep. Would it not be altogether too dreadful if people kept on chattering while asleep? Hence speech ceases at that time. And what makes us speak is nurtured during the time between falling asleep and awaking by beings belonging to the Hierarchy of the Archangeloi.

If we disregard the sleep-walker, who is also in an abnormal condition, human beings are quiet while asleep. They do not walk, they grasp no objects, they do not move. That which pertains to man's waking life as forces which call forth the movements out of his will is nurtured, between going to sleep and awaking, by beings belonging to the Hierarchy of the Archai.

By comprehending the manner in which the hierarchical beings above the human kingdom – Angels, Archangels, Archai – approach the ego and astral body, approach the entire human being during sleep, we can also understand how the little child masters the three activities of walking, speaking, and thinking. We recognize how it is the work of the Archai that brings to the little child, as he masters the dynamics of life, as he masters the faculty of walking and handling objects, what the human being has experienced, between death and a new birth, by coming into contact with spirit and soul beings. Now, the counterpart of these experiences comes forth with the learning to walk of the little child. It is the Archai, the primeval powers, who transmit to the child that learns how to walk the counterpart of all the spiritual movements emanating, between death and a new birth, from spirit and soul beings.

It is the Archangels that transmit what the human being experiences, between death and a new birth, by means of revelation; they are at work when the child masters speech. And the Angels carry down the forces developed by the human being when, out of the whole world ether, he gathered the substance for his etheric body. The Angels, bringing down these forces, mould their counterparts within the thought-organs, which are plastically formed in order that the child may learn thinking by means of language.

You must keep in mind that Anthroposophy does more than look at the physical world and say: it is based on something spiritual. This would be much too easy. By such a way of thinking, we could acquire no real conception of the spiritual world. Someone who is determined to repeat in philosophic terms that the physical world rests on a spiritual foundation would be like a person who, when walking across a meadow, is told by his companion: look, this flower is a dandelion, these are daisies, and so forth. The first person, however, might reply: indeed, I am not interested in these names; here I see flowers, *just* flowers in the abstract. Such a person would be like a philosopher who recognizes only the pantheistic spiritual element but refuses to discuss the concrete facts, the particular formations of the spiritual.

What we are given by Anthroposophy shows us how the divine spiritual dwells everywhere in life's single formations. We look at the way in which the child passes from the clumsy stage of crawling to that of walking. Looking in admiration and reverence at this grandiose world phenomenon, we see in it the work of the Archai, who are active when the experiences we undergo between death and a new birth are transformed into their earthly shape.

We follow the process through which the child produces speech out of his inner self; we follow the activity of the Archangels; and, when the child begins to think, the activity of the Angels. And all this has a deeply significant, practical side. In our materialistic age, many people have ceased to regard words as something genuinely spiritual. More and more, people use words only for the purpose of naming physical objects in the outer world. Think how many people in the world are unable to form the slightest conception of spiritual things; this is because the words have no spiritual significance for them and are used merely in connection with physical objects.

For many people, speech itself has assumed a materialistic character. It can be used only in connection with physical things. Undeniably, we live within a civilization making language, more and more, into an instrument of materialism. And what will be the consequence?

The consequence will become apparent to us if we look, with regard to language, at the connection between the waking and the sleeping state. While we remain awake during the day, we talk with others. We make the air vibrate. The way in which the air vibrates transmits the soul content which we wish to convey. The soul impulses of our words, however, live in our inner being. Every word corresponds to a soul impulse, which is the more powerful the more our words are imbued with idealism; the more we are conscious of the spiritual significance contained in our words. Anyone aware of these facts will clearly recognize what lies behind them. Think of a person who uses words in a merely materialistic sense. During the day, he will not differ greatly from others whose words contain an idealistic, spiritual element, who know that words must be given wings by the spirit. At night, however, the human being takes the soul and spirit element of language, together with his ego and astral body, into the spiritual world. He returns again to his spiritual origin.

Those possessing only a materialistic speech cannot establish a connection with the world of the Archangels. Those still possessing an idealistic speech are able to establish this connection with the world of the Archangels.

The tragedy inherent in a civilization whose materialism is expressed even by its language has the consequence that the human being, by letting his language become wholly materialistic, may lose the nightly connection with the world of the Archangels. For the genuine spiritual scientist, there lies indeed something heart-breaking in present-day civilization. People who forget more and more to invest their words with a spiritual content lose their rightful connection with the spiritual world, with the Archangels. And this terrifying fact can be perceived only by someone envisaging the true nature of the sleeping state.

It is impossible to become a real anthroposophist without rising above mere theory. We may remain perfectly indifferent while developing theories on June bugs, earth worms, and cells. Such theories shall certainly break nobody's heart. For the way in which June bugs and earthworms grow out of a cell is not apt to break our heart. But if we acquire anthroposophical knowledge in all its fullness, we look into the depths of man's being, of man's evolution, of man's destiny. Thus our heart will ever be interlinked with this knowledge. The sum of this knowledge will be deposited in the life of our feelings, our emotions. Hence we partake of the whole world's feelings, and also of the whole world's volition.

The essence of Anthroposophy consists in the fact that it grasps not only the human intellect but the whole human being. Thereby it illuminates, with the forces of feeling and sentiment, the destinies of culture and civilization, as well as the destinies of single persons.

We cannot take part genuinely in human experiences on earth unless looking also at the other side, the spiritual side, as it is unveiled to us through our knowledge of the sleeping state that leads us back into the spiritual world. Thus spiritual science can be truly at one with human life, understood in its spiritual and ultimately its social, religious and ethical significance.

This spiritual science is to become real science which leads to wisdom. Such life-giving science is greatly needed by mankind, lest it fall into deeper and deeper decline, instead of making a new beginning.

V. The Working of Karma in Life after Death

Berne, 15 December 1912

MUCH THAT will be considered today has been spoken about previously but we shall discuss it from new aspects. The spiritual worlds can only become fully intelligible if we consider them from the most varied viewpoints. Life between death and a new birth has been described in many different ways. Today our considerations will deal with much that has concerned me recently in the sphere of spiritual investigation.

We remember that as soon as we have gone through the Gate of Death we experience the Kamaloca period, during which we are still intimately connected with our feelings and emotions, with all the aspects of our soul life in the last earthly embodiment. We gradually free ourselves from this connection. Indeed, we no longer have a physical body after death. Yet, when the physical and etheric bodies have been laid aside, our astral body still possesses all the peculiarities it had on earth, and these peculiarities of the astral body, which it acquired because it lived in a physical body, also have to be laid aside. This requires a certain time and that marks the period of Kamaloca. The Kamaloca period is followed by experiences in the spiritual world or Devachan.[7] In our writings it has been characterized more from the aspect of what man experiences through the different elements spread out around him. We shall now consider the period between death and a new birth from another side. Let us begin with a general survey.

When man has gone through the Gate of Death he has the following experience. During life on earth he is enclosed within his skin, and outside is space with things and beings. This is not so after death. Our whole being expands and we feel that we are becoming ever larger. The feeling of being here in my skin with space and surrounding things out there is an experience that we do not have after death. After death we are inside objects and beings. We expand within a definite spatial area. During the Kamaloca period we are continually expanding, and when this expansion reaches its end, we are as large as the space within the orbit of the moon. The fact of dwelling within space, of being concentrated in one point, has quite a different meaning after death than during physical existence. All the souls who dwell simultaneously in Kamaloca occupy the same space circumscribed by the orbit of the moon. They interpenetrate one another. Yet this interpenetration does not mean togetherness. The feeling of being together is determined by quite other factors than filling a common spatial area. It is possible for two souls who are within the same space after death to be quite distant from one another. Their experience may be such that they need not know of one another's existence. Other souls, on the other hand, might have close, intimate connections and sense each other's presence. This depends entirely on inner relationships and has nothing to do with external spatial connections.

In later phases when Kamaloca has come to an end, we penetrate into still vaster realms. We expand ever more. When the Kamaloca phase draws to a close, man leaves behind him, as if discarded, everything that during his physical existence was the expression of his propensities, longings and desires for earthly life. Man must experience all this but he must also relinquish it in the moon-sphere or Kamaloca. As man lives on after death, and later recalls the experiences in the moon-sphere, he will find all his earthly emotions and passions inscribed there, that is, everything that developed in his soul life as a result of his positive attraction to the bodily nature. This is left behind in the moon-sphere and there it remains. It cannot be erased so easily. We carry it with us as an impulse but it remains inscribed in the moon-sphere. The account of the debts, as it were, owing by every person is recorded in the moon-sphere.

As we expand farther we enter a second realm that is called

the Mercury-sphere in occultism. We shall not represent it diagrammatically, but the Mercury-sphere is larger than the moon-sphere. We enter this sphere after death in the most varied ways. It can be accurately investigated by means of spiritual science. A person who in life had an immoral or limited moral disposition lives into the Mercury-sphere in a completely different way from one who was morally inclined. In the Mercury-sphere the former is unable to find those people who die at the same time, shortly before or after he did, and who are also in the spiritual world. He so enters into the spiritual world that he is unable to find the loved ones with whom he longs to be together. People who lack a moral disposition of soul on earth become hermits in the Mercury-sphere. The morally inclined person, however, becomes what one might call a sociable being. There he will find above all the people with whom he had a close inner connection on earth. This determines whether one is together with someone. It depends not on spatial relations, for we all fill the same space, but on our soul inclinations. We become hermits when we bring an immoral disposition with us, and sociable beings if we possess a moral inclination.

We encounter other difficulties in connection with sociability in the moon-sphere during Kamaloca but by and large whether a human being becomes a hermit or a sociable being there also depends on the disposition of his soul. A thorough-going egoist on earth, one who only indulged his urges and passions, will not easily find in the moon-sphere the people with whom he was connected on earth. A person who has loved passionately, however, even if it were only physically, will nevertheless not find himself completely alone, but will find other individuals with whom he was connected. In both these spheres it is generally not possible to find human beings apart from those with whom one has been connected on earth. Others remain unknown to us. The condition for meeting other people is that we must have been with them on earth. Whether or not we find ourselves with them depends on the moral factor. Although they lead to a connection with those we have known on earth, even moral strivings will not carry us much farther beyond this realm. Relationships to the people we meet after death are characterized by the fact that they cannot be altered.

We should picture it as follows. During life on earth we always have the possibility of changing a relationship with a fellow human being. Let us suppose that over a period of time we have not loved someone as he deserved. The moment we become aware of this we can love him rightly, if we have the strength. We lack this possibility after death. Then, when we encounter a person, we perceive far more clearly than on earth whether we have loved him too little or unfairly, but we can do nothing to change it. It has to remain as it is. Life-connections bear the peculiar quality of a certain constancy. Because they are of a lasting nature, an impulse is formed in the soul by means of which order is brought into karma. If we have loved a person insufficiently over a period of fifteen years, we shall become aware of it after death. It is during our experience of this that we bring about the impulse to act differently in our next incarnation on earth. We thereby create the impulse and the will for karmic compensation. That is the technique of karma.

Above all, we should be clear about one thing. During the early phases of life after death, namely during the moon and Mercury periods (and also during subsequent periods that will shortly be described), we dwell in the spiritual world in such a way that our spiritual life depends on how we lived on earth in the physical world. It not only is a question of our earthly consciousness. Our subconscious impulses also play a part. In our normal waking state on earth we live in our ego. Below the ego-consciousness lies the astral consciousness, the subconscious sphere. The workings of this sphere are sometimes different from our normal ego-consciousness without our being aware of it.

Let us take an actual example that occurs quite frequently. Two people are on the friendliest terms with each other. One develops an appreciation for spiritual science while the other, who previously appeared quite complacent towards it, comes to hate spiritual science. This animosity need not pervade the whole soul. It may only be lodged in the person's ego-consciousness, not in his astral consciousness. As far as his astral consciousness is concerned, the person who feeds his animosity still further might in fact have a longing and a love for the spirit of which he is unaware. That is quite possible. There are contradictions of this kind in human nature. If a person investigates his astral consciousness, his subconscious, he might well find a concealed sympathy for what in his waking consciousness he professes to hate. This is of particular importance after death because then, in this respect, man becomes truly himself. A person may have brought himself to hate spiritual science during a lifetime, to reject it and everything connected with it, and yet he may have a love for it in his subconscious. He may have a burning desire for spiritual science. The fact of not knowing and being unable to form thoughts of his memories can result in acute suffering during the period of Kamaloca because during the first phase after death man lives mainly in his recollections. His existence is then not only determined by the sorrow and also the joy of what lives in his ego-consciousness. What has developed in the subconscious also plays a part. Thus man becomes truly as he really is.

Here we can see that spiritual science rightly understood is destined to work fruitfully in all spheres of life. A person who has gone through the Gate of Death is unable to bring about any change in his relation to those around him, and the same is true of the others in relation to him. An immutability in the connections has set in. But a sphere of change does remain that is in the relationship of the dead to the living. Inasmuch as they have had a relationship on earth with those who have died, the living are the only ones who can soothe the pain and alleviate the anguish of those who have gone through the Gate of Death. In many cases such as these, reading to the dead has proved fruitful.

A person has died. During his lifetime for one reason or another he did not concern himself with spiritual science. The one who remains behind on earth can know by means of spiritual science that the deceased has a burning thirst for spiritual science. Now if the one who remains behind concerns himself with thoughts of a spiritual nature as if the dead were there with him, he performs a great service to him. We can actually read to the dead. That enables the gulf that exists between the living and the dead to be bridged. The two worlds, the physical and the spiritual, are severed by materialism. Consider how their union will take hold of life itself! When spiritual science does not remain mere theory but becomes a life impulse as it should, there will not be separation but immediate communication. By reading to the dead we can enter in immediate connection with them and help them. The one who has avoided spiritual science will continue to feel the anguish of longing for it unless we help him. We can assist him from the earth if such a longing is at all present. By this means the living can help the dead.

It is also possible for the dead to be perceived by the living, although in our time the living do little to bring about such connections. Also in this respect spiritual science will take hold of life, will become a true life elixir. To understand in which way the dead can influence the living let us take the following as our starting point. What does man know about the world? Remarkably little if we only consider the things of the physical plane with mere waking consciousness. Man is aware of what happens out there in front of his senses and what he can construe by means of his intellect in relation to these happenings. Of all else he is ignorant. In general he believes that he cannot know anything apart from what he observes by means of sense perception. But there is much else that does not happen and yet is of considerable importance. What does this mean?

Let us assume that we are in the habit of going to work at eight o'clock every morning. On one occasion, however, we are delayed by five minutes. Apart from the fact that we arrive five minutes late, nothing unusual has happened apparently. Yet, upon closer consideration of all the elements involved, we might become aware that, precisely on that day, if we had left at the correct time we would have been run over. That means that had we left at the right time we would no longer be alive.

Or what is also possible and might have occurred is that a person might have been prevented by a friend from sailing on the *Titanic*.[8] He might feel that had he sailed he surely would have been drowned! That this was karmically planned is another matter. But do think, when you consider life in this way, of how little you are in fact aware. If nothing of what might have taken place has happened, then you are simply unaware of it. People do not pay attention to the countless possibilities that exist in the world of actual events.

You might say that surely this is of no importance. For the outer events it matters little, yet it is of importance that you were not killed. I would like to draw your attention to the fact that we might have known that there was a high probability of being killed if, for instance, we had not missed the train that was involved in a major accident. One cannot mention all possible cases and yet they happen constantly on a small scale. Certainly, for the external course of events, we only need know what can be observed.

Let us assume that we definitely know that something would have happened had we not missed the train. Such a knowledge makes an inner impression on us, and we might say that we have been saved in a remarkable way by good fortune. Consider the many possibilities that confront people. How much richer would our soul lives be if we could know all the things that play into life and yet do not happen! Today people only consider the poverty-stricken sequence of what has actually occurred.

It is as if one were to consider a field with its many ears of wheat and reflect that from it a relatively small number of seeds will be sown. Countless others will not sprout and will go in another direction. What might happen to us is related to what actually occurs as the many grains of wheat that do not sprout are related to those that sprout and carry ears. This is literally so, for the possibilities in life are infinite. Moments in which especially important things for us in the world of probability are taking place are also particularly favourable moments for the dead to draw near. Let us suppose that a person left five minutes early, and as a result his life was preserved. At a particular moment he was saved from an accident, or it might also happen that in such a manner a joyful event escaped him. A dream picture that imparts a message from the dead can enter life at such moments. But people live crudely. As a rule, the finer influences that constantly play into life go unheeded. In this respect, spiritual science refines the feelings and sensations. As a result, man will sense the influence of the dead and will experience a connection with him. The gulf between the living and the dead is bridged by spiritual science that becomes a true life elixir.

The next sphere after death is the so-called Venus-sphere. In this sphere we become hermits if on earth we have had an irreligious disposition. We become sociable spirits if we bring a religious inclination with us. Inasmuch as in the physical world we are able to feel our devotion to the Holy Spirit, so in the Venus-sphere shall we find all those of a like inclination towards the divine spiritual. Human beings are grouped according to religious and philosophic trends in the Venus-sphere. On earth it is so that both religious striving and religious experience still play a dominant part. In the Venus-sphere the grouping is purely according to religious confession and philosophic outlook. Those who share the same world-conception are together in large, powerful communities in the Venus-sphere. They are not hermits. Only those are hermits who have not been able to develop any religious feeling and experience.

For instance, the monists, the materialists of our age, will not be sociable, but lonely beings. Each one will be as if encaged in the Venus-sphere. There can be no question of a Monistic Union because by virtue of the monistic conception each member is condemned to loneliness. The fact that each will be locked in a cage in this sphere is not something that has been theoretically cooked up. It is mentioned so that souls may be brought to an awareness of reality as compared to the fanciful theories of monism that have been elaborated on earth. In general we can say that we come together with those of the same world-conception, of the same faith as ourselves. Other confessions are hard to understand in the Venus-sphere.

This is followed by the sun-sphere. Only what bridges the differences between the various religious confessions can help us in the sun-sphere. People do not find it easy to throw bridges from one confession to another because they are so entrenched in their own views. A real understanding for one who thinks and feels differently is particularly difficult. In theory such an understanding is often claimed, but matters are quite different when it is a question of putting theory into practice.

One finds, for instance, that many who belong to the Hindu religion speak of a common kernel in all religions. They in fact, however, only refer to the common kernel of the Hindu and Buddhist religions. The adherents of the Hindu and Buddhistic religions speak in terms of a particular egoism. They are caught in a group egoism.

One might insert here a beautiful Estonian legend about group egoism that tells of the origin of languages. God wished to bestow the gift of language on humanity by means of fire. A great fire was to be kindled and the different languages were to come about by having people listen to the peculiarities of the sounds of the fire. So the Godhead called all the peoples of the earth to assemble so that each might learn its language. Prior to the gathering, however, God gave preference to the Estonians and taught them the divine-spiritual language, a loftier mode of speech. Then the others drew near and were allowed to listen to how the fire was burning, and as they heard it they learned to understand the various sounds. Certain peoples preferred by the Estonians came first when the fire was still burning quite strongly. When the fire was reaching its end the Germans had their turn, for the Estonians are not particularly fond of the Germans. In the feebly crackling fire one heard, *'Deitsch, peitsch; deitsch, peitsch'* (German, whip). Then followed the Lapps of whom the Estonians are even less fond. One only heard, *'Lappen, latschen'* (Lapp, lash). By that time the fire was reduced to mere ashes, and the Lapps brought forth the worst language of all because the Estonians and the Lapps are deadly enemies. Such is the extent of the Estonians' group egoism.

A similar group egoism is true of most peoples when they speak of penetrating to the essential core common to all religious creeds. In this respect Christianity is absolutely not the same as all the other creeds. If, for example, the attitude in the West was comparable to that toward the Hindu religion, then old Wotan would still reign as a national god. The West has not acknowledged a ruling divinity to be found within its own area, but one outside it. That is an important difference between it and Hinduism and Buddhism. In many respects, western Christianity is not permeated by religious egoism. Religiously it is more selfless than the eastern religions. This is also the reason why a true knowledge and experience of the Christ impulse can bring man to a right connection with his fellow human beings, irrespective of the confessions they acknowledge.

In the sun-sphere between death and rebirth it is really a matter of an understanding that enables us not only to come together with those of a like confession, but also to form a relationship with mankind as a whole. If sufficiently broadly understood in its connection with the Old Testament religion, Christianity is not one-sided. Attention has been drawn previously to something of considerable importance that should be recognized. You will recall that one of the most beautiful sayings of Christ, 'Ye are Gods,' is reminiscent of the Old Testament. Christ points to the fact that a divine spark, a god, dwells in every human being. You are all gods; you will be on a par with the gods.

It is a lofty teaching of Christ that points man to his divine nature, that he can become like God. You can become Godlike, a wonderful and deeply moving teaching of Christ! Another being has used the same words, and it is indicative of the Christian faith that another being has done so. At the opening of the Old Testament Lucifer approaches man. He takes his starting point – and therein lies the temptation – with the words, 'You shall be as Gods.' Lucifer at the beginning of the temptation in Paradise and later Christ Jesus use the same words! We touch here upon one of the deepest and most important aspects of Christianity, because this indicates that it is not merely a matter of the content of the words but of which being in the cosmic context utters them. In the last Mystery Drama it had to be shown that the same words have a totally different meaning according to whether spoken by Lucifer, Ahriman or the Christ.[9] We touch here upon a deep cosmic mystery, and it is important that we should develop an understanding for the words, 'Ye are Gods' and 'Ye shall be as Gods,' uttered on one occasion by the Christ, on the other by Lucifer.

We must consider that between death and rebirth we also dwell in the sun-sphere where a thorough understanding of the Christ impulse is essential. We must bring this understanding along with us from the earth, for Christ once did dwell in the sun but, as we know, He descended from the sun and united Himself with the earth. We have to carry Him up to the sun period, and then we can become sociable beings through the Christ impulse and learn to understand Him in the sphere of the sun.

We must learn to discriminate between Christ and Lucifer, and in our time this is only possible by means of Anthroposophy. The understanding of Christ that we bring with us from the earth leads us as far as the sun-sphere. There it acts as a guide, so to speak, from human being to human being, irrespective of creed or confession. But we encounter another being in the sun-sphere who utters words that have virtually the same content. That being is Lucifer. We must have acquired on earth an understanding of the difference between Christ and Lucifer, for Lucifer is now to accompany us through the further spheres between death and rebirth.

So you see, we go through the moon-, Mercury-, Venus-, and sun-spheres. In each sphere we meet, to begin with, what corresponds to the inner forces that we bring with us. Our emotions, urges, passions, sensual love, unite us to the moon-sphere. In the Mercury-sphere we meet everything that is due to our moral imperfections; in the Venus-sphere, all our religious shortcomings; in the sun-sphere, everything that severs us from the purely human.

Now we proceed to other spheres that the occultist terms the spheres of Mars, Jupiter and Saturn. Here Lucifer is our guide and we enter into a realm that bestows new forces upon us. Just as here we have the earth below us, so there in the cosmos we have the sun below us. We grow into the divine-spiritual world, and as we do so we must hold fast in memory what we have brought with us of the Christ impulse. We can only acquire this on earth and the more deeply we have done so, the farther we can carry it into the cosmos. Now Lucifer draws near to us. He leads us out into a realm we must cross in order to be prepared for a new incarnation. There is one thing we cannot dispense with unless Lucifer is to become a threat to us, and that is the understanding of the Christ impulse, of what we have heard about Christ during our life on earth. Lucifer approaches us out of his own accord during the period between birth and death, but Christ must be received during earthly life.

We then grow into the other spheres beyond the sun. We become ever larger, so to speak. Below us we have the sun and above, the mighty, vast expanse of the starry heavens. We grow into the great cosmic realm up to a certain boundary, and as we grow outward cosmic forces work upon us from all directions. We receive forces from the mighty world of the stars into our widespread being.

We reach a boundary, then we begin to contract and enter

again into the realms through which we have travelled previously. We go through the sun-, Venus-, Mercury-, and
moon-spheres until we come again into the neighbourhood of
the earth and everything that has been carried out in the
cosmic expanse has concentrated itself again in an embryo
borne by an earthly mother.

That is the mystery of man's nature between death and a
new birth. After he has gone through the Gate of Death he
expands ever more from the small space of the earth to the
realms of moon, Mercury, Venus, sun, Mars, Jupiter and
Saturn. We have then grown into cosmic space, like giant
spheres. After we as souls have received the forces of the
universe, of the stars, we contract again and carry the forces
of the starry world within us. This explains out of spiritual
science how in the concentrated brain structure an imprint of
the total starry heavens may be found. In fact, our brain does
contain an important secret.

We have yet another mystery. Man has gathered himself
together, incarnated in a physical body to which he comes by
way of his parents. He has journeyed so far during his
expansion in cosmic space that he has recorded his particular
characteristics there. As we gaze from the earth upward to the
heavens, there are not only stars but also our characteristics
from previous incarnations. If, for instance, we were ambi-
tious in previous earth lives, then this ambition is recorded in
the starry world. It is recorded in the Akasha Chronicle, and
when you are here on the earth at a particular spot, this
ambition comes to you with the corresponding planet in a
certain position and makes its influence felt.

That accounts for the fact that astrologers do not merely
consider the stars and their motions but will tell you that here
is your vanity, there is your ambition, your moral failing, your
indolence; something you have inscribed into the stars is now
working out of the starry worlds onto the earth and determines your destiny. What lives in our souls is recorded in the
vastness of space and it works back from space during our life

on earth as we journey here between birth and death. If we truly understand them, these matters touch us closely, and they enable us to explain many things.

I have concerned myself a great deal with Homer. Last summer during my investigations into the conditions between death and rebirth I came upon the immutability of the connections after death. Here, in a particular passage, I had to say to myself that the Greeks called Homer the blind poet because he was such a great seer. Homer mentions that life after death takes place in a land where there is no change. A wonderfully apt description! One only learns to understand this through the occult mysteries. The more one strives in this direction, the more one realizes that the ancient poets were the greatest seers and that much that is secretly interwoven in their works requires a considerable amount of understanding.

I would like to mention something that happened to me last autumn and which is quite characteristic. At first, I resisted it because it was so astonishing, but it is one of those cases where objectivity wins. In Florence we find the tombs of Lorenzo and Giuliano de Medici by Michelangelo. The two brothers are portrayed together with four allegorical figures. These figures are well known, but at a first visit it occurred to me that something was not quite right with this group. It was clear to me that the one described as Giuliano is Lorenzo, and vice versa. The figures, which can be removed, had obviously been interchanged on some occasion and it has gone unheeded. That is why the statue of Giuliano is said to be that of Lorenzo, and vice versa. But I am really concerned here with the four allegorical figures.

Let us first deal with this wonderful statue, 'Night'. It cannot be understood simply in terms of an allegory. If, however, knowing about the etheric body and imagining it in its full activity, one were to ask, 'What is the most characteristic gesture corresponding to the etheric body when it is free from the astral body and ego?' the answer would be the gesture as given by Michelangelo in 'Night'. In fact, 'Night' is so moulded that it gives a perfect representation of the free, independent etheric body, expressed by means of the forms of the physical body when the astral body and ego are outside it. This figure is not an allegory, but represents the combination of the physical and etheric bodies when the astral body and ego are outside them. Then one understands the position of the figure. It is historically the truest expression of the vitality of the etheric body.

One comes to see the figure of 'Day' as the expression of the ego when it is most active and least influenced by the astral, etheric and physical bodies. This is portrayed in the strange gesture and position of Michelangelo's 'Day'. We obtain the gesture of the figure 'Dawn' when the astral body is active, independent from the physical and etheric bodies and the ego, and of 'Dusk' when the physical body is active without the other three members.

I struggled long against this piece of knowledge and to begin with thought it quite absurd; yet the more one goes into it, the more it compels one to recognize the truth of the script contained in these sculptures. It is not that Michelangelo was conscious of it. It sprang from his intuitive creative power. One also understands the meaning of the legend that tells that when Michelangelo was alone in his studio, the figure 'Night' became endowed with life and would move around freely. It is a special illustration of the fact that one is dealing with the etheric body. The spirit works into everything in art as in the evolution of humanity. One learns to understand the world of the senses only if one grasps how the spirit works into sensible reality.

There is a beautiful saying by Kant. He says, 'There are two things that have made a specially deep impression on me, the starry heavens above me and the moral law within me.' It is particularly impressive when we realize that both are really one and the same. Between death and rebirth we are spread out over the starry realms and receive their forces into ourselves, and during our life in a physical body the forces we have gathered are active within us as moral impulses. Looking up to the starry heavens we may say that we dwell among the forces that are active out there during the period between death and rebirth. This now becomes the guiding principle of our moral life. The starry heavens outside and the moral law within are one and the same reality. They constitute two sides of that reality. We experience the starry realms between death and rebirth, the moral law between birth and death.

When we grasp this, spiritual science grows into a mighty prayer. For what is a prayer but that which links our soul with the divine-spiritual permeating the world. We must make it our own as we go through the experiences of the world of the senses. Inasmuch as we strive consciously towards this goal, what we learn becomes a prayer of its own accord. Here spiritual knowledge is transformed immediately into feeling and experience, and that is how it should be. However much spiritual science might work with concepts and ideas, they will nevertheless be transformed into pure sensations and prayer-like feelings. That is what our present time requires. Our time needs to experience the cosmos by living into a consideration of the spirit in which the study itself takes on the nature of a prayer. Whereas the study of the external physical world becomes ever more dry, scholarly and abstract, the study of spiritual life will become more heartfelt and deeper. It will take on the quality of prayer, not in a one-sided sentimental sense but by virtue of its own nature. Then man will not know merely as a result of abstract ideas that the divine that permeates the universe is also in him. He will realise as he advances in knowledge that he truly has experienced it during life between the last death and a new birth. He will know that what he experienced then is now in him as the inner riches of his life.

Such considerations, related as they are to recent research, help us to gain an understanding of our own development. Then spiritual science will be able to transform itself into a true spiritual life-blood. We shall often speak further about these matters in the future.

VI. Inward Experiences after Death

Stuttgart, 23 November 1915

WHEN WE approach the mystery of death we must always bear in mind, above everything else, that it is indeed necessary for a characterization of the spiritual worlds to change the meaning contained in the words which are cut out for our ordinary world, for the ordinary physical world.

The dead, the so-called dead person, enters the spiritual world, and, as we have repeatedly explained, in the spiritual world things present an aspect which is fundamentally different from that of the physical world. Not only a spiritual-scientific insight but also the ordinary common sense pertaining to the physical world might induce us to believe that when the dead person enters the spiritual world through the portal of death the first thing which takes place there is the loosening of his physical body from that which constitutes his other human being within the physical body. This is, of course, quite a commonplace truth. But today we shall contemplate the inner experiences of the dead in the sense in which they can be investigated by spiritual science; we shall contemplate processes which should be borne in mind when describing the portal of death and tracing the path between death and a new birth.

The one who remains behind here, on the physical plane, will feel: 'That part which was enclosed within the physical frame of the deceased abandons him, and it abandons the friends whom he has left behind.' He will feel that the dead departs for another world.

The first perception of the dead person is that he, too, is being abandoned by those who are still dwelling upon the earth, and also by his physical body. Between birth and death this body was the instrument of his perceptive faculties, of his thinking, feeling and of his capacity for willing. (These descriptions are based, as already stated, on spiritual-scientific investigations.) Hence, his first perception is that those who were about him, who were connected with him, depart from him. And this perception is, to begin with, connected with processes which we have often described, namely, that the earth itself departs, as it were, and it is the departing earth which takes away the physical frame from the one who is passing through the portal of death. It is indeed almost as if the dead would acquire the feeling that he is remaining behind, that he remains behind a movement which he did not perceive at all while he lived upon the earth; he feels that he remains behind the earth's own movement. He feels that the earth is going away from him and with it everything which surrounded him upon the earth. He also feels that he is beginning to form part of an entirely different world, but it is a world which enables him to perceive something he had not seen before; namely, that his bodily frame, the bodily frame which has been given to him, is closely connected with the earth, and even with the movements of the earth. He feels, as it were (although this is expressed inadequately), that he can no longer follow the path of the earth and of its spirits, and for this reason they abandon him. He feels that he is left behind in a kind of greater state of repose, and that he begins to form part, as it were, of a more reposeful world. This perception which the dead person has, the perception of being abandoned particularly by the physical bodily frame, by everything he has experienced through other human beings and in common with them during the life between birth and death, constitutes the foundation of many things. During his earthly life, the possession of his physical frame was, so to speak, an obvious thing to him. What he now perceives is, therefore, an entirely new experience, and we shall see that there is a difference according to whether a person dies a so-called natural death through illness or old age, or a violent death; for instance, the kind of death which so many people must encounter today. Certain differences corresponding to the different cases must, therefore, be borne in mind.

The perception of being abandoned by that which was obviously our property during our life on earth brings about the circumstance that an entirely new factor arises in the life of the soul; something arises within the soul's life which could not be known during our existence in a physical body. The first thing which arises in the soul's life is, I might say, a reversal of its feelings toward life. Here upon the earth we feel that life is given to us from outside, that our life depends upon the vital forces which we receive from the earth, from the external world. But now this earth and all that it used to give us departs, as it were, and this inevitably produces the feeling that the vitalizing force now flows from within. The first experience is, therefore, the perception that the vitalizing force comes from within, that we vitalize ourselves. It is a transition from the state of passivity in which we have lived, to a certain state of activity. We ourselves vitalize what we now are. We dwell within our own self. What we have once known as the world, departs from us; the element in which we now live, by filling it out entirely with our own self, produces within itself the vitalizing force; it vitalizes itself.

Concretely speaking, it produces what I have often called the panorama of life, a surging life containing all we have experienced between birth and death. The pictures of this life rise up before our soul. Our whole past life between birth and death rises up, as it were, like a powerful dream, from the very point where we ourselves are standing. But vital forces are needed for the production of this picture, so as to make it into something which is more than a dream. It would really be a dream, a passing dream, had we not grown aware of the following fact: 'The bodily frame loosens itself from the soul-spiritual', and had not this experience given us new, revitalized forces? The dream becomes filled with life. What would otherwise be nothing but a surging, dark world of dream-pictures is thus filled with life streaming out of one point: it becomes a living world, a living panorama of life. And we ourselves are the vitalizing source of the dream which thus arises.

This is the first experience immediately after death. It takes place so that man is hardly aware of having abandoned his former state of consciousness; he simply realizes that something new has arisen, coming, as it were, from the central point of his being. It is something which begins to spread and which is avoided by that life to which he merely gave himself up passively until now. What he did not know between birth and death he now knows, namely, that thoughts, which otherwise surge up and down like a dream dreamt by the ego, can be alive. This is what he now knows. And from his former estranged state of life he now begins to penetrate into this life of his own. He experiences the true meaning of the fact that something which becomes connected with him takes hold of his innermost being. What used to be a mere picture of life, not life itself, now takes hold of his thoughts, of his thinking. And while he penetrates into this conception, another conception gradually arises. We may describe it as follows: He penetrates with his own life into sounds resounding through the panorama of life, and he connects these sounds with the whole universe. I have already described these things from a more general aspect, but we should consider them more and more accurately, in order to penetrate into the mysteries of the world.

At first, this innermost dream of life becomes filled with life. The dream itself becomes a living universe, a living cosmos. We experience how that which constituted our own self is now taken up by the cosmos, it becomes a part of the cosmos, part of something which is no longer the earth. For what pertains to the earth is something we have experienced between birth and death. The next experience is that we begin to feel how intimately the cosmos permeates what we thus are, as a part of the cosmos. We feel as if an inner light were to rise and throw its light upon what we once were. All this streams into the panorama of our life and resounds through it, as it were.

Then begins a process which severs from us that part which constitutes our etheric body – for all the other processes described above take place while we are still connected with our etheric body. A process takes place which we may designate as the loosening, the severing of the etheric body.

The experience which we now have, this perception of the panorama of life and its permeation with substances, with the sound and light-substances of the cosmos, resembles our incorporation in the human nature of the physical body when we enter life through birth. Just as here upon the earth the human substances given to us by the earth become incorporated, as it were, with man's soul being, so after we have passed through the portal of death the cosmic substance incorporates itself, that which corresponds to the universe incorporates itself.

This experience which we have just described is a necessity. And if we investigate in a truly spiritual scientific way the life between death and a new birth we shall realize the significance of these first experiences after passing through the portal of death, the significance which they have for the whole life between death and a new birth.

During our physical life on earth (I have repeatedly emphasized that we must realize this clearly) we acquire our ego-consciousness through the fact that we live in our physical body. I repeat: our ego-consciousness, not our ego. For we receive the ego from the Spirits of Form, and this is an entirely different matter. But we acquire our ego-consciousness through the fact that we are submerged in the physical body. The ego-consciousness which we have during our waking life on earth is something which we should contemplate very clearly. We can do this best of all by considering the following: imagine that you are moving about in space. You do not feel anything, but suddenly you hit against something. The external world comes into contact with you, yet you become aware of yourself. Within you, you will experience this contact with the external world; the external world makes you grow conscious of yourself; you can feel yourself because you have collided with the external world.

Indeed, we acquire our ego-consciousness because we come into contact with the external world. Of course, this does not only take place through our sense of touch, for even when we open our eyes we hit against something; namely, we come into contact with the external light. And when sounds reach our ear, we become aware of ourselves because our sense of hearing is struck by sounds.

We also grow aware of ourselves through the fact that every morning we come out of the spiritual world and dive into the physical world. We dive into our physical body. This diving into our body, that is to say this collision of our ego and astral body with our etheric body and our physical body, produces our ego-consciousness. This explains the lack of ego-consciousness in the world of dreams, for we need this collision with the physical and etheric body in order to acquire our ego-consciousness.

We need this collision in order to have a clear, wide-awake ego-consciousness. The human being who passes through the portal of death is deprived of his physical body. He can no longer produce his ego-consciousness in the same way as during his life between birth and death. If this ego-consciousness were not produced in some other way, he would have to pass through his life between death and a new birth unconscious of his ego. The way in which ego-consciousness is now produced is as follows: after having passed through the portal of death, everything we have experienced within the immediate region of the etheric body remains; it is there constantly, throughout the time between death and a new birth.

Also in this connection the experience in the spiritual world between death and a new birth is the very opposite of the physical experience which we have here, between birth and death. In the physical world, under normal conditions, it is not possible to remember the moment of birth, for memory begins later. Man does not remember his birth; this lies, so to speak, in a greater distance of time, further back than the path

which memory can tread. What the human being now experiences inwardly, from the other side, from the side of death,
remains throughout the life between death and a new birth;
the soul does not lose it. The experience of death remains just
as surely as the experience of birth vanishes when the human
being enters the physical world. In the physical world, the
human being living in a physical body does not look back as
far as his birth, but throughout the time between death and a
new birth he looks back upon death. This looking back upon
death, this encounter with the experience of death, is what
produces ego-consciousness between death and a new birth.
We owe our ego-consciousness to that circumstance. The
contemplation of death – if it is terrible at all – is only terrible
when seen from the standpoint of physical experience; it
terrifies and frightens us only if we look upon it from that side.
But the dead see it from the other side. And seen from that
other side it is indeed not terrible at all to know that the
moment of death constantly remains, as it were, throughout
the life between death and a new birth. Even if death means
destruction when seen from the physical standpoint of life, it
is the most glorious, lofty and beautiful thing of all when seen
from the other side of life, where it can always be seen. There,
it constantly bears witness to the victory of the spirit over
matter, to the self-creative vital power of the spirit. In the
spiritual worlds our ego-consciousness, therefore, arises when
we begin to feel the self-creative, vital power of the spirit.

In the spiritual worlds we acquire our ego-consciousness
because we ourselves constantly produce it within us, because
we never appeal to an extant life, but because we continually
call into being our own self, and because this process of
producing our own being makes us come into contact, as it
were, with ourselves, by going back into time as far as the
moment of death.

We are, therefore, also able to explain how our ego-
consciousness, the consciousness of our own self, is produced
between death and a new birth. This experience, which we

gain soon after death, has a great significance: it is the birth of our ego-consciousness. And this first experience differs according as the human being has reached, let us say, a more mature age and has passed through the portal of death in a natural way, or has died at a tender age, or in the prime of life. And we may say (of course, this is not pedantically exact) that in regard to the differences in this sphere the thirty-fifth year of life has a very special significance. When young people pass through the portal of death in the prime of life – at present this takes place in thousands of cases, and we shall see how this is modified still more by the fact that death hits them from outside – when a human being passes through the portal of death in the prime of life, he will then see the picture of his life and its vitalizing processes (as described above) differently than if he had passed through the portal of death after his thirty-fifth year of life.

We may more or less say, although it is, of course, difficult to find the appropriate words for similar conditions, that one who dies in the prime of life has the following experience and he will say to himself: 'The dream-picture of your life rises up, and you vitalize it from out of the central point of your life. But while you pour your own vitalizing forces out on this life-picture something else stands behind this picture of your life, something which is like a remainder from the world out of which you have come when you passed through birth!'

When a child dies, the picture of its life will be very short. When a six-year-old child dies, the picture of its life cannot contain much. But behind this picture, overshadowing it, as it were, from behind, many things appear which form part of the child's experiences in the spiritual world before its birth, or; to use an old German expression (Goethe used it), before it 'grew young'.[10] This is a beautiful expression which is no longer used. And when a child dies, that has not yet stored up memories, a child that has not yet reached the moment when it is able to remember past things, it will not be able to have such a life-picture with which it grows familiar in a direct and immediate way, as would be the case with a person who dies later. The child's life-picture would, instead, contain, slightly modified, that which surrounded the child before its birth. We may say: the contemplation of certain things which we have experienced before birth and which have remained behind from the spiritual world disappears in our after-death retrospection when we have gone beyond the thirty-fifth year of life. We should never be tempted (I am saying this in parenthesis) to yield to a thought which is not at all devoid of danger – and I wish to emphasize this – the thought of whether it is better for us to die before our thirty-fifth year or to die after our thirty-fifth year and to have certain experiences which we shall also describe. We should not follow this train of ideas, we should not cherish these thoughts, but we should think instead: 'Let us leave it to our karma, in the strictest meaning of the word, when we are to pass through the portal of death.' It is important to understand these things.

When we have passed beyond our thirty-fifth year of life and die, then, of course, we do not have the possibility of still seeing some of the things which have remained behind from our preceding spiritual life before birth. These are obscured but the picture of our life arises nevertheless. We have a strong feeling that we produce it from within, that we ourselves spin and weave it, as it were, and that this woof becomes filled with life.

As far as the life-picture is concerned, there is an essential difference between a death which takes place before the thirty-fifth year and one which takes place after the thirty-fifth year. Before the thirty-fifth year the picture of our life still possesses to a great extent a character which makes it approach us just as if it came from outside, from a spiritual world, and as if we were merely sending out to it our own experiences. After the thirty-fifth year, the picture of our life at first resembles a void, it is as if something dark came towards us from outside, and we bring towards this darkness the experiences which we have acquired during our earthly life, but this fact will not in any way diminish the vitality which is kindled in it. The inner experience is, however, modified through the fact that in the one case it resembles the approach of a *fata morgana*, towards which we go, while in the other case our own individual world is borne into the cosmic world. All this has a great significance for our life, as we shall see tomorrow. This significant karmic process, that our physical body is torn away from physical life at a certain age of life, is most important for the manner of life after death, and it is intimately connected with our whole karma.

Then comes a time – we already know this – when we begin to feel: 'Now you have completely left the earthly sphere!' Roughly speaking we may say: while we are passing through the portal of death we feel that the earthly body is going away from us. Our friends, the people with whom we have been associated, go away from us. The experiences which we have had in common with them go away from us. For a while we are left alone, alone with our experiences. Naturally, our life-dream contains everything we have experienced with other people; we look upon it as something which they have engraved upon us, but we see it so that we experience these past times within us, and within us we vitalize this life-dream. We also feel as if the earth were going away from us, but that we still live in the sphere from which the earth receives its light, in the sphere which belongs to the earth. We also experience the laying aside of our etheric body so as to feel: 'Now you have not only abandoned the earth and its substances, but also the immediate environment of the earth, namely, the light; you have also abandoned the densest substantiality of the earth which prevented you from hearing the music of the spheres. You have lost the habit (this is perhaps the last impression, and a very important one, which then remains constantly) of allowing the external light to throw light upon you and your environment.' In parenthesis, I wish to say that it is a very foolish idea to think that, in flying away from the earth to the sun, we always fly through light. Materialistic scientists have this fantastic notion. The belief that the sun spreads light in the manner described in physics, that the light passes through the world's spaces and falls upon the earth, is one of the worst superstitions. After death we realize this, for when we grow aware of the fact that we have abandoned our etheric body, we know that the light of the sun, which exists here, in physical life, only exists in that sphere which belongs to the earth. We have the perception: 'You are no longer disturbed by that light. Now it is the inner conviction of this light which begins to spread in the world which is at first filled with sounds. The inner light can only shine because the external light no longer disturbs the inner light!'

And now, with the laying aside of the etheric body, we begin to enter that world which has so often been called the Kamaloca world. Let us call it the soul world; for, after having experienced the inner vitalizing force, followed by a process resembling an inner permeating of our being with sounds, after feeling entirely alone with our own self and being filled with light from within, something arises which is like being filled with *warmth from within*. Here on earth we are filled with warmth, with heat, because we take up heat from outside – and in a physical body we feel that we cannot do otherwise – but now we begin to be filled with heat from within. This process of being filled with warmth, with heat, takes place so as to make us feel: 'In the element in which you now live you are able to call forth within you the same feeling which you once had when you experienced that heat had an effect upon you.' This feeling now fills the life-picture with heat, with warmth, and thus we enter a completely new element. We feel that the etheric body is beginning to leave us. And this is the entrance into the world which has purposely been named the Region of Burning Desires in my book *Theosophy*, because the heat which arises from within is at the same time passion; it is a streaming, flowing passion, producing itself; it is the experiencing of the will element.

Mingled with it is something which remains for a certain

length of time – we can only describe these things more accurately by and by – namely, the experiencing of the soul-world in the form of a retrospective experiencing of life. We go backwards from our experience of death towards our birth. And we now experience once more, from the other side, everything we have experienced here, during our physical life. But we do not experience it in the same way in which we have experienced it here, in the physical world, for we experience it in a *moral way*. We experience it in such a way (let us take this example) that if we have hurt another person at a certain moment between birth and death, we may at that time have felt what we have done, but not the pain which the other person has felt. Now we pass through this moment, but we do not feel what we ourselves have experienced in the form of anger or antipathy; we now pass through this experience with the other person's feelings. I might say that our experience spreads over the results of the deeds which we have done between birth and death. We penetrate with our living experience into the results and effects of our deeds. This constitutes, as it were, the foundation of our life between death and a new birth. Our experiences in the soul-world gradually enable us to penetrate into what we have brought about during our existence between birth and death; we gradually dive down into this. Indeed, just as here upon the earth we gradually become familiar with Nature from our childhood, just as here we begin to perceive Nature, to understand Nature, so during the time after death we begin to penetrate into the effects and results of our own deeds, into the consequences of our own thoughts and words – in short, into the whole world of effects; we flow out into the world of effects. Of course, *spiritual beings* now gradually begin to emerge from this foundation; they are beings belonging to the higher hierarchies and to the elemental world. Just as here we do not merely experience Nature, for animals, plants and minerals appear upon the foundation of Nature, so spiritual beings appear in our retrospective experience when we dive into the consequences of our deeds;

spiritual beings who live in the spiritual world emerge from this experience which makes us enter in a living way into the results of our deeds, and this experience is really the true foundation of our world. And just as here in the physical world we encounter physical beings, so we encounter there, among the spiritual beings of the elemental kingdoms and of the higher hierarchies, the souls of those who have died before us and dwell in the spiritual world, or the souls of those who are still embodied in a physical body, and with whom we have been connected on earth. All this vitalizes our foundation of life, this *melting away of our being into the world of our own deeds* vitalizes the foundation of our life.

And in a way we can perceive a certain difference between, let us say, our perception of a soul that still dwells upon the earth, or of a soul that has already passed through the portal of death. The dead, of course, knows whether he is facing one or the other kind of soul. When the departed is facing a soul that is still dwelling in an earthly body, he feels that the soul approaches him more from outside, that this picture, or imagination, forms itself of its own accord. In the case of a soul that already belongs to the disembodied souls, the experience which arises is far more active. In that case we also feel that the soul is coming towards us but we ourselves must form the picture for this soul. The departed friend approaches us with his being but we ourselves must form his image. One who is still alive brings his picture towards us when we look down upon him.

And now we experience with a certain moral note that which we may call our deeds; that is to say, the consequences of what we have done, thought or willed. We dive down into these deeds; we penetrate into them. And we penetrate into them in a certain definite way. Thus we say, for instance (since we have this experience): 'You have hurt someone, and now you feel what the other one has felt through the fact that you have pained him!' This becomes our own experience; we ourselves experience what the other person has passed through in the physical world. We have this experience. And in having this experience a force rises up from our inner being, entirely as if it were born out of an inner elemental necessity, a force which makes us say: 'You must compensate for this! You must make amends!' Indeed, you can make the following comparison. A mosquito flies towards you; you shut your eyes; you do something under a certain impression. But now, after death, you experience the cause, the motive of what you have done and you reply to this by calling forth within you the force which makes amends for your deed, which counterbalances it; that is to say, you wish to counterbalance, to make amends for what the other person has felt as a result of your offence. In other words: when you experience this, when you pass through this experience retrospectively in the soul-sphere, you take up within you a force which induces you to annul the pain which the other person has felt through you. This produces the desire to be with him again during a subsequent life on earth in order to make amends for what you have done to him. During this retrospective experience all the forces arise which produce karma; all the forces are taken up which create a compensation through karma.

Thus, already during these first years or decades after passing through the portal of death, we produce karma; karma takes its course. And just as it is true that the seed contains a force of growth which unfolds later in the blossom, so it is also true that now, after passing through the portal of death, a root-force lives in the dead which remains for the whole life between death and a new birth; then, in a new life on earth or during a later life on earth, this force produces, as it were, a karmic compensation for what he has done. Thus the will arises which then becomes the unconscious will bringing into effect karma.

Let us now observe another thing more closely, which is important for the knowledge of this picture of life which arises between death and a new birth. We may observe this if we cast our glance once more upon the reciprocal relationships of earthly life here upon the earth, relationships which are well known to us in their external appearance and which we have studied from several aspects in regard to their inner mysteries – I mean the reciprocal influence of the waking life of daytime and the sleeping life of the night.

Let us consider, then, from a particular aspect, waking and sleeping. Seen from outside, sleep consists in that we are inside our ego and astral body, and outside our physical and etheric body. If the life of sleep is not permeated in a certain way by the life of dreams, it remains, to begin with, unconscious, but it is not inactive, not devoid of activity. On the contrary! Sleeping life is inwardly a far more active life than the waking life of the soul, even though during our normal life on earth it remains, at first, unconscious; it is far more active than the waking life of the soul. The waking life of the soul is so intensive only because the activity of the ego and of the astral body encounters a resistance in the etheric body and in the physical body, and this mutual repelling of the ego and astral body on the one hand, and of the physical and etheric body on the other hand, produces, as it were, continual collisions which assume for us the form of our waking life of daytime, whereas, during our normal life on earth, we are not able to call up in our consciousness the continual, but intensive, activity of our life during the night. In this life there is no collision with the physical and etheric bodies, hence it does not rise up in our consciousness. The daytime life is, in itself, a weaker form of life; we are simply more conscious of it because it continually hits upon the etheric body and the physical body. Its collision with these bodies, this striking upon them as on a drum, this is what we perceive. The more intensive activity of sleep-life takes on an indefinite form but it cannot strike upon anything, and for this reason it remains unconscious.

With what do we occupy ourselves during our sleeping life? When dreams arise during our normal life, they are not the true activity which we develop during our sleeping life but, in reality, they are an image of this activity resulting from our recollections of ordinary life. The images of dream-life arise because life spreads its carpet over the true inner activity, and thus we can

INWARD EXPERIENCES AFTER DEATH

perceive many things in dreams. The ego and the astral body are livingly active when we dream; when their activity comes into contact with the etheric body, when we hit upon the etheric body, then dreams arise. But in dreams we make use of life's physical memories in the etheric body, thus rendering visible the activity of the ego and of the astral body, which would otherwise remain invisible. We shall be able to understand a dream only if we look upon the characteristic course of its pictures, if we learn to understand these pictures. Dreams should first be read in the right way; they should first be interpreted in the right way. Then they will indeed point to the significant reality and activity of the ego and of the astral body during sleep. This activity which we unfold during sleep can thus reveal itself to a serious and worthy form of spiritual research.

In what does this activity consist, which goes on from the moment of falling asleep to the moment of waking up? This activity consists in that we live through once more, inwardly and far more intensively, the experiences of the day; we become, as it were, our own judges; we judge the experiences of the day. This may sound trivial, nevertheless it is deeply true: during our normal state of consciousness we penetrate into our daytime experiences; we allow the events which take place about us to flow away. But during the night we consider the events of the day far more seriously, far more significantly, through our ego and our astral body, through our ego and our soul. We weigh and examine these events in regard to their cosmic value. We are engaged in finding out their significance within the whole connection of the world. An immensely deep, inner conscientiousness in the way of considering life permeates the activity which is carried on from the moment of falling asleep to the moment of waking up. But, of course, during normal life this remains unconscious. And all that the human being experiences every night by passing once more through his day-life is very significant as a preparation for the life which begins after having passed through the portal of death.

Let us consider, with the aid of a normal physical way of

looking upon life, this continuous existence between birth and death.

We may say that we are able to go back in memory through life up to a certain moment. In reality, we do not remember our whole past life, for in the evening we remember what took place until the morning of that day; there, the thread of memory breaks; then comes the preceding day, and then again the night which we cannot remember. Thus our memory reaches back, but our recollections are like links of a chain, alternately a white link and a black link. During our life between birth and death, we cannot remember the nights.

Now it is characteristic that when we live in the soul-land we are able to remember particularly the way in which we have passed through the events of the day backwards during the nights – night after night. Here, during our physical life, we remember our days; in the soul-land we remember the same things, but we remember the way in which we have worked and lived through our days during the nights. We go backwards in memory through the nights.

This enables us to have an insight into the way in which we experience life in soul-land. If we try to realize this in detail, we shall find that this is as follows: we have met someone on a certain day of our life. We have experienced this or that in connection with this meeting. We have these experiences with him not only during the day, but we have them again during the night, and also during the following nights, as a kind of reminiscence. We experience this inwardly in our ego and astral body. Everything we have experienced here in our daytime consciousness, we experience again in our night consciousness.

The way in which we experience these things in our night consciousness supplies the foundation for the way in which we must cope with them in the soul world. We live through our nights backwards. This is a very significant truth of spiritual research, and can again and again remind us of the fact that spiritual investigation is not as many people think it to be.

Many people think that upon entering the spiritual world the spiritual investigator immediately becomes acquainted with the spiritual world, and with everything there. This belief is just as simple as to think that if a person has walked over the earth he is well acquainted with the whole earth. He may be well acquainted with certain parts of the earth, but he will know nothing whatever about certain other parts. Similarly, a person who knows the spiritual world from one definite standpoint, may not know everything concerning the spiritual world. The knowledge of the spiritual world is gained after a long, patient investigation. For this reason it is so difficult to speak about spiritual science, because we continually encounter this prejudice. When spiritual-scientific lectures are delivered and questions are answered after a lecture, people ask information about all kinds of things. These questions are asked from the following standpoint: if someone has, for instance, learnt to know a certain number of minerals and plants, one can ask him questions about the mysteries of the animal kingdom, for if he knows one thing he must also know the other!

Undoubtedly every detail relating to the spiritual world must be grasped through patient work. In the spiritual world we must, as it were, wait until the one or the other thing reveals itself. From my books *Occult Science* and *Theosophy* you were able to gather that I have spoken of the approximate length of the so called Kamaloca life, of the life in the soul world.[11] From a certain aspect it is undoubtedly possible to speak in this way. But the spiritual investigator may reach another standpoint in a certain definite connection, and this can really be compared with travels through many countries. Just as one travels from land to land, so the spiritual investigator comes from one sphere into the other; he can thus reach another standpoint, and from this standpoint the following question arises: in what does the night-activity of the ego and of the astral body consist? And the reply to this question is: the life during the night can be considered so as to see in it a repetition, an elaboration, of the daytime experiences. The following question can then be asked: what is the aspect of life in the soul world, in order that we may know that in this soul world we live through our nights? I have indicated that the life in the soul world lasts about one third of our earthly life. If we live through our nights, how long would our life in the soul world last? Well, here upon the earth we spend about one third of our life in sleep. Some people sleep more and others less, but as a rule we sleep through about one third of our earthly life.

You see, such are the immensely significant impressions which can be gained in regard to the verification of spiritual science! For in spiritual science we find that in one case we may obtain something from a certain definite standpoint, giving us an insight into the spiritual world. A truth is thus revealed. Someone may question this truth. Now we examine things from another standpoint and reach exactly the same truth! This could be seen in the case of the nights, of the retrospective experiences during the night. A truth could thus be verified. And this inner agreement is a most important criterion. Where spiritual science is pursued earnestly and seriously, You will always find that the same thing is sought from various points of view, and that the same truth results from different standpoints. When human beings will be able to feel the truth-value contained in this manner of approaching spiritual truths and of finding these spiritual truths, when they will be able to feel this inner verification of spiritual science, then they will also feel that the truths which can be discovered in this sphere are immensely more true than all the things which can be investigated in the physical world. This is the essential and important thing to be borne in mind: here, during our physical life on earth, we are able to remember the experiences acquired during our waking daytime consciousness; but during the time in which we pass through the soul world we are able to remember the things which we continued to elaborate in the night upon the foundation of the experiences gained during our waking daytime consciousness.

In order that we may approach in a productive, really productive, way the significant truths which we shall consider tomorrow, let us recall what I have already mentioned from another standpoint in regard to the great events of our time.

When a human being passes through the portal of death in such a way that his life has, so to speak, been closed abruptly from outside, or if he has died in the prime of life, then the separation from his etheric body sets in very soon after his passage through the portal of death. This etheric body would, however, still have possessed the power of bestowing external vital forces for the rest of life. Normally, with his etheric body, the human being receives forces which can provide him with vital power until he grows quite old. If life closes suddenly, these forces remain. And these forces also exist in the etheric body which has been laid side. Just as in the physical world no forces are lost, or they merely undergo a transformation, so also these forces of the etheric are not lost, but remain – they really remain. Try to apply this to concrete facts. Try to think: when someone dies in his youth, in the prime of life, he leaves to the world what he still possessed in his etheric body as vital forces which he himself could have used. Try to imagine this still more concretely. Take the case of a man who has been hit by a bullet, let us say in his twenty-fifth year. He will leave to the world the etheric forces of life which he might have used for the rest of a long life from his twenty-sixth year onwards. This remains, this is a gift of the dead to the spiritual atmosphere of life in which we dwell; we are surrounded by these forces. And these forces contain the feelings of sacrifice with which the human being who has died in this way has permeated his etheric forces. This remains. And the successors do not realize at all how, in reality, they live in the forces which are left behind by their predecessors, how these forces surround them and how they permeate our spiritual life-forces. We do not take any notice of what is thus left behind by the departed at a time like the present, when so many etheric bodies well suited for life are given to the spiritual atmosphere of the earth in a comparatively short time.

Let us cast our glance upon that which is revealed to us by these deep connections enabling us to have an insight into the spiritual world and to see the spirit, not only in an abstract, indistinct and trivial way (in the world of the senses it is indistinct and dim) but so that we discover in it concretely a spiritual element, a spiritual essence. In addition to the course of destiny in the case of human beings who have passed through the portal of death, we see the beings of the higher Hierarchies, the beings of the elemental world; but we also see what remains inwardly connected with the earth, namely what has remained behind in the etheric bodies. This will be active in a concrete way; the unused etheric forces which are left to the children of the earth by those who encounter death upon the great battlefields of life's events will exercise a concrete influence. These forces will unite themselves with what is brought towards these seeds by the children of the earth in the form of an understanding for the future. Let us consider this and repeat the words which we have frequently spoken at the conclusion of a lecture:

> Aus dem Mut der Kämpfer,
> Aus dem Blut der Schlachten,
> Aus dem Leid Verlassener,
> Aus des Volkes Opfertaten –
> Wird erwachsen Geistesfrucht,
> Lenken Seelen geistbewusst
> Ihren Sinn ins Geisterreich!

> From the courage of the fighters,
> From the blood of the battles,
> From the sufferings of the abandoned,
> From the nation's deeds of sacrifice,
> Shall grow out a spiritual fruit,
> If souls lead, in spirit-consciousness,
> Their hearts and minds into the spirit-realm.

VII. The Moment of Death and the Period Thereafter

Leipzig, 22 February 1916

THE TIME in which we live reminds us daily and hourly of death, this significant event in human life; it reminds us of man's passage through the portal of death. For only in the light of spiritual science does death become a real event in the true meaning of the word, because spiritual science shows us the eternal forces that are active within us, that pass through births and deaths and take on a special form of existence between birth and death, in order to assume another form of existence after their passage through the portal of death. In the light of spiritual science, death becomes an event, instead of being merely the abstract end of life (only a materialistic world-conception can look upon death as the end of life); it becomes a deep and serious event within the whole compass of human life. Even from our own ranks, dear friends of ours have left us in order to pass through the portal of death, chiefly as a result of the present historical events, but also for other reasons, and so it may perhaps be particularly appropriate just now to say a few things on death, on this great event, and on the facts of human life that are connected with it.

Explanations have often been given in our spiritual-scientific lectures on the life between death and a new birth, so that we were able to gain many essential facts, particularly in regard to this subject. The course which spiritual science has followed up to now will have shown you that in every single case it can only speak of things from one definite standpoint, so that a more accurate knowledge can gradually be acquired by speaking of things repeatedly and throwing light upon them from many points of view. Today I shall therefore add to the facts that you already know in connection with this subject a few things that may be useful to our comprehension of the world as a whole.

Through spiritual science, we consider, to begin with (and that is a good thing), the human being such as he stands before us, here in the physical world, as an expression of his whole being. We must depart first of all from the manner in which the human being presents himself to us in the physical world; and for this reason, I have frequently pointed out that we obtain, as it were, a general view of man's whole being if we contemplate him so that we first take, as a foundation, his physical body which we learn to know externally in the physical world through our senses and the scientific dissection of what we perceive through the senses. We then proceed by studying that form of organization which we designate as our etheric body: this already possesses a supersensible character and cannot, therefore, be contemplated with the aid of the ordinary intellect, which is bound to the brain, and is consequently also inaccessible to our ordinary science. The etheric body is an organism having a supersensible character, concerning which we may say that it was already known to men such as Immanel Hermann Fichte, son of the great thinker Johann Gottlieb Fichte, to Troxler and others. Indeed, man's etheric body can only be grasped through imaginative knowledge owing to its supersensible character; but as far as imaginative knowledge is concerned, it *can* be contemplated externally, just as the physical-sensory body can be contemplated externally through our ordinary sensory knowledge.

We then ascend in our contemplation to the astral body. The astral body in man cannot be contemplated in an external-sensory manner in the same way in which we contemplate the physical body through our external senses, or in the same way in which we contemplate our etheric body through our inner sense; the astral body is something that can only be experienced inwardly. We must experience it inwardly, and in order to experience it we must be within it. The same thing applies to the fourth member which must be grasped in the physical world, to the ego. With these four members of human nature we build up our whole being.

Past lectures showed us that what we designate as man's physical body is a very complicated structure, formed during long periods of development, that passed through the stages of Saturn, the Sun and the Moon;[12] also the evolution of the Earth contributed to this development of the physical body, from the very beginning of earthly existence up to our time. A complicated process of development therefore built up our physical body.

That form of contemplation which is, to begin with, accessible to us in the physical world merely sees the external aspect of everything that lives within the physical body. Even ordinary science merely sees this external aspect. We might say: our ordinary physical contemplation and ordinary science, in the form in which it now lives in the world, merely know of the physical body as much as we would know of a house if we would only go round it outside, without ever going inside, so that we would never learn to know what it is like inside, nor what people live in it.

Of course, those who stand upon the foundation of ordinary science, in the usual materialistic meaning, will argue: 'We are thoroughly acquainted with the interior of the physical body! We know what it is like, because we have frequently studied the brain inside the skull when dissecting corpses; we have frequently studied the stomach and the heart.' This interior, however, that can thus be studied from outside, this spatial interior, is not what I mean when I speak of man's inner being. Even this spatial interior is nothing but an external thing. Indeed, in the case of the physical body, this spatial interior is far more external than the real spatial interior.

This must sound strange. But our sense-organs – you know this from other descriptions contained in our spiritual science

– were formed already during the Saturn period and we carry them on the surface of our body. Spatially speaking, they are outside. Nevertheless, they were built by forces that are far more spiritual than those that formed our stomach or everything that exists, spatially speaking, inside our body. What is inside our body is built up by the least spiritual of forces. Strange though it may sound, I must nevertheless point out that we really speak of ourselves in an entirely mistaken manner – upside down, we might say. Since we live on the physical plane, it is natural to speak in that way; nevertheless the way in which we speak of ourselves is quite wrong. We should really designate the skin of our face as our interior, and the stomach as our exterior. This would lead us far closer to the truth! It would lead us closer to the real truth if we were to say: we eat in such a way that we send the food out of us; when we send food into our stomach, we really send it out, we do not send it into our body, as we generally say at the present time. The more our organs lie on the surface, the more spiritual are the forces from which they come; and the more they lie inside our body, the less spiritual are the forces that gave rise to them.

The descriptions that were given so far in our spiritual science enable you to grasp this with a certain ease. If you carefully remember the descriptions of spiritual science, you will no doubt remember what it says in regard to the Moon stage of development, namely, that something split off during the Moon stage of development, and that something also split off during the Earth-development; it went out into the world's spaces from the Saturn, Sun and Moon stages of development. A very strange thing is connected with this splitting-off process, namely, we were turned inside out! Our inside became our outside and our outside became our inside. During the Saturn and Sun periods, our human countenance, which is now turned towards the outer world, was really turned towards our inner being. Of course, this was only the case during the early stages of development; but even during a part of the Moon period, during the Moon existence, the foundation of the inner organs which we now possess was still formed from outside. Since that time, we have really been turned inside out, like an overcoat that can be turned. We should bear in mind that many supersensible facts are connected with our physical body. Its whole structure is supersensible; the supersensible world has formed it, and when we look upon the physical body as a whole, it merely shows us its external aspect.

If we now come to the etheric body, we shall find that it is neither visible nor accessible to the physical-sensory contemplation. But when the human being passes through the portal of death, it becomes all the more important. The time through which the human being now passes, the first days after his death, are particularly important as far as the etheric body is concerned. But we must learn to think differently, even in regard to the physical body, if we wish to grasp in the right way all that we encounter after our passage through the portal of death.

You already know (for you can observe this even in the physical world) that when we pass through the portal of death we lay aside our physical body, as we generally say. We lay aside our physical body. Through decomposition or cremation (the only difference between these two processes lies in the length of time that they take up) the physical body is handed over to the elements of the earth. Now we might think that the physical body simply ceases to exist for those who have passed through the portal of death. But this is not the case, in this meaning. For we can hand over to the earth only those parts of our physical body that come from the earth itself. We cannot, however, hand over to the earth that part of our physical body that comes from the Old Moon existence, nor that part which comes from the Old Sun existence or from the Old Saturn existence. For those parts that come from the Old Saturn existence, from the Sun existence, from the Moon existence, and even from a great portion of the

Earth existence, are supersensible forces. These supersensible forces contained in our physical body, of which only the external part is accessible to our sensory contemplation, as explained just now – where do these supersensible forces go to after we have passed through the portal of death? As stated, we hand over to the earth, we return to the earth, only that part of our physical body – of that most wonderful structure which exists in the world, to begin with, as a form – we return to the earth only what the earth has given to the physical body. And where is the other part when we have passed through the portal of death? The other part withdraws from the one that sinks down into the earth, as it were, through the process or decomposition or cremation; the other part is taken up by the whole universe.

If you now think of everything you can at all imagine in the environment of the earth, including the planets and the fixed stars, if you imagine this in the most spiritual form, this spiritually conceived idea would give you the place where the spiritual part of our physical body abides after death. Only a portion of this spiritual part, a portion contained in the element of warmth, separates and remains with the earth. But every other spiritual part of our physical body is borne out into the spaces of the universe, into the whole cosmos.

Where do we go to when we abandon our physical body? Where do we dive down? Through our death, we go out with lightning speed into that which forms our physical body from out of all the supersensible forces. Imagine that all the constructive forces that have worked upon your physical body, ever since the time of Old Saturn, were to stretch themselves into infinity in order to prepare the place in which you live between death and a new birth. Between birth and death, all this is drawn together, I might say, within the space enclosed by your skin; it is merely drawn together.

When we are outside our physical body, we experience something that is of the utmost importance for the whole subsequent life between death and a new birth. I have often mentioned this. This experience is of opposite character to the corresponding experience during our life here, upon the physical plane. During our life upon the physical plane we cannot look back as far as the hour of our birth; we cannot look back upon it with the aid of our ordinary cognitive power. There is not one person who can remember his own birth, nor look back upon it. The only thing we know is that we were born, in the first place, because we have been told so by others, and in the second place, because all the other human beings that came to the earth after us were also born, so that we infer from this that we, too, were born. But we cannot pass through the real experience of our own birth.

Exactly the opposite is the case with the corresponding experience after death. Whereas, during our physical life, the immediate contemplation of our birth can never rise up before our soul, the moment of death stands before our soul throughout our life between death and a new birth, if we only look upon it spiritually. We must realize that we then look upon the moment of death from the other side. Here, on earth, death has a terrifying aspect only because we look upon it as a kind of dissolution, as an end. But when we look back upon the moment of death from the other side, from the spiritual side, then death continually appears to us as a victory of the spirit, as the Spirit that is extricating itself from the physical. It then appears as the greatest, most beautiful and significant event. Moreover, this experience kindles that which constitutes our ego-consciousness after death. Throughout the time between death and a new birth we have an ego-consciousness that not only resembles but far exceeds that which we have here during our physical life. We would not have this ego-consciousness if we could not look back incessantly, if we would not always see – but from the other side, from the spiritual side – that moment in which our spiritual part extricated itself from the physical. We know that we are an ego only because we know that we have died, that our spiritual has freed itself from our physical part. When we cannot contemplate the moment of death, beyond the portal of death, then our ego-consciousness after death is in the same case as our physical ego-consciousness here upon the earth when we are asleep. Just as we know nothing of our physical ego-consciousness when we are asleep, so we know nothing concerning ourselves after death if we do not constantly have before us the moment of death. It stands before us as one of the most beautiful and loftiest moments.

You see, even in this case we must set about thinking in an entirely different way of the spiritual world than of the sensory-physical world. If we indolently remain with the thoughts which we have in connection with the physical-sensory world, it will be impossible for us to grasp the spiritual in any way more precisely. For the most important thing after death is that the moment of death is viewed from the other side. This kindles our ego-consciousness on the other side. Here, in the physical world, we have, as it were, one side of ego-consciousness; after death, we have the other side of ego-consciousness. I explained just now where we should look for the supersensible part of our physical body after death. We should seek this physical body in the shape of a relation of forces, of an organism of forces, as a cosmos of forces, within the whole world. This physical essence prepares the place through which we must pass between death and a new birth.

Within our physical body, which is so small in comparison with the whole world, our skin really encloses a microcosm, something that is, in reality, a whole world. Trivially speaking, I might say that this world is merely rolled together and that afterwards it unrolls again and fills out the universe, with the exception of one tiny space that always remains empty.

Between death and a new birth we really exist everywhere in the world; we live in it with that part which, here on earth, lies at the foundation of our physical body in the form of supersensible forces. We are everywhere, except in that one place. This remains empty. It is the space enclosed by our skin, the space which we take up in the physical world. This remains empty.

Yet we constantly look upon this empty space. That is to say, we look upon our own self, from outside; we look into a concavity. This remains empty. It remains empty to such an extent that a fundamental feeling rises up in connection with it. Namely, we do not contemplate things in an abstract manner, we do not simply stare at them, but our contemplation is connected with a powerful inner life-experience, with a mighty experience. It is connected with the fact that when we contemplate this emptiness, a feeling rises up in us, a feeling that accompanies us throughout our life between death and a new birth and constitutes a great deal of what we generally designate as our life beyond. It is the feeling that there is something in the world which must again and again be filled out by us. And then we acquire the feeling: 'I exist in the world for a definite purpose, which I, alone, can fulfil.' Thus we learn to know our place within the world. We feel that we are building stones, without which the world could not exist. This is what arises through the contemplation of that empty space. When we gaze at it, we are overcome by a feeling telling us that we stand within the world as something that forms part of it.

All this is connected with the further development of our physical body. The more elementary forms of description only enable us to explain schematically, as it were, a reality of the spiritual world that really requires to be explained in the form of images. In order to rise gradually to those concepts which penetrate more deeply into the reality of the spiritual world, we must first have those images.

We know that our next experience is a kind of retrospective memory that lasts for days. But this retrospective memory is inappropriately designated (but nevertheless with a certain right) as a retrospective memory, for we have before us now, for a few days, something that resembles a tableau, or a panorama, woven out of all we have experienced during our past life. It does not, however, rise up in the same way in which an ordinary memory rises up in our physical body. You see,

the memories that live in our physical body are of such a kind
that we draw them out of our memory. Memory is a force that
is connected with our physical body. Our recollections rise up
in the form of thoughts; through the power of memory we
draw them out successively within the stream of time. But the
retrospective memory after death is of such a kind that
everything that occurred during our early life now surrounds
us simultaneously, as if it were a panorama. Our life-experiences now rise up in the form of imaginations. We can only say
that we now live, for whole days, within these experiences.
What we experienced just before death and what we experienced during our childhood stand before us simultaneously in
powerful pictures. A panorama of our life, a life-picture,
stands before us and it reveals, simultaneously, in a woof
woven out of the ether, what normally occurs successively
within the stream of time. Everything that we now see before
us lives in the ether.

We feel, above all, that we are now surrounded by something that is alive. Everything within it lives and weaves. And
then we experience that it resounds spiritually, that it shines
forth spiritually and gives warmth spiritually.

We know that this life-tableau disappears after a few
days. What makes it cease and what is the essence of this
life-tableau?

If we study the true essence of this life-tableau, we must
really say: everything that we have experienced during our life
is woven into it. How did we experience these things? In the
form of thoughts connected with our experiences. Everything
that we experienced in the form of thoughts and concepts is
contained in this picture of our life.

In order to grasp this concretely, let us now say: during our
earthly life we lived together with another human being, we
spoke with him and, in speaking with him, his thoughts
communicated with our thoughts. We received love from
him, we allowed his soul to influence us and experienced all
this inwardly. In this manner we shared the experiences of the

person we lived with. He lived and we lived, and through him we experienced something. What we experienced through him now appears to us woven into this etheric life-tableau. It is the same thing that constitutes our memories. Think, for instance, of the moment, ten or twenty years ago, when you first met him and experienced something through him. Imagine that this memory now rises up before you, but that you do not remember it in the same way in which you would remember things during your ordinary life. The ordinary memories are grey and faded, but now you remember things in such a way that they rise up within you as LIVING memories; you see your friend standing before you in exactly the same way in which he stood before you during the real experience.

Here, on earth, we are often very dreamy and what we experience upon the physical plane in a living and hearty manner becomes dulled and loses its vitality. But when we pass through the portal of death, when our experiences rise up before us in the life-tableau, they are no longer dull and lifeless but exist there in the original freshness and vitality which they possessed when we passed through them during our earthly life. In this form they become interwoven with our life-tableau; in this form we experience them after death for whole days.

In regard to the physical world, we have the impression that our physical body falls away from us when we die; in a similar way we now have the impression that our etheric body too falls away from us after a certain number of days, but it does not fall away from us in the same way in which our physical body falls away, for it becomes interwoven with the whole universe, with the whole world. It lives in the world and stamps its impressions upon the whole world while we are experiencing our life-tableau. What we thus have before us in the form of a life-tableau has now been handed over to the external world: it lives in our surroundings and has been taken over by the world.

During those days we have an important and impressive experience in this connection. For, after death, our experiences do not merely resemble the memories which we have during our earthly life but they are in every way substance for new experiences. Even the manner in which we grasp our ego, through the fact that we constantly look back upon our death, is a new experience, for our earthly senses do not enable us to experience anything similar. This can only be grasped through the knowledge of initiation. But even what we experience during the days in which we are surrounded by this life-tableau, by this etheric life that frees itself from us and becomes interwoven with the universe, even what we experience in this manner is impressive and lofty; it is an overwhelming and powerful experience for the human soul.

You see, during our physical life on earth, we face the world: we face the mineral, vegetable, animal and human kingdoms. They enable us to experience what our senses are able to experience, what our intellect, that is bound to the brain, obtains through the sense-experiences, what our feelings, that are connected with our vascular system, experience: we experience all these things here on earth.

But in reality, and from a loftier standpoint, we human beings are extremely great dunces (excuse this expression!), gigantic dunces, between birth and death. In regard to the wisdom of the great world, we are fearfully stupid if we believe that here on earth, when we experience something in the manner described and bear it along in the form of memories, everything is finished; we are fearfully stupid if we think that our experiences are finished when we take them up in this manner as human beings. For while we experience things, while we form concepts and feelings rise up in our experiences, the whole world of the Hierarchies is active within this process through which we acquire our experiences; the Hierarchies live and weave in it.

When we face a human being and look into his eyes, then the spirits of the Hierarchies, the Hierarchies themselves, the work of the Hierarchies, live in our gaze and in what is sent towards us through the gaze of the other human being. Our experience merely shows us the external aspect of things for, in reality, the Gods work within our experiences. We think that we only live for our own sake; yet the Gods work out something through our experiences; they obtain from them something that they can weave into the world. We form ideas, we have feeling experiences; the Gods take them up and communicate them to their world. And when we die, we know that the purpose of our life is to give the Gods the opportunity to spin out of our life this woof coming from our etheric body and to hand it over to the whole universe. The Gods gave us the chance to live in order that they might spin out something for themselves, thus enriching the world.

This is an overwhelming thought. Every one of our strides is the external expression of an event connected with the Gods; it forms part of that woof which the Gods use for their plan of the world and which they leave to us only until we pass through the portal of death. After our death they take it away from us and incorporate with the universe these, our human, destinies. Our human destinies are, at the same time, the deeds of Gods, and the form in which they appear to us human beings is merely their outward aspect. This is the significant, important and essential fact which we should bear in mind.

What we acquire inwardly, during our earthly life, through the fact that we can think and have feelings, whom does this belong to after our death? Whom does it now belong to? After our death it belongs to the universe. We look back upon our death, and in the same way we now look back with that part which remains to us, namely, with our astral body and our ego, upon that which has become interwoven with the universe, with the world. During our earthly life we bear within us what thus becomes interwoven with the universe after our death; we bear it within us as our etheric body. But now it is spun up and becomes interwoven with the world. And we now look upon it, we contemplate it. After our death, we look upon it in the same way in which we experience it inwardly here on earth. It now lives in the world outside. Just as here on earth we see stars, mountains, rivers, so after our death we see, in addition to what our physical body has become with lightning speed, also that part of our own experiences which has become interwoven with the universe. That part of our own experiences which now incorporates with the whole world-structure is reflected in those members which we still possess, in our astral body and in our ego; it is reflected in the same way in which the external world is reflected here on earth in our physical organs and through our physical being.

While this is reflected in us we acquire something that we cannot acquire during our earthly life, something that we shall only acquire later on, during the Jupiter period, in the form of a more external, physical impression. Now we acquire it spiritually, through the fact that our etheric being outside makes an impression upon us. This impression which is thus made upon us is, to begin with, a spiritual one; it is made in the form of images; in its image-character it is, however, the prototype of what we shall one day possess upon Jupiter: namely, the Spirit-Self.

A Spirit-Self is therefore born to us through the fact that our etheric part becomes interwoven with the universe; this Spirit-Self comes to birth spiritually, not in the form in which we shall have it later on, upon Jupiter.

The etheric body has now detached itself, so that we now have the astral body, the ego and the Spirit-Self.

The astral body and the ego therefore remain to us from our earthly life.

You already know that our astral body, in the earthly form in which it was subjected to us, remains with us for a long time after death. The astral body remains with us because it is permeated with all those things that only pertain to the earthly-human life, and because it cannot immediately expel this. We now pass through a time during which we can only cast off little by little what has become of our astral body as a result of our earthly life.

You see, here on earth we can only experience, in regard to the astral body, one half at the most of everything through which we pass. We really experience only half of what takes place in every one of our experiences. Let us take an example. Imagine – this applies both to good and to evil thoughts and actions – but let us take as an example an evil action. Imagine that you say something bad to another person and that your words hurt him. When we say something unkind we only experience that part which concerns us personally; we only experience the feelings that prompted us to say those evil words. This is the soul-impression which we gather when we say bad and unkind things. But the other person to whom we addressed our unkind words has an entirely different impression; he has, as it were, the other half of the impression and feels hurt. The second half of the impression lives in him. What we ourselves experience during our physical life on earth is one thing, and what the other person experiences is another thing.

Now imagine the following. After our death, when we pass backwards through our life, we must once more live through everything that other people, outside, have experienced through us. As we go backwards through our life, we experience the effects of our thoughts and actions. Between death and a new birth we therefore pass through our life by going through it backwards. And when we have gone back as far as our birth, we are ripe for the moment when also that part of our astral body may be cast off which is permeated with earthly things. It abandons us, and a new state of existence begins for us when we have cast off our astral body.

The astral body always kept us connected, I might say, with the earth; it maintained this connection in all our experiences. When we pass through our astral body – not in a dreamy condition, but by living through our earthly experiences backwards – we are still connected with our earthly life; we

still stand within our earthly existence. Now that we have cast
off – but this is not the right expression; it is, however,
impossible to use another one – now that we have cast off our
astral body, we are quite free of all that pertains to the earth
and we live in the real spiritual world.

A new experience now sets in. This casting-off of the astral
body is, again, merely one aspect of the whole experience; the
other aspect is an entirely different one. When we have passed
through our earthly experiences and no longer have our astral
body, we feel, as it were, inwardly filled and permeated with
– we cannot say with material – but with spirit; then we really
feel that we are in the spiritual world and the spiritual world
rises up within us. In former times it rose up before us in the
outer world when we contemplated the universe and saw our
own etheric body interwoven with the universe. But now it
rises up within us; we now experience it inwardly. And our ego
rises up within us as a prototype of what we shall possess
physically only upon Venus; our ego rises up as a prototype of
the Life-Spirit.

We now consist of Spirit-Self, Life-Spirit and ego.

Just as here on earth we live in a rather dreamy state from
our birth until that moment of our childhood in which we
acquire self-consciousness, which is the earliest moment of
life that we can recall, so we now lead a form of life that is fully
conscious, indeed more conscious and higher than our earthly
life. However, we experience a purely spiritual life, only when
we have detached ourselves from our astral body, from our
astral life, retaining only that part of our astral which permeates us inwardly. Consequently, we are, from that time
onwards, spirits among spirits.

Now another important and essential experience rises up.
During our life in the physical world we carry on our work, do
this or that thing and have experiences in connection with all
these things. Our experiences are, however, not limited to the
physical world; simultaneously and in connection with them,
we also experience something else. Although the expression

which I shall now use for these simultaneous experiences is just an ordinary, more general expression, let me nevertheless use this word; while we experience these things, we grow tired, we get used up. This is constantly the case: we grow tired. Although our weariness is eliminated for our next state of consciousness through the fact that we sleep, or rather, through the fact that we rest during our sleep, this elimination, or adjustment, is nevertheless only a partial one, for we know, of course, that during our life we gradually become used up, we grow older, and our strength gradually dwindles. Consequently, we also grow tired in a wider sense. When we grow older, we know that we cannot adjust everything by sleeping. Thus we wear out our strength, we grow tired, during our life on earth.

Indeed, we are now able to view this problem from another aspect. After our preceding explanation, we can now advance this problem in a different way; we can ask: why do the Gods allow us to grow weary? The fact that here on earth we get tired and wear out our strength gives us something that is really most significant for our whole life. Let us, however, grasp the idea that we get tired, in a wider sense than the usual one. Let us place it clearly before our soul.

You will grasp it best of all if you imagine it in the following way. Ask any one of those present: do you know anything concerning the interior of your head? Probably only a person who is suffering from a headache would answer that at the present moment he does know something concerning the interior of his head. He alone would feel what the inside of his head is like; all the others would not feel it.

We can feel our organs only when they are not quite in order; we are then to some extent aware of their existence through our feelings. As a rule, we only have a more general feeling of our physical body, and this feeling increases when anything is out of order. But when we only have this general feeling, we know very little concerning the interior of our body. Those who suffer from bad headaches know a little more concerning the inside of their head than an anatomist, who is merely acquainted with the head's vessels. In growing more and more tired, during the course of our life, we acquire an ever stronger feeling in regard to the body's interior, its spatial interior.

Consider the fact that the more weary we grow, the more the infirmities of life arise, for instance the infirmities of old age. Our life consists in that we gradually begin to feel and to sense our physical body. We learn to sense this physical part of our being because it becomes hardened within us and because it pushes itself, as it were, into our being. Just because it develops so slowly we regard it, I might say, as an insignificant feeling. Its real significance could be gauged if we could feel (excuse this trivial expression, but it conveys what I wish to say) in the pink of health, like an exuberantly healthy child, and immediately afterwards, for the sake of comparison, like an old man of 80 or 85, whose limbs have grown fragile. This would enable us to experience that feeling more strongly, simply because it develops so slowly. Yet growing weary is a real process. At first, it does not exist at all, for a child is full of exuberant vitality. But later on, fatigue gradually begins to drown the vital forces, and then the process of getting tired breaks through. We have the possibility of growing weary, and during this process (even though it only gives us, let us say, a dim feeling of our body's inner structure), during this process something takes place within us, something really takes place within us.

Our life in the physical world only shows us the outer aspect of deep, significant and lofty mysteries. The fact that this dim, insignificant feeling of growing weary accompanies us throughout our life, so that we are able to feel the inner structure of our body, is merely the outer aspect of something that becomes interwoven with us; it is wonderfully woven out of pure wisdom, a complete woof of pure wisdom.

While we thus grow weary during our life and begin to experience ourselves inwardly, a delicate knowledge becomes

interwoven with us, a knowledge of the wonderful constitution of our organs, of our inner organs. Our heart grows tired,
yet this weariness means that a knowledge of the heart's
structure becomes interwoven with us, a knowledge of how
the heart is built from out of the universe. Our stomach gets
tired – most of all, when we spoil it by eating too much – yet
during this process that tires the stomach, an image of wisdom
from out of the cosmos is woven into us, and this image shows
us how the stomach is built up.

The lofty, wonderful structure of our organism, of this
great work of art, arises within us in the form of an image. But
this image only comes to life when we cast off that part of our
astral body which is bound to the earth. What now lives within
us, what now fills us as Life-Spirit, is the wisdom connected
with our own being, it is the wisdom connected with the
wonderful structure of our inner being and this wisdom now
lives in us.

Now begins a time in which we compare, as it were, what
fills us in the form of Life-Spirit from out of the wisdom of our
inner being with the etheric woof that has already been woven
into the universe. Our task is now to compare how one thing
fits in with the other, and we then build up, in the form of an
image, our inner being; we give it the shape which it should
have during our next incarnation.

This is how we begin, but little by little our life approaches
the Midnight, which you will find described in one of the
Mystery Plays, in *The Soul's Awakening*. Particularly after the
World-Midnight we are engaged in a work that consists in
that we now participate in the world's creative work; we call
into life what we afterwards enjoy here. During our life
between death and a new birth we share in the work, we
participate in the weaving of the Gods' images. We have the
privilege of sharing in a divine task, in what the Gods aimed
at when they placed man into the world. We are allowed to
prepare our next incarnation.

Of course, this is not only connected with processes that

exclusively and egoistically concern our own being, for all manner of other processes take place as well. This may be evident particularly from the following:

If we gradually succeed in experiencing, in spiritual contemplation, this wonderful process – which is, above all, far higher than the one which takes place on earth, when summer and winter alternate, or when the sun rises and sets and when all that takes place which occurs in the form of earthly work – then something occurs in the spiritual world finally leading to our earthly incarnation, to human existence. This is a lofty, heavenly process, which has not only an external significance but a deep significance for the whole world.

We also encounter something else when we contemplate this process. It may sound strange to say this but, you see, the higher mysteries at first necessarily appear strange in the light of a physical-sensory contemplation. What rises up before our soul in connection with these mysteries must move us. The more it moves us, the better it is, for these things, the very nature of these things, should not approach our soul so that we remain dry and indifferent. They should not be taken up in such a way that we remain indifferent, dry and cool; but they should, instead, give us a soul-impression of the loftiness and greatness of the divine-spiritual world.

We can say: if anybody would undertake to present a spiritual science in such a dry way that it does not take hold of our whole being, and so that we do not gain an impression of the loftiness and greatness of the divine-spiritual that pulses and weaves through the world – if, after all these descriptions, we would live on indifferently and dryly, then we would be born without heads, in accordance with the present conditions of the world and in spite of everything we know! We would be born without heads! The structure of our head is something that we are unable to build. In its whole structure the human head is such a lofty image of the universe that the human being would be unable to form it, even with the aid of that life-wisdom which is woven into him; he would be unable to prepare it for the next incarnation. All the divine Hierarchies must co-operate in this work. Your head, this slightly irregular and somewhat transformed sphere, is a real microcosm, a true image of the great world-sphere. Within it lives, within it is collected, everything that exists outside in the universe. All the forces that are active in the different Hierarchies co-operate in order to produce the head. And when we begin to shape our next incarnation, from out the wisdom which we collected during the process of growing weary, all the Hierarchies co-operate and influence this activity in order to embody in us, as an image of the whole wisdom of the Gods, what afterwards becomes our head.

While all this occurs, our physical, hereditary stream is being prepared generations ahead here upon the earth. Just as after our death we can only hand over to the earth what comes from the earth, so our parents and grand-parents only give us that part of our being which pertains to the earth. Our earthly part is merely our exterior; it is merely the external expression within this earthly part. Woven into it is, in the first place, everything that we ourselves are able to weave in the manner described, and what all the Hierarchies of the Gods weave, before we gain a connection (through conception) with that which enwraps us and clothes us about when we enter the physical plane.

I explained to you that the more of this lofty knowledge we take up in our feelings the better it will be for us. Just consider the fact: we use our head. In so far as we live in materialism, we generally have not the slightest idea that whole Hierarchies of Gods are at work in order to produce our head, in order to mould that which lies, spiritually, at the foundation of our head, so that we are able to live. If we grasp this, in the meaning of a spiritual-scientific knowledge, it will spontaneously be filled with feelings of gratitude and thankfulness towards the whole universe.

Consequently, what we acquire through spiritual science should incessantly continue to increase and raise our feelings.

In the sphere of spiritual science, our sentient life should more and more hold pace with our cognitive work. It is not good to remain behind with our feelings. Whenever we learn to know a new and higher portion of spiritual science, we should be able to unfold, I might say, more and more reverent feelings towards the world's mysteries, which finally lead to the mysteries of man. A true progress in spiritual science really lies in this purifying, spiritual warmth of our feelings.

Let me mention one more thing, because it completes all that we have contemplated in this lecture. Here, in the physical world, we gradually grow accustomed to life by having, to begin with, the dull consciousness of childhood. At first we only recognize our mother and, little by little, we learn to know other people. As we grow accustomed to life in the physical world, we believe that we are constantly coming across new people. As far as our physical consciousness is concerned this is, in fact, true. But when we pass through the portal of death we have a real, true connection with all the souls that we encountered during our earthly life. They rise up again before our spiritual eye. The souls with whom we were connected during our earthly life and that crossed the portal of death before us, we find these souls, as it were. The words 'to find' really applies to physical conditions, but we may use it here to define that living way in which souls approach other souls. This 'finding' of the souls that crossed the portal of death before us should, however, be imagined in such a way that we approach them, as it were, in an opposite manner from the one in which we approach human beings here on the physical plane.

On the physical plane we encounter human beings so that we first approach them physically, and then we gradually become acquainted with their inner being. Their inner being unfolds only when we penetrate into their inner life. Hence, what we experience inwardly in connection with a human being is the result of that which develops from out of our own inner life. When we ourselves have crossed the portal of death and encounter the souls that have passed through the portal of death before us, we know to begin with: there is that particular soul. We can feel it, we know that it is there. Now we must, however, surrender our whole inner being to the first impression that arises, to the first most abstract impression. Here on earth we should allow other human beings to exercise their influence upon us; but in the spiritual world we must surrender our inner being, and we must now build up the image, the imagination, ourselves. The imaginative element, what we can look upon, this we must gradually build up. You may have an idea of the soul's experiences after death if you imagine that you do not see it all, but that you take hold of it... and as you gradually encompass it with your grasp, you form an image, you build up an image for yourself. You must therefore build up in inner activity the image of the soul whom you encounter. You realize, as it were: 'I am now facing a soul – what soul is it? It is the soul...' (and this knowledge rises out of your own soul) 'towards whom I had the feelings of a son towards his mother.' And you begin to feel: 'I experience myself together with this soul.' Now you begin to build its spiritual form. You must be active within it, and then it develops into an image. Through the fact that you build this image together with the other soul, you are united with that dead person even before you begin to form its spiritual shape. In this manner you are united with everything with which you were united during your earthly life; that is to say, you now experience these things in their own world. You must discover them by awakening within you the power of vision, so that you may look upon them, but this requires activity on your part.

It is not the same with souls that still dwell in their physical body, with souls that are still alive when we die. Even here on earth we encounter them in the form of images. After death we look down upon them on the earth and do not need to build up their image, for they already face us as images. The souls of those still on the earth may of course weave into these images something that can become spiritual warmth and nourishment for the dead, namely, the image which they are able to form through their thoughts for the dead, through their lasting love and memory, or – we know this, as spiritual scientists – by their reading something to the dead.

You see, all this extends the human gaze so that it penetrates, really penetrates, into the real world. If this rises up before our soul, we begin to realize how little we know of the spiritual world. This was not always the case. Only the completely materialistic people of modern times boast of the great extent of their knowledge. But we know that in the past human beings were clairvoyant and that this ancient, atavistic clairvoyance was lost only because certain qualities had to be acquired which disappeared in the midst of an existence connected with a materialistic world. If a real materialist, a thoroughly materialistic thinker, approaches us, he will, of course, say: 'It is nonsense to speak of an ancient clairvoyance, or that people had a special knowledge in the past.' But if we would only open our physical eyes a little as we pass through the world, we would very soon discover the falsity of such an argument! It is not even so long ago that people used to know more than they do at the present time.

You know, for we have often considered this matter – but let me mention it again at the conclusion of this lecture – that Lucifer and Ahriman have a share in our spiritual existence. We also know that in the Bible Lucifer is symbolized as a Serpent, as the Serpent on the Tree. The physical serpent, such as we see it today, and as modern painters always paint it when they depict the Paradise Scene, is not a real Lucifer; it is only his outer image, his physical image. The real Lucifer is a being that remained behind during the Moon-stage of evolution. He cannot be seen upon the earth among physical objects. If a painter wishes to paint Lucifer's real aspect he would have to paint him so that he can be grasped as an etheric form, through a kind of inner clairvoyant form of contemplation. He would then appear in the shape in which he works upon us; he would show that he is not connected with our head or with our organism in so far as these are exclusively formed by the earth, but that he is connected with the continuation of our head, with the spinal cord. A painter who knows something through spiritual science would therefore paint Adam and Eve, the Tree, and on the Tree the Serpent, but this serpent would only be a symbol and it would have a human head. If we were to come across such a painting today, we would assume that the painter has, of course, been able to paint this picture through spiritual science.

Probably such a painting may even be found here in Leipzig; but people do not go about with open eyes, they go through the world with bandaged eyes. In the Art Gallery of Hamburg there is a painting of the Middle Ages by Master Bertram, setting forth the Paradise Scene. In that painting, the Serpent on the Tree is painted correctly, as described just now. That picture can be seen there. But other painters have also painted the Paradise Scene in that way. What may we gather from this? That in the Middle Ages people still knew this, they knew it to the extent of being able to paint it. In other words: it is not so long ago that human beings were pushed completely on to the physical plane.

The course of man's spiritual history as related by materialistic thinkers, is, after all, nothing but an outer deception, because they think that man always had the aspect which he assumed in the course of the past few centuries, whereas it is not so long ago that he used to look into the spiritual world with the aid of his ancient clairvoyance. He had to abandon the spiritual world because he was not free, and in order to acquire full freedom and his ego-consciousness it was necessary that he should leave the spiritual world. Now he must once more find his way into the spiritual world.

Spiritual science therefore prepares something very important and essential: namely, that we may once more penetrate livingly into the spiritual world. Again and again let us conjure up in our soul the necessity of feeling that this small number of men that is now living in the very midst of a materialistic world and is led through its karma to the possibility of grasping mankind's most important task for the future – that this small number of human beings is called upon to fulfil important, most important, tasks through its soul-life. We should realize without any pride, we should realize modestly and humbly, the great difference between a soul that is gradually finding its way into the spiritual world, and all the people outside, who have not the slightest idea of this, who are, above all, not willing to have any idea of it. This fact should not merely arouse in us discouraging and painful feelings, but produce feelings that incite us to continue our work with increasing energy and to work faithfully within the stream of spiritual science, to which we were led through our karma.

When we were together last I also mentioned that when a human being passes through the portal of death before having lived through the whole of his life, then that part which is given to him in the form of an etheric body has not been used up completely. When a human being passes through the portal of death in his youth, then his etheric body might still have worked for years upon his physical body. But these forces do not get lost; they are still there. I also mentioned that in the present time, through the fact that every day and every hour death so numerously approaches mankind, many, many etheric bodies that might still have worked for a long time upon their physical bodies here on the physical plane are handed over to the spiritual-etheric world and hover in it. The forces that might, for decades, have provided for the physical body, become spiritual forces that co-operate in the spiritual development of humanity. Thus a time will come when these forces that constitute these etheric bodies, can be used for the spiritual progress of humanity; but this time will only come if here on earth there will be human souls who are able to understand this.

When the terrible events of the present shall have passed

over the earth and there will be peace once more, then the souls of those who are still living on the earth in human bodies will have the possibility of grasping something of the fact that all those who have gone into the spiritual world before their time have their etheric bodies in that world and that they can ray their forces into the earth. It will be necessary that this fact be grasped by these souls. These souls can then co-operate in that spiritual progress which is rendered possible particularly through the many deaths of self-sacrifice.

Imagine what it would mean if spiritual science were to disappear, and if no one were to have any comprehension for all that is being prepared in the spiritual world through these deaths of self-sacrifice! Imagine what this would mean! In that case, all those forces would become the property of Beings who would use them for other purposes than those for which they should be used, in accordance with the plan and resolution of the Gods who follow the right course of development.

This is an admonition that also comes from the events of our time, an admonition to the effect that we should stand fully within all that which constitutes the spiritual world. For even these events of our time have their spiritual aspect. What they reveal outwardly, in the form of blood, death and sacrifices, is the external expression of an inner spiritual course of events, which should, however, be grasped in the right spirit.

Of this I wish to remind you again and again, with the words that conclude our present considerations:

> From the courage of the fighters,
> From the blood of battles,
> From the sufferings of the abandoned,
> From the nation's deeds of sacrifice,
> Shall grow out a spiritual fruit,
> If souls lead, in spirit-consciousness,
> Their hearts and minds into the spirit-realm.

VIII. The Lively Interchange between the Living and the Dead

Bergen, 10 October 1913

As we are together here for the first time, I want to speak in an aphoristic way of matters pertaining to the spiritual world. Such matters are better and more easily expressed by word of mouth than in writing. This is not only because the prejudices existing in the world make it difficult in many respects to commit to writing everything that one so gladly conveys to *hearts* devoted to Anthroposophy, but it is also difficult because spiritual truths lend themselves better to the spoken word than to writing or to print.

This applies very specially to spiritual truths of a more intimate kind. For these things to be written down and printed always goes rather against the grain, although in our day it has to be done. It is always difficult to allow the more intimate truths relating to the higher worlds themselves to be written down and printed, precisely because writing and printing cannot be read by the spiritual Beings of whom one is speaking. Books cannot be read in the spiritual world.

True, for a short period after death books can still be read through remembrance, but the Beings of the higher Hierarchies cannot read our books. And if you ask: do these Beings then not want to learn how to read? – I must tell you that according to my experience they show no desire at present to do so because they find that the reading of what is produced on the earth is neither necessary nor useful to them.

The spiritual Beings begin to read only when human beings on the earth read books – that is to say, when what is contained in the books *comes to life in the thoughts of men.* Then the spiritual Beings read in these thoughts; but what is written or printed is like darkness for the Beings of the spiritual worlds. And so when something is committed to writing or to print, one has the feeling that communications are being made behind the back of the spiritual Beings. This is a feeling which a person of modern culture may not wholly share, but every true occultist will experience this feeling of distaste for writing and print.

When we penetrate into the spiritual worlds with clairvoyant vision, we see it to be of particular importance that knowledge of the spiritual world shall spread more and more widely during the immediate future, because upon this spread of spiritual science will depend a great deal in respect of a change that is becoming increasingly necessary in man's life of soul. If with the eyes of spirit we look back over a period measured by centuries only, we find something that may greatly astonish those who have no knowledge of these things. It is that intercourse between the living and the dead has become more and more difficult, that even a comparatively short time ago this intercourse was far more active and alive.

When a Christian of the Middle Ages, or even a Christian of more recent centuries, turned his thoughts in prayer to the dead who had been related or known to him, his prayers and feelings bore him upward to the souls of the dead with much greater power than is the case today. For the souls of the dead to feel warmed by the breath of the love streaming from those who looked upwards or sent their thoughts upward to them in prayer was far easier in the past than it is today – that is, if we allow external culture to be our only guide.

Again, the dead are cut off from the living more drastically in the present age than they were a comparatively short time ago, and this makes it more difficult for them to perceive what is astir in the souls of those left behind. This belongs to the evolution of humanity, but evolution must also lead to a rediscovery of this connection, this real intercourse between the living and the dead.

In earlier times the human soul was still able to maintain a real connection with the dead, even if it was no longer a fully conscious one, because for a long time now human beings have ceased to be clairvoyant. In even more ancient times the living were able to look upwards with clairvoyant vision to the dead and to follow the happenings of their life. Just as it was once natural for the soul to be in living relationship with the dead, so it is possible today for the soul to re-establish this intercourse and relationship by acquiring thoughts and ideas about the spiritual worlds. And it will be one of the practical tasks of anthroposophical life to ensure that the bridge is built between the living and the dead.

In order that we may really understand one another, I want to speak first of certain aspects of the mutual relationship between the living and the dead, starting with a quite simple phenomenon which will be explained in accordance with the findings of spiritual investigation. Souls who sometimes practise a little self-contemplation will be able to observe the following (and I believe that many have done so). Let us suppose that someone has hated another person in life, or perhaps it was, or is, merely a question of antipathy or dislike. When the person towards whom hatred or antipathy was directed dies, and the other hears of his death, he will feel that the same hatred or antipathy cannot be maintained. If the hatred persists beyond the grave, sensitive souls will feel a kind of shame that it should be so. This feeling – and it is present in many souls – can be observed by clairvoyance. During self-examination the question may well be asked: why is it that this feeling of shame at some hatred or antipathy arises in the soul, for the existence of such hatred was never at any time admitted to a second person?

When the clairvoyant investigator follows in the spiritual worlds the one who has passed through the Gate of Death and then looks back upon the soul who has remained on the earth, he finds that, generally speaking, the soul of the dead has a very clear perception, a very definite feeling, of the hatred in the soul of the living person. The dead sees the hatred – if I may speak figuratively. The clairvoyant investigator is able to confirm with all certainty that this is so. But he can also perceive what such hatred signifies for the dead. It signifies an obstacle to the good endeavours of the dead in his spiritual development, an obstacle comparable with hindrances standing in the way of some external goal on earth. In the spiritual world the dead finds that the hatred is an obstacle to his good endeavours. And now we understand why hatred – even if there was justification for it in life – dies in the soul of one who practises a little self-contemplation: the hatred dies because a feeling of shame arises in the soul when the one who was hated has died. True, if the person is not clairvoyant he does not know the reason for this, but implanted in the very soul there is a feeling of being observed; the man feels: the dead sees my hatred and it is an actual hindrance to his good endeavours.

Many feelings rooted deeply in the human soul are explained when we rise into the worlds of spirit and recognize the spiritual facts underlying these feelings. Just as when doing certain things on earth we prefer not to be physically observed and would refrain from doing them if we knew this was happening, so hatred does not persist after a person's death when we have the feeling that we ourselves are being observed by him. But the love or even the sympathy we extend to the dead eases his path, removes hindrances from him.

What I am now saying – that hatred creates hindrances in the spiritual world and love removes them – does not cut across karma. After all, many things happen here on earth which we shall not attribute directly to karma. If we knock our foot against a stone, this must not always be attributed to karma – not, at any rate, to moral karma. In the same way it is not a violation of karma when the dead feels eased through the love streaming to him from the earth, or when he encounters hindrances to his good endeavours.

Something else that will make an even stronger appeal in connection with intercourse between the dead and the living is the fact that in a certain sense the souls of the dead too need nourishment; not, of course, the kind of nourishment required by human beings on the earth, but of the nature of spirit-and-soul. By way of comparison, just as we on the earth must have cornfields where the grain for our physical sustenance ripens, so must the souls of the dead have cornfields from which they can gather certain sustenance which they need during the time between death and a new birth. As the eye of clairvoyance follows the souls of the dead, the souls of sleeping human beings are seen to be cornfields for the dead. For one who has this experience in the spiritual world for the first time, it is not only surprising but deeply shattering to see how the souls living between death and a new birth hasten as it were to the souls of sleeping human beings, seeking for the thoughts and ideas which are in those souls; for these thoughts are food for the souls of the dead and they need this nourishment.

When we go to sleep at night, the ideas and thoughts which have passed through our consciousness in our waking hours begin to live, to be living beings. Then the souls of the dead draw near and share in these ideas, feeling nourished as they perceive them. When clairvoyant vision is directed to the dead who night after night make their way to the sleeping human beings left behind on earth – especially blood-relations but friends as well – seeking refreshment and nourishment from the thoughts and ideas that have been carried into sleep, it is a shattering experience to see that they often find nothing. For as regards the state of sleep there is a great difference between one kind of thought and another.

If throughout the day we are engrossed in thoughts connected with material life, if our mind is directed only to what is going on in the physical world and can be achieved there, if we have given no single thought to the spiritual worlds before passing into sleep but often bring ourselves into those worlds by means quite different from thoughts, then we have no nourishment to offer to the dead. I know towns in Europe where students induce sleepiness by drinking a lot of beer! The result is that they carry over thoughts which cannot live in the spiritual world. And then when the souls of the dead approach, they find barren fields; they fare as our physical body fares when famine prevails because our fields yield no crops. Especially at the present time much famine among souls can be observed in the spiritual worlds, for materialism is already very widespread. Many people regard it as childish to occupy themselves with thoughts about the spiritual world but thereby they deprive souls after death of needed nourishment.

In order that this may be rightly understood, it must be stated that nourishment after death can be drawn only from the ideas and thoughts of those with whom there was some connection during life; nourishment cannot be drawn from those with whom there was no connection at all. When we cultivate Anthroposophy today in order that there may again be in souls a spirituality which can be nourishment for the dead, we are not working only for the living, or merely in order to provide them with some kind of theoretical satisfaction, but we try to fill our hearts and souls with thoughts of the spiritual world because we know that the dead who were connected with us on earth must draw their nourishment from these thoughts. We feel ourselves to be workers not only for living human beings, but workers too in the sense that anthroposophical activity, the spread of anthroposophical life, is also of service to the spiritual worlds. In speaking to the living for their life by day, we promote ideas which, bringing satisfaction as they do in the life by night, are fruitful nourishment for the souls whose karma it was to die before us. And so we feel the urge not only to spread Anthroposophy by the ordinary means of communication, but deep down within us there is the longing to cultivate Anthroposophy in communities, in groups, because this is of real value.

As I have said, the dead can draw nourishment only from souls with whom they were associated in life. We therefore try to bring souls together in order that the harvest-fields for the dead may become more and more extensive. Many a human being who after death finds no harvest-field because all his family are materialists, finds it among the souls of anthroposophists with whom he had had some connection. That is the deeper reason for working together in communities, and why we are anxious that the dead should have been able before death to know anthroposophists who are still occupied on the earth with spiritual things; for when these people are asleep the dead can draw nourishment from them.

In ancient times, when a certain spirituality pervaded the souls of human beings, it was among religious communities and blood-relatives that help was sought after death. But the power of blood-relationship has diminished and must be replaced by cultivation of the spiritual life, as is our endeavour. Anthroposophy can therefore promise that a new bridge will be built between the living and the dead and that through it we can mean something real to the dead. And when with clairvoyant vision today we sometimes find human beings in the life between death and a new birth suffering because those they have known, including their nearest and dearest, harbour only materialistic thoughts, we recognize how necessary it is for cultural life on earth to be permeated with spiritual thoughts.

Suppose, for example, we find in the spiritual world a man who died fairly recently, whom we knew during his life on earth and who left behind certain members of his family also known to us. The wife and children were all of them good people in the ordinary sense, with a genuine love for one another. But clairvoyant vision now reveals that the father, whose wife was the very sun of his existence when he came home after heavy and arduous work, cannot see into her soul because she has not spiritual thoughts either in her head or in her heart. And so he asks: where is my wife? What has become of her? He can look back only to the time when he was united with her on earth, but now, when he is seeking her most urgently of all, he cannot find her. This may well happen. There are many people today who believe that as far as consciousness is concerned the dead have passed into a kind of void, who can think of the dead only with materialistic thoughts, not with any fruitful thoughts. In the life between death and rebirth a soul may be looking towards someone still on earth, someone who had loved him, but the love is not combined with belief in the soul's continued existence after death. In such a case, at the very moment after death when this desire arises to see one who was loved on earth, all vision may be extinguished. The living human being cannot be found, nor can any link be established with him, although it is known that he could indeed be contacted if spiritual thoughts were harboured in his soul.

This is a frequent and sorrowful experience for the dead. And so it may happen – this can be seen by clairvoyant vision – that many a human being after death encounters obstacles in the way of his highest aims on account of the thoughts of antipathy by which he is followed, and he finds no consolation in the living thoughts of those to whom he was dear on earth because owing to their materialism they are hidden from his sight.

The laws of the spiritual world, perceived in this way by clairvoyant vision, hold good unconditionally. That this is so is shown by an example which it has often been possible to observe. It is instructive to see how thoughts of hatred, or at least antipathy, take effect even if they are not conceived in full consciousness. There are school-teachers of the type usually known as 'strict', who are unable to gain the affection of their pupils; in such cases, of course, the thoughts of antipathy and hatred are formed half innocently. But when such a teacher dies it can be seen how these thoughts too – for they persist – are obstacles in the way of his good endeavours in the spiritual world. After the teacher's death it is not often that a child or young person realizes that his hatred ought to cease, but he nevertheless preserves the feeling of how the teacher tormented him. From such insights a great deal can be learnt about the mutual relationships between the living and the dead.

I have been trying to lead up to something that can become a fundamentally good result of anthroposophical endeavour – namely, *reading to the dead*. It has been proved in our own Movement that very great service can be rendered to the souls of those who have died before us by reading to them about spiritual things. This can be done by directing your thoughts to the dead and, in order to make this easier, you can picture him as you knew him in life, standing or sitting before you. In this way you can read to more than one soul at a time. You do not read aloud, but you follow the ideas with alert attention, always keeping in mind the thought: the dead are standing before me.

That is what is meant by reading to the dead. It is not always essential to have a book, but you must not think abstractly and you must think each thought to the end. In this way you are able to read to the dead.

Although it is more difficult, this can be carried so far that if in the realm of some particular world-conception – or indeed in any domain of life – thoughts have been held in common with the soul of the dead and there has been some degree of personal relationship, one can even read to a soul with whom the connection has been no closer than this. Through the warmth of the thoughts directed to him, he gradually becomes attentive. Thus it may be of real use to read to distant associates after their death.

The reading can take place at any time. I have been asked what is the best hour of the day for such reading, but it is quite independent of time. All that matters is to think the thoughts through to the end; to skim through them is not enough. The subject-matter must be worked through word by word, as if one were reciting inwardly. Then the dead read with us. Nor is it correct to think that such reading can be useful only to those who have come into contact with Anthroposophy during their lifetime. This is by no means necessarily so.

Quite recently, perhaps not even a year ago, one of our friends, and his wife too, felt a kind of uneasiness every night. As the friend's father had died a short time previously, it struck him at once that his father was wanting something and was turning to him. And when this friend came to me for advice, it was found that the father, who during his lifetime would not listen to a word about Anthroposophy, was feeling an urgent need after his death to know something of it. Then, when the son and his wife read to the father the lecture-course on the Gospel of St John which I once gave in Cassel, this soul felt deeply satisfied, as though lifted above many disharmonies that had been experienced shortly after death.[13]

This case is noteworthy because the soul concerned was that of a preacher who had regularly presented the views of his religion to other people, but after death could only find satisfaction by being able to share in the reading of an anthroposophical elucidation of the Gospel of St John. It is not essential that the one whom we wish to help after death should have been an anthroposophist in his lifetime, although in the nature of things very special service will be rendered to an anthroposophist by reading to him.

A fact such as this gives us a view of the human soul quite different from the one usually held. There are factors in the souls of human beings of far greater complexity than is generally believed. What takes its course consciously is actually only a small part of man's life of soul. In the unconscious depths of his soul there is a great deal going on of which he has at most a dim inkling; it hardly enters at all into his clear waking consciousness. Moreover, the very opposite of what a person believes or thinks in his upper consciousness may often be astir in his subconscious life. A very frequent case is that one member of a family comes to Anthroposophy and the brother or the husband or the wife become more and more hostile to it, often scornful and rabidly opposed. Great antipathy to Anthroposophy then develops in such a family and life becomes very difficult for many people because of the scorn and even anger of friends or relatives.

Investigation of these latter souls often reveals that in their subconscious depths an intense longing for Anthroposophy is developing. Such a soul may be longing for Anthroposophy even more intensely than someone who in his upper consciousness is an avid attender of anthroposophical meetings. But death lifts away the veils from the subconscious and balances out such things in a remarkable way. It often happens in life that a person deadens himself to what lies in the subconscious; there are people who may have an intense longing for Anthroposophy –

but they deaden it. By raging against Anthroposophy they deaden this longing and delude themselves by repudiating it. But after death the longing asserts itself all the more forcibly. The most ardent longing for Anthroposophy often shows itself after death in the very people who have raged against it in life. Do not, therefore, refrain from reading to those who were hostile to Anthroposophy while they were alive, for by this reading you may often be rendering them the greatest service imaginable.

A question often raised in connection with this is: 'How can one be sure that the soul of the dead person is able to listen?' Admittedly, without clairvoyance, it is difficult to be sure of this, although one who steeps himself in thoughts of the dead will in time be surprised by a feeling that the dead person is actually listening. This feeling will be absent only if he is inattentive and fails to notice the peculiar warmth that often arises during the reading. Such a feeling can indeed be acquired, but even if this proves not to be possible it must nevertheless be said that in our attitude to the spiritual world a certain principle always applies. The principle is that when we read to one who has died, we help him under all circumstances if he hears us. Even if he does not hear us, we are fulfilling our duty and may eventually succeed in enabling him to hear. In any case we gain something by absorbing thoughts and ideas which will quite certainly be nourishment for the dead in the way indicated. Therefore under no circumstances is anything lost. Actual experience has shown that in fact this awareness of what is being read is extraordinarily widespread among the dead, and that tremendous service can be rendered to those to whom we read the spiritual wisdom that can be imparted to us today.

Thus we may hope that the wall dividing the living from the dead will become thinner and thinner as Anthroposophy spreads through the world. And it will be a beautiful and splendid result of Anthroposophy if in a future time people come to know – but as actual fact, not in theory only – that in reality it is only a matter of a transformation of experience when we ourselves have passed through so-called death and are together with the dead. We can actually enable them to share in what we ourselves experienced during physical life. A false idea of the life between death and rebirth would be indicated if the question were asked: 'Why is it necessary to read to the dead? Do they not know through their own vision what those on earth can read to them? Do they themselves not know it far better?' This question will of course be asked only by one who is not in a position to know what can be experienced in the spiritual world. After all, we can live in the physical world without acquiring knowledge of it. If we are not in a position to form judgements about certain things, we have no real knowledge of the physical world. The animals live together with us in the physical world, but do not know it as we ourselves know it. The fact that a soul after death is living in the spiritual world does not mean that this soul has knowledge of that world, although he is able to behold it. The knowledge acquired through Anthroposophy can be acquired only on the earth; it cannot be acquired in the spiritual world. If, therefore, beings in the spiritual world are to possess knowledge, it must be learnt through those who themselves acquire it on earth. It is an important secret of the spiritual worlds that the soul can be in them and behold them, but that knowledge of them must be acquired on the earth.

At this point I must mention a common misconception about the spiritual worlds. When a human being is living in the spiritual world between death and a new birth, he directs his longing to our physical world somewhat as a physical human being directs his longing to the spiritual world. A human being between death and a new birth expects from people on the earth that they will show and radiate up to him knowledge that can be acquired only on the earth. The earth has not been established without purpose in spiritual world-existence; the earth has been summoned to life in order that there may come into being that which is possible nowhere else. Knowledge of the spiritual worlds – which means more than vision, more than a mere onlooking – can arise only on the earth.

I said before that the beings of the spiritual worlds cannot

read our books, and I must now add that what lives in us as
Anthroposophy is for the spiritual beings, and also for our
own souls after death, what books here on earth are for
physical man – something through which he acquires knowledge of the world. But these books which we ourselves are for
the dead, are *living* books. Try to feel the importance of these
words: we must provide reading for the dead!

In a certain sense our books are more long-suffering, for
they do not allow their letters to vanish away into the paper
while we are reading them, whereas, by filling our minds with
material thoughts which are invisible in the spiritual worlds,
we people often deprive the dead of the opportunity of
reading. I am obliged to say this because the question is often
raised as to whether the dead themselves are not capable of
knowing what we are able to give them. They cannot be,
because Anthroposophy can be grounded only on the earth
and must be carried up from there into the spiritual worlds.

When we ourselves penetrate into the spiritual worlds and
come to know something about the life there, we
encounter conditions altogether different from those
prevailing in physical life on earth. That is why it is so very
difficult to describe these conditions in terms of human
words and human thoughts. Any attempt to speak concretely
about them often seems paradoxical.

To take one example only, I am able to tell you of a human
soul after death together with whom it was possible – because
of his special knowledge – to make certain discoveries in the
spiritual world about the great painter Leonardo da Vinci,
particularly about his famous picture *The Last Supper* in
Milan. When one investigates a spiritual fact in association
with such a soul, this soul is able to indicate many things
which ordinary clairvoyance might not otherwise have found
in the Akasha Chronicle. The soul in the spiritual world is
able to point them out, but can do so only if there is some
understanding of what this soul is trying to convey. Something very noteworthy then comes to light.

Suppose that in company with such a soul one is investigating how Leonardo da Vinci created his famous picture. Today the picture is hardly more than a few patches of colour. But in the Akasha Chronicle one can watch Leonardo as he painted, one can see what the picture was once like – although this is not an easy thing to do. When the investigation is carried on in company with a soul who is not incarnate but has some connection with Leonardo da Vinci and his painting, one perceives that this soul is showing one certain things – for example, the faces of Christ and of Judas as they actually were in the picture. But one perceives, too, that the soul could not reveal this unless at the moment when it is being revealed there is understanding in the soul of the living investigator. This is a *sine qua non.* And only at the moment when the soul of the living investigator is receptive to what is being disclosed does the discarnate soul itself learn to understand what is otherwise merely vision. To speak figuratively: after something has been experienced together with such a soul – something that can be experienced only in the way described – this soul says to one: you have brought me to the picture and I feel the urge to look at it with you. (The soul of the dead says this to the living investigator because of the latter's desire to investigate the picture.) Numerous experiences then arise. But a moment comes when the discarnate soul is either suddenly absent or says that it must depart. In the case of which I have just told you, the discarnate soul said: up to now the soul of Leonardo da Vinci regarded with approval what was being done, but does not now desire the investigation to continue.

My object in telling you this is to describe an important feature of the spiritual life. Just as in physical life we know that we are looking at this or that object – we see a rose, or whatever it may be – so in the spiritual life we know: this or that being is seeing us, watching us. In the spiritual worlds we have the constant feeling that beings are looking at us. Whereas in the physical world we are conscious that we are observing the world, in the spiritual world the experience is that we ourselves are being observed, now from this side, now from that. We feel that eyes are upon us all the time, but eyes that also impel us to take decisions. With the knowledge that we are or are not being watched by eyes in favour of what we ought or ought not to do, we either do it or refrain. Just as we reach out to pick a flower that delights us because we have seen it, in the spiritual world we do something because a being there views it favourably, or we refrain from the action because we cannot endure the look that is directed at it. This experience must become ingrained in us. In the spiritual world we feel that we ourselves are being seen, just as here in the physical world we feel that we ourselves are seeing. In a certain sense, what is active here is passive in that other world, and what is active there is passive here.

From this it is obvious that quite different concepts must be acquired in order to understand correctly descriptions of conditions in the spiritual world. You will therefore realize how difficult it is to coin in words of ordinary human language descriptions of the spiritual world that one would so gladly give. And you will realize too how essential it is that for many things the necessary preparatory understanding shall first have been created.

There is only one other matter to which I want to call attention. The question may arise: why does anthroposophical literature describe in such a general sense what happens directly after death, in Kamaloca and in the realm of spirits (Devachan) and why is so little said about individual examples of clairvoyant vision? For it may well be believed that to observe a particular soul after death would be easier than to describe general conditions. But it is not so. I will use a comparison to explain this.

It is easier for rightly developed clairvoyance to survey the broad, general conditions – such as the passage of the human soul through death, through Kamaloca and upwards into Devachan – than to perceive some particular experience of an individual soul. In the physical world it is easier to have knowledge of phenomena that are subject to the influences of the great movements of the celestial bodies and more difficult in the case of irregular phenomena caused by those movements. Every one of you will be able to predict that the sun will rise tomorrow morning and set in the evening; but it is not so easy to know exactly what the weather will be. The same holds good for clairvoyance. The knowledge of conditions usually portrayed in the descriptions of the spiritual worlds – conditions which are first perceived in clairvoyant consciousness – is to be compared with the knowledge of the general course taken by the heavenly bodies. And one can always count upon the fact that the data of such knowledge will generally prove correct.

Particular happenings in the life between death and rebirth are like the weather conditions here on the earth – which are, of course, also subject to law, but difficult to know with certainty. At one place one cannot be sure what kind of weather there is at another. Here in Bergen it is difficult to know what the weather is in Berlin, but not the positions of the sun or the moon. A special development of the faculty of clairvoyance is required to follow the course of an individual life after death, for to do this is more difficult than to follow the general course taken by the human soul.

On the right path, knowledge of the general conditions is acquired first, and only at the very end – if the necessary development has been achieved through training – knowledge of what would seem to be the easier. A person may have been able for some time to see conditions in Kamaloca or Devachan quite correctly and yet find it extremely difficult to see what time it is on the watch in his pocket. Things in the physical world present the greatest difficulty of all to clairvoyance.

In acquiring knowledge of the higher worlds it is exactly the opposite. Errors occur here because a certain natural clair-voyance still exists; this clairvoyance is unreliable and prone to all kinds of aberrations, but it may long have been present without its possessor having clairvoyant sight of the general conditions described in Anthroposophy, which are easier for the trained clairvoyant.

IX. The Human Being's Experiences Beyond the Gates of Death

Düsseldorf, 17 June 1915

IT HAS often been observed that our spiritual-scientific Movement does not only aim to adopt in a theoretical way the concepts and ideas which spiritual science can provide; it is concerned, rather, that the results of spiritual research should enter deeply into the inmost gestures and impulses of our feeling life. We must, of course, take our starting-point from the study of these results – this is the only way to make them our own. But we should not regard spiritual science in the same way as other sciences, in which it is possible merely to remain knowledgeable about this or that fact. Rather, it should work upon our soul so that various regions of our feeling-life are altered by its influence. The concepts, ideas and images which we encounter in spiritual science should rouse and stir our inmost soul, should unite with our feelings so that we learn not only to see the world in a different way, but also to feel differently. The spiritual scientist should actually find his way through certain life-situations quite differently than would otherwise be possible. Only when he can do this has he really achieved what spiritual science can offer us.

We live in difficult times: death, that most important concern of spiritual science, appears before our eyes, souls and hearts in innumerable instances; to some it comes close, to others very close indeed. The spiritual scientist should be able to keep spiritual science alive in his heart even during these difficult times. He should have a different relationship to the events of these times than is possible for someone else, even when they touch him very closely. One person may, of course, need consoling, another may need encouragement; but both of them can find these in spiritual science. Only when this can be so have we rightly understood the true intention of spiritual science.

The fact that spiritual science enables us to feel quite differently than we otherwise would about certain things must move and affect us. If you peruse much of what has already been said in the context of our spiritual science about the mystery of death, you will understand what I wish to say today; I do not, though, intend merely to repeat myself, but also wish to add to earlier observations. We do not only need to think differently about death, we also need to feel differently about it. The mystery of death is connected with the deepest mysteries of the world. We must be quite clear that we lay aside, when we pass through the gates of death, every faculty which allows us to perceive and gain knowledge in the physical world, everything which enables us to experience the outer world. We lay aside these senses when we enter the spiritual world, we have them no longer. This fact alone should prove to us that we need to make efforts to think in a different way from the way we have learned to think through our senses, when we think about the sense-free world.

We do, however, have a kind of reference point for such experience; something akin to conditions in the spiritual world penetrates our ordinary life between birth and death. Our dream experiences do not come to us through our senses. The senses really have nothing to do with them. And yet they come to us in images which sometimes remind us of the life we lead through the senses. In dream images we have, albeit in a weak form, a reflection of the imaginative world we encounter in spiritual existence between death and a new birth. We have imaginative perception after death; we experience through images. In the sense-world we may see, for example, a red colour, and ask: 'What lies behind this colour?' The answer will be: 'Something which exists in space, something made of matter.' A red colour will also appear to you in the spiritual world, but behind it is nothing material, nothing which would give a material impression in the ordinary sense. Behind this red is, rather, a soul-spiritual being. What is behind it is the same that you experience within your soul as your world. One could put it like this: from the sense-impression of a colour we descend into the outer, physical material world; from imaginative perception, on the other hand, we rise up higher and higher through regions of the spiritual world. And now we must be quite clear – I have particularly emphasized this in the latest edition of *Theosophy* – that such imaginative perceptions do not come towards us in the same way as sense-impressions of the physical world. They are there, certainly, but we encounter them as experiences. It is quite justified to call these imaginative perceptions 'red' or 'blue', but they are different from sense-impressions of the physical world. They are much more inward; we are connected to them in a far more inward way. You are separate from the red colour of the rose; but you feel yourself united with, and contained within, the red colour in the spiritual world. When you perceive red in the spiritual world, you are in the presence of a spiritual being whose will is unfolding, actively shining out, manifesting in this colour. Yet you feel yourself contained within this will; and this feeling and experience of within-ness is what you, quite naturally, perceive as red. Physical colour is like a frozen, solidified spiritual experience. This is just one example of the way we must learn to think differently about many things, must alter the quality and nature of our concepts, if we really wish to encompass the spiritual world with our understanding.

Then we must also be clear that the relationship in the spiritual world between 'imaginations' and the spiritual beings from whom they originate – who, for example, express themselves through colours – is a different relationship from the one between colours and entities in the sense-world. The rose is red – that is a property of the rose. But when a spirit comes near to us and we are aware, in the way that has just been described, that it is radiating red, this red is not a property of the spirit in the same way that the red belongs to the rose. It is, rather, a kind of manifestation of the spirit's inner intention, a script which the spirit inscribes into the spiritual world. And one must fathom and discern the meaning of these imaginations. The activity necessary for this can only be compared, in the physical world, with its ahrimanic reflection in the process of reading. We perceive the red colour of the rose to be its property. In the spiritual world we do not simply observe red, but we interpret it – not at all, I must repeatedly warn, in any fantasizing way. Our soul discovers naturally that it has encountered a sound, a sign, something which must be deciphered or read, through which it can then understand what is meant. The spirit means something when it manifests as red or blue or green; or as C or G sharp. One begins to speak with the spirit, to decipher its script. Our ordinary cultural life is actually based on the fact that such things, which have a deep wisdom in the spiritual world, are also transplanted into the outer world. One can justifiably speak of an 'occult reading', for whoever develops clairvoyant consciousness and enters the spiritual world perceives these imaginations, and through reading them can look upon the essence of the souls living in the spiritual world. Not only colour experiences are perceived but also other impressions, some of which are reminiscent of sense-impressions and others which are new, existing only in spiritual regions.

Such an activity, which is a purely soul-spiritual one, is under the sway of spiritual beings who are progressing and developing in a right way. Here in the physical world Ahriman creates a reflection of what I have described. The reading of an outer script in the physical world is an ahrimanic reflection of occult reading. At the time of its invention, printing was quite rightly felt to be an ahrimanic art, a 'black art', as it was called. One must not believe that it is possible somehow to escape the clutches of Lucifer and Ahriman; they have to exist within worldly culture. It is just a question of finding an equilibrium, finding a middle way between their continual pull. If someone wished to remain quite untouched by Ahriman, he would have to forgo learning to read. But it is not a question of fleeing Ahriman and Lucifer; instead we must develop the right relationship to them, in spite of the fact that their powers surround us. As long as we know that we follow what has so often been described as the Christ impulse living within us, and as long as we embrace those spiritual feelings which enjoin upon us to follow Christ through our will, then we may also read. We can then also experience – and will do so, if it accords with our karma – that reading originated with Ahriman; then we will see this ahrimanic art in the right light. If we do not experience this then we may well speak loud praises of ahrimanic culture, of the progress and glory of ahrimanic culture as represented, for example, by reading.

But all such things also bring responsibilities which need to be honoured. Particularly in our present time, much can be cited in defence of, or in opposition to, any point of view. We really have, these days, what can be termed a flood of warring literature. Every day brings not only new pamphlets but also books which make statements such as: 'This country has such and such a percentage of people who are illiterate.' To sanction and adopt this sort of information would not be in keeping with the responsibility borne by someone familiar with spiritual science. If I wished, for example, to illuminate the worst qualities of a particular country as part of my descriptions of our times, and in order to do so would say: 'The number of people in this country who cannot read and write is such and such a percentage,' then I would not be speaking in a proper spiritual-scientific way. Only those things should be spoken of which are in harmony with one's sense of responsibility towards occult obligations. You can see from this example that spiritual science lays obligations upon us and must really enter into life in this deeper sense. If ever the spiritual researcher says things which others also say, you will be able to see that they are said in a quite different

context, which is the important thing. This is why much of
what is described by spiritual science will seem strange to
someone unfamiliar with it, since he is used to thinking in
other ways; he will no doubt sometimes say to himself: this
spiritual science calls white black and vice versa! And in fact
this is sometimes quite necessary, since many ideas and
concepts which one develops in the physical world have to be
radically altered when one rises into the spiritual world.

Let us from this point of view consider one of the most
important, mysterious conceptions which we must glean
from our impressions of the physical world – that of death. In
the physical world the human being always sees death from
one side only; he sees human life developing up to the point
at which a person dies, that is, at which the physical body falls
away from the higher aspects of human nature and decays
within the physical world. The human being viewing death
from the perspective of the physical world really sees it from
one side only. To see death from the other side means to see
it in a quite opposite light, in a radically different way.

When we enter physical life at birth we experience a time
in which we have not yet attained the peak of physical
consciousness. You know that we cannot remember the first
years of our life with our normal physical consciousness.
No one can remember their birth with this normal consciousness. It can be said that physical consciousness dictates
that one's own birth must be forgotten. Birth and the first
years of life are forgotten. When, between birth and death,
we look back at our life, we can only remember back to a
certain point. The point at which memory breaks off is
not our physical birth; there is a period during which we
have experiences which we cannot later remember. No one
can know that he was born. He can only conclude it by
observing the births of other human beings. If a scientific
researcher wished only to accept what he could see, then
he would find it impossible – if he wanted to be logical – to
prove his own birth. One can only perceive one's own birth

through clairvoyance. Otherwise one can only infer it.

Exactly the opposite is true of death. All through the time between death and a new birth, the moment of death stands before the eye of the soul as the most vivid and vital impression. But you must not think that this is a painful memory. Then you would have to believe that the person who has died looks back upon the same aspect of death which you perceive in the physical world, upon decay and dissolution. But in reality he sees death from the other side: he sees death as the most beautiful experience of all. There is nothing more beautiful in the human being's normal experience of the spiritual world than his perception of death. This victory of the spirit over matter, this spiritual light shining up out of the darkness of matter, is the most significant and mightiest thing that can be experienced during the life which the human being passes through between death and a new birth.

When, after death, the human being lays aside the etheric body and gradually emerges into full consciousness – which is accomplished not long after death – then he no longer has the same relationship to himself which he had here in the physical world. The human being on earth is unconscious of himself while asleep; when he awakes, he becomes aware that he has a Self, an 'I'. After death it is somewhat different, for his self-awareness reaches a higher stage. I will describe to you in a moment how it alters. He also experiences in the spiritual world something like a reflective awareness of himself, of his 'I'. It is a similar experience to the one of remembering and contemplating oneself when one wakes up in the morning. But this self-contemplation is achieved by looking back to the moment of death. In order to perceive our 'I' between death and a new birth we look back at our death and can then say: 'You are myself, you are an "I", for you really died!'

This is the most significant thing: one looks back upon the victory of the spirit over the body at the moment of death, which is the most beautiful experience that one can have in the spiritual world. And as one looks back one becomes aware of one's Self in the spiritual world. This is – it is not quite correct to say like an awakening – a contemplation of oneself through perceiving one's death. Therefore it is so important that the human being is really able to look back at the moment of death with the full consciousness he develops after death. It is enormously important that he should not dream through what he perceives, but can fully understand it. We can, in fact, prepare ourselves for this during life by trying to practise self-knowledge. Spiritual science really exists in order to give the human being access to the self-knowledge which he needs. It is, after all, a way of leading the human being out into his larger Self, that Self through which he is part of the whole world. I said that consciousness after death was somewhat different from consciousness here in the physical world. I could depict for you the nature of post-death consciousness in the following way:

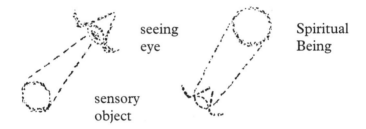

seeing
eye

Spiritual
Being

sensory
object

Let us say that we have here an eye and there an object. How do we become conscious that there is an object outside us? Because the object makes an impression upon our eye. As it does so, we get to know something about the object. The object is outside us in the world and makes an impression upon our senses; we take the image and concept which we then form of it into ourselves, into our soul. The object is outside us. The idea of it which we then form is given to us by it. In the spiritual world it is different. And because I am unable to depict it to you in any other way, I would like to draw what I always refer to as the 'eye of the soul' in the form of an eye, although it is not strictly speaking correct. This eye of the soul of the human being after death does not, for instance, see an Angel or another human soul which is also in the spiritual world in the same way as he sees a flower in the physical world; rather, this eye of the soul has the characteristic – and let us not take a human soul, but a being of the higher Hierarchies – that when an Angel, an Archangel Being is present, the eye is not conscious of seeing an Angel outside itself, but is, instead, aware of being seen by the Angel. It is the exact opposite of the physical world. We live out into the spiritual world by means of becoming aware that we are known by the beings of the higher hierarchies, that they think us. We feel ourselves embedded in them, we feel ourselves compre-hended by Angels, Archangels and Spirits of Personality, just as the realms of minerals, plants and animals feel themselves comprehended by us.

In the case of other human souls, we have both the feeling that we can be seen by them and that our seeing enters into them. Of all other Beings of the higher Hierarchies we have the feeling that we are perceived, thought and pictured by them. By virtue of this perception, thinking and picturing, we are contained within the spiritual world. Then, as we roam as soul through the spiritual world – much as we roam through the physical world – we have the feeling of relating everywhere to Beings of the higher Hierarchies, just as we relate in the physical world to mineral, plant and animal kingdoms. The difference is that we need constantly to reflect that we have a Self, which we do by looking back to our death and saying to ourselves: 'That is you!" We have a continual awareness of this; it is constantly in our consciousness.

What I am describing today is intended to supplement the various conceptions which are elaborated in my lecture-cycles and books. I am here describing more an inwardly felt experience, in contrast to the more outward approach in *Theosophy,* for example. Only by perceiving these things feelingly can one properly develop the right sensitivity to-wards them and towards the spiritual world as a whole.

It is self-knowledge which helps us forward, which makes us strong for life between death and a new birth. I became particularly vividly aware of this recently when I had, on several occasions, the task of speaking at the cremations of friends of our Movement. I always felt it necessary to say something which was intimately connected with the character, with the Self, of the one who had passed through the gates of death. What inspired me, gave me the intuition to convey to those who had died something connected with their being? Anything which strengthens the forces of self-knowledge is a help to those who have just died. By speaking, immediately after death, before their consciousness has fully woken, of the attributes which they feel within themselves, one can impart a degree of strength to them. This strength is what they need in order to gradually develop the possibility of looking back at the moment of death, in which their whole being appears concentrated in the form it achieved between birth and death. One helps the dead by sending them thoughts immediately after death which remind them of their characteristics and experiences. Their forces of self-knowledge are nurtured if one does this. And if one is able, clairvoyantly, to enter into the soul of such a dead person, then one can sense the soul's yearning to hear something about the way he was, the life he lived or his chief qualities and attributes. You can, I am sure, understand that just as here on earth the life of every person is different from that of every other, so it is the same for those who have passed through the gates of death. The life of every soul is different from every other between death and a new birth. Each soul's life is, you could say, a new revelation; one can always only delineate specific individual attributes.

Now, I would like to give a concrete example of what I have been describing.

Some time ago, in Dornach, a member of our Society who had reached a fairly advanced age took leave of the physical plane. He had passed his life in diligent, caring, thoughtful work; for a good number of years he had been whole-

heartedly united with our spiritual-scientific convictions and
had impressed and engraved them into his own soul. In the
last period of his physical existence, this person had become
wholly united with our world-outlook in his feelings and
perceptions. You know that when the human being passes
through the gates of death he first of all lays aside the physical
body; for a while he still carries the etheric body with him,
then he lays this, too, aside. Then comes a time during which
he only slowly and gradually achieves the consciousness
which will be his between death and a new birth. Immediately
after death the human being is in his etheric body. At this
stage, as we know, he looks back and experiences his whole
life in a great tableau. In particular, the powerful impulses of
his soul emerge all of a sudden and can manifest quite
differently from the way they did during life.

During life the human being is in many respects bound
within the confines of his physical body. At death we immediately overcome the body's weight, solidity and constraint,
which weaken the clarity of many soul-impulses. We still
possess the etheric body and have therefore not yet lost the
memory of our past life. In this world of images we see first of
all the scenes of our previous life, but then the particularly
strong impulses of our soul. If someone, during life, has
powerfully united himself with the impulses of spiritual
science to the point of feeling and experiencing them in a most
inward way within his soul, then after death he can unfold and
develop these impressions in a quite different way; for his soul
now has the supple, flexible, yielding etheric body at its
service, which is no longer constrained by the physical body.
One could observe this particularly well in the case of the
person of whom I spoke just now: quite shortly after death,
once he had succeeded in wholly transposing himself into his
soul, he was able to pour out what had lived in him as spiritual-
scientific impulses. During life he would not, of course, have
expressed himself in the way he did now. But because the
etheric body was still there, he could clothe in physical words

what he wished to say. What he had taken into himself through spiritual science became the voice and expression of his soul while he remained within the supple etheric body. And I found it necessary, a few days later at the cremation of this person, to speak the particular words which rang out from the being of his soul, which belonged not to me but to him:

> I will carry into world-expanse
> My feeling heart, that it may grow
> warm in the fire of holy powers;
>
> I will weave in world-thoughts
> My own thinking that it may grow
> In the light of eternally unfolding life;
>
> I will plunge into depths of soul
> My yielding thoughts that they may grow
> Strong for humanity's true aims;
>
> I strive for the tranquillity of God
> Through life's cares and toils,
> Preparing myself for the higher Self;
>
> Seeking active, vigorous peace
> Sensing world-being in my being
> I wish to fulfil humanity's task;
>
> Then I may live in expectancy,
> Following the star of my destiny
> Which shows me my place in Spirit-Land.

Here, clothed in words, were the after-death feelings of a soul imbued with spiritual science. Then followed a time which everyone more or less passes through after death; it cannot really be called a time of sleep, for after we have laid aside the etheric body we are immediately fully immersed in the spiritual world, but are blinded by its abundance. We cannot take it all in. We must first adapt the forces we have brought with us, adjust them to correspond with the spiritual world: we must attune ourself. We see too much after death; consciousness is present, but we must harmonize it, tone it down to correspond with the forces we have acquired. Then we begin to be able to find our bearings and really live in the spiritual world. So it is not quite correct to say that our consciousness awakens after a while; we really have too much consciousness and must tone it down to the point at which it is bearable. That is the moment of awakening. When the soul I am speaking of had laid aside its etheric body, it entered, therefore, into this condition of not being able to bear the light of spirit. But it had a great deal of strength; you can glean this from the words which I just read. This strength gradually became quite permeated by powers of feeling and willing which the soul had imbued with spiritual science. Therefore, shortly after death, it was able to arrive at a state of consciousness which it could bear. If I was going to describe everything which a soul begins to experience at this stage, there would, of course, be a great deal to describe. I can only describe parts of it, certain aspects. For us, it is naturally of great significance to observe what connects such souls to our Movement. We can also learn about the overall connection of human souls with the whole world after death, but can best observe the nature of life after death in souls who have been as close to us as this soul of whom I speak. This particular soul, then, as it orientated itself and came to clear consciousness, could be observed taking part in our meetings; yes, really taking part in our meetings. This involvement became fully-fledged at an Easter festival in Dornach this year, when the attempt was made to impress upon our dear friends in Dornach the profound nature of the meaning of Easter. This soul was present there and took part, just as it had previously taken part in our conferences with inward warmth. And it wished also to express itself, just as many who still inhabit their physical bodies wish to speak about what they have heard. It wished to express itself. And the remarkable thing is that it again expressed itself in words, so that it could be understood; expressed in words how its experience of our Easter lecture is related to its own continuing, everlasting life. What it expressed was something like an addition to the verses received at the time of its death. This addition, which now issued from its consciousness, went as follows:

> In human souls I will direct
> feeling of spirit, so that it readily
> wakens the word of Easter in the heart;
> Together with human spirits I will think
> the warmth of soul, so that they powerfully
> can feel The Risen One;

One can see that this soul wishes to continue working with the people it was connected to in our spiritual-scientific Movement. It wishes to dedicate itself to them so that the message of Easter can awaken in their hearts – which was also my aim in the Easter lecture – and so that they can develop the right feeling for what we call in spiritual science, 'The Risen One'. Even more significant than this, however, was what came to expression in the following three lines, which was particularly beautiful and deeply moving.

In those Easter lectures and in various other lectures which were given then, I tried time after time – as I have done on many other occasions – to draw attention to the significance that spiritual science has not only for this earthly life, but also for the whole universe. Whoever passes through the gates of death can experience this, can understand the significance of what is being accomplished by spiritual science. That is why I advise so many people, whose dear ones have passed through the gates of death, to read to them or speak to them about the teachings of spiritual science; for these have meaning and relevance not only for souls living in a physical body

– they are also very significant for disembodied souls. What is expressed in spiritual-scientific words nourishes them like spiritual air, like a spiritual water of life; or one could also say that they perceive light coming up to them from us below. For us, this light is, as it were, symbolic, for we hear words and receive them in our soul as thoughts; but the dead see it really as spiritual light.

Now it is very significant that this particular soul, who had often heard these things spoken of, wished to say clearly: 'I have understood this and it is really so!' For its words in this respect were:

> To the world of appearance of death shines up
> Spiritual knowledge's bright earth-flame...

This soul now sees as actuality what it once heard. It wishes to say: 'What you speak below, shines up like a flame.' And it expresses this by saying 'earth-flame'. But why does it speak of the 'world of appearance' of death? If you think about it, you will understand. The soul had often heard the world described as 'maya' or 'appearance' and so now it says: 'On earth I lived in the world of appearance of the senses; now I live also in a world of appearance in which I must seek to perceive real being:'

> To the world of appearance of death shines up
> Spiritual knowledge's bright earth-flame;

and then comes something which strengthens the soul:

> The Self becomes world-eye and ear.

'World-ear' is meant. The soul means that the whole Self becomes something like a mighty sense-organ, an organ of perception for the whole world. In this beautiful way the one who has died shows how he has become aware of the truth of the teachings of spiritual science. It is characteristic of this particular soul that it wishes to express itself immediately after death in order to say: 'Yes, I am now able to confirm that what I learned on earth was true and right.'

These words from a soul in the spiritual world were of some importance to me, since they came perhaps two weeks or so after another pleasing event had occurred.

Friends of our Movement lost a fairly young son in this present war, who had voluntarily gone into battle. The young man was killed. Before his death he had begun to have a certain interest in spiritual science. He was only seventeen or eighteen years old. It could be seen after a while that the soul of this young man – and many souls now passing through the gates of death, as a result of this war, come fairly quickly to consciousness – approached his parents, really came close to his parents. And it was as if he said – it could really be heard: 'Now I want to tell you, I want you to really understand that it is clear to me that what I often heard in your house about spiritual science, about spiritual light and spiritual beings, is true. What I then heard is now a help to me.'

I do not tell you this because I wish it to seem something out of the ordinary, but because it shows the nature of the connection between the earthly and the spiritual life. There is, however, one interesting thing about it which I would like to mention. After giving a lecture in one of our branch-meetings, I went to see the parents of this young man and told them of what had occurred; I told them also on which night the young man had approached his parents and I conveyed to them the words he had spoken to their souls. Then the father said: 'That is very remarkable. I very seldom have dreams, but on this same night I dreamed of my boy; he appeared to me and wished to tell me something, but I did not understand what he said.'

People outside our Movement will find such things strange; therefore it is best to keep them, as far as possible, within our own circles. But it is nonetheless important that we ourselves explore such matters in detail, for our knowledge is built up upon the foundation of these various separate experiences of the spiritual world. And we will only develop a concrete and detailed picture if we do not merely confine ourselves to listening to fine theories about the spiritual world, but also make spiritual science vital and vivid within us. Then we will be able to bear it when the spiritual world is spoken of in just the same way as reasonable people speak of their experience in the sense-world. Spiritual science can only become truly alive in us – and it should, it should really come alive within us – when we gain life by means of it, rather than just a body of knowledge. By means of it we must span the chasm which arises through materialism and which must grow ever wider and wider, the chasm between the physical sense-world which we experience from birth to death, and the spiritual world in which we live between death and a new birth. Then we can eventually learn also to become true citizens of the spiritual world. What is important is that we learn to feel that whoever has passed through the gates of death has only assumed another form of life; we should feel towards him as towards someone who has been obliged to emigrate to a far-away country, to which we are going to follow him at a later date. Therefore we have nothing worse to bear than a time of separation. But this must be vividly felt and experienced through spiritual science. If you will only form a picture composed of single, concrete facts, then you will see that these facts agree and accord with one another, even for someone who cannot perceive the spiritual world: and on this basis one can have belief before one has developed such perception; not a blind belief, not dependent on an authority, but a belief carried by a feeling which goes deeper than critical knowledge – by the human soul's original, innate feeling for truth.

X. From a Memorial Speech

Dornach, 29 June 1923

WE MUST be clear in our inmost soul that what we experience
in physical existence, and in our soul-life as well, is bound up
with our outer senses and with what our powers of reason and
understanding gather from sense-impressions. But neither
these senses nor anything which our reason deduces from
them can follow us into post-earthly existence. At our physical death we give back our outer senses to earthly existence.
A few days after physical death we give back to the etheric
world what our understanding has gleaned from outer sense-
impressions. It all melts away from us; and from then on we
are obliged to live fully in what, during earthly life, is hidden
in the darkness of the unconscious.

The human being spends part of his earthly life in the
condition which he experiences between waking up and
falling asleep. In this condition he is filled by what comes to
him in sense-impressions and through his powers of reason;
and by everything which, in the form he experiences it here on
earth, is extinguished at death. Every day the human being
also encounters the other side of existence, between falling
asleep and waking up again. What is experienced during this
time is not accessible to earthly consciousness, is hidden in
the darkness of the unconscious, and may seem to many to be
of little importance for earthly existence; but these experiences become fully conscious once the human soul has passed
through the gates of death, and then appear as the most
significant of all earthly life. What lives in us as unconscious
experience here on earth remains with us during the long
period between our death and a new earthly life.

The greatest possible difference exists in our relationship

to outer nature between what we perceive, observe and think here on earth and what we see once we have passed through the gates of death. Whoever believes that he can, in a waking state, with his physical senses and his earthly reasoning, exhaustively investigate what is hidden within the manifestations of nature, is mistaken, for he knows only the least part of it. Nature has a quite other aspect, one which we live within between falling asleep and waking up, which is deeply concealed from waking consciousness and which truly represents another side of our existence. The aspect of nature revealed to our earthly senses and understanding is very different indeed from the other aspect which is revealed to our eternal soul and spirit.

Whoever can properly understand this radical difference, whoever can see the degree to which nature presents two quite different aspects – on the one hand appearing to our senses as despiritualized and soulless, on the other hand revealing an unending wealth of spiritual beings – can also understand what a huge difference there is between a human being clothed in a physical body and one who has laid aside the physical and etheric garments and lives on in his soul-spiritual aspect beyond the gates of death. But the radical difference also extends to our relationship with this human being. We encounter another human being in earthly life, we share experiences with him here on earth. His experiences inscribe themselves into our earthly thoughts, form part of our memory. During our life on earth we carry, in our memory, this other person in us and with us. But every time we see him again we are affected not only by our earthly memory of him, but also by what streams livingly from his soul and pours itself into this memory. You only need to think how your memory of someone is enlivened when you encounter him in person; how much more vivid for earthly thought is what streams out from him into this memory, than the memory itself.

And now he departs from physical earth existence and

leaves us. We retain the memory of him, but from the moment of his death onwards he can add nothing more to this memory which might enliven or transform it. We retain a memory, just as we retain thoughts about outer nature when we observe it with our physical senses, grasp it with our physical understanding. In this mode of knowledge the phenomena of nature do not, themselves, add anything to our thinking since we keep our thoughts as objective as possible in order to truly reflect what is there; we cannot allow ourselves to be led astray by any modifying influence which life might have upon them. But just as the other aspect of nature is different from the one revealed to our senses and earthly understanding, so a human being who has become for us a mere earthly memory is different from what he was when he enlivened this memory, day in day out or from time to time. From the moment of death onwards, this human being is removed from our sight and experience into the other side of existence.

In sleep we inhabit the realm of nature beings who are inwardly spiritually alive, in contrast to the dead countenance of nature presented to our earthly senses. In the same way, the human being who has become merely a memory for our earthly perception now lives in the other realm of existence which, during sleep, we experience in the darkness of unconsciousness.

Yes, my dear friends, just as a physical human being appears before us, enlivening our thoughts and influencing our emotions as we experience him in waking earthly consciousness, so the human being who has departed from physical existence is experienced by us in sleep – unconsciously, it is true, but nevertheless in an equally real way; he approaches us and exists together with us. He enters into the realm of our sleeping consciousness to the same degree that he has disappeared from our waking consciousness. And if we human souls are aware, as a result of anthroposophical understanding, that we must learn to ascribe to sleep a quite different orientation and direction than we are familiar with in our waking lives, then we will have a feeling for what this means.

If we were always able only to live within physical time, in which later events follow on from earlier ones, we would never be able to experience the reality of the spirit. This can only be experienced when we can reverse life's usual forward direction. In the realm of the spirit all life runs in the opposite direction, however paradoxical that may seem to physical thinking. The wheel of life fastens together and closes. The end ultimately joins together with the beginning.

Such a concept appears unbelievable to earthly human beings because they have come so far adrift from any spiritual perspective. Yet in even the shortest sleep we experience time running backwards, which is the way forward to the realm of spirit out of which the world originated.

And even the belief of older civilizations, that at death human beings return to their ancestors, is more correct than the concept which we have in our apparently so enlightened time.

Every night when we take the path to the spirit, in the opposite direction from the physical, those who have died before us are the ones whom we follow after. Every night when we enter the spiritual world, the beings of the higher Hierarchies who never incarnate upon earth, are – to speak metaphorically – nearest the front, and then behind them come those souls with whom we had connections of destiny and who passed through the Gate of Death before us. We follow them; even though we are unconscious, we truly follow them in our unconscious thoughts for that part of the way which is given to us in every period of sleep.

And if we manage to keep alive and awake the memory of our dear ones who have died, if we can keep our thoughts of them constantly and vividly before us during our waking life, then the memory-pictures we lovingly carry within us will enable the dead to have an influence upon our world, to pour their will into it, so that their will lives on in the will of those who are still alive.

But if we manage to continually re-enliven our memory of the dead during our waking life, this will also accompany us and have an effect during sleep. It makes a difference to the dead if we enter sleep from a life in which we have forgotten them, or from a life in which we have continually called their image lovingly before our soul. The dead experience and feel what we bring into the spiritual world every time we fall asleep. Their souls perceive the images which we bring every day into the spiritual world through the gates of sleep. We can enable the dead, when we sleep, to unite their perception with the images of them which we faithfully preserve and guard. In this way we can enable the will of the dead to unite with our will through the thoughts and faithful memories of them which we uphold when we are awake. So we can learn to truly live with those who have died.

The dead will then find us worthy of living with them. And then a right and true human community can arise, which is only instinctive and involuntary within the physical world; it can become a soul-community even within the physical world if soul connections are not loosened or destroyed when earthly life is extinguished, if soul-connections can remain in spite of the fact that outer earthly connections are loosened and dissolved. This means that the human soul affirms the reality of the spirit and does not detract from it by giving himself over only to the physical, sense-world. We can enable ourselves to live as freely in soul-spiritual realms as we are compelled and constrained within physical sense existence.

Every death, especially that of a dear friend, can remind us of this, can activate our will; can awaken us, not to a mere dead memory, but to a living, enduring, feeling memory.

XI. On the Connection of the Living and the Dead

Berne, 9 November 1916

IT IS one of the aims of our spiritual-scientific endeavour to form concrete ideas of how we, as human beings upon earth, live with the spiritual worlds, even as we are connected through the physical body – its experiences and perceptions – with the physical world.

At the present stage of our studies we may well take our start from what is already known to us – what has already come before our souls during these years. Here, for instance, is the world of our sense-perceptions, the world to which we direct our will-impulses for which the physical body mediates – that is to say, our actions. Immediately behind it, as you know, there is the elemental world. That is the next world behind this one. It is not a question of the name; we might have named it differently. To gain clear and living ideas of these supersensible worlds we must at least enter into some of their peculiarities. We must try to recognize what they are for us as human beings. For in truth our whole life between birth and death – and also our subsequent life which takes its course between death and a new birth – depends on our co-existence with the various worlds that are spread out around us. We call the 'elemental world' that world which can only be perceived by what we know as 'imaginations'. Hence we may also call it the 'imaginative world'. In ordinary human life, under ordinary conditions, man cannot lift into consciousness his imaginative perceptions – his perceptions of the elemental world. Not that the imaginations are not there, or that in any given moment of our sleeping or waking life we are not in relation to the elemental world, receiving imaginations from it. On the contrary, imaginations are perpetually ebbing and flowing in us. Though we are unaware of it, we constantly receive impressions from the elemental world. Just as when we open our eyes or lend our ears to the outer world we have sensations of colour and light, perceptions of sound, so do we receive continual impressions from the elemental world, giving rise to imaginations – in this case, in our etheric body. Imaginations differ from ordinary thought in this respect. In ordinary, every-day human thoughts, only the head is concerned as an instrument of conscious assimilation and experience. In our imaginations, on the other hand, we partake with almost the whole of our organism – albeit, it is our etheric organism. In our etheric organism they are constantly taking place – we may refer to them as unconscious imaginations, since it is only for an occultly trained cognition that they rise into consciousness. Moreover, though they do not enter our consciousness directly in every-day life, they are by no means without significance for us. No, for our life as a whole they are far more important than our sense-perceptions, for we are united far more intensely and intimately with our imaginations than with our sense-perceptions.

From the mineral kingdom, as physical human beings, we receive few imaginations. We receive more through all that we develop by living with the plant-world and with the animal. But the greater part, by far, of what lives as imaginations in our etheric body is due to our relations to our fellow human beings, and all that these relations entail for our life as a whole. In fact, our whole relation to our fellow human beings – our whole attitude towards them – is fundamentally based on imaginations. Imaginations always result from the way we meet another human being, and though, as I said, to ordinary consciousness they do not appear as imaginations, nevertheless they make themselves felt in the sympathies and antipathies which play such an overwhelming part in our life. To a greater or lesser degree, we develop sympathies and antipathies with all that approaches us as human beings in this world. We have our vague undefined feelings, slight inclinations or disinclinations. Sometimes our sympathies grow into friendship and love – love which can be so enhanced that we think we can no longer live without this or that human being. All this is due to the imaginations which are perpetually called forth, in our etheric body, by our life with our fellow human beings. In fact we always carry with us in life something that cannot quite be called memory – for it is far more real than memory. We bear within us – shall we say – these enhanced memories or imaginations which we have received from all the impressions of the human beings with whom we have ever been, and which we go on receiving all the time. We bear them within us, and they constitute a goodly portion of what we call our inner life. I mean not the inner life that lives in clear, well-defined memories, but that inner life which makes itself felt in our prevailing mood and feeling and outlook – our outlook on the world itself, or on our own life in the world. We would go past the world around us coldly and we would live with our contemporary world indifferently if we did not unfold this imaginative life by living together with other beings – and notably with other human beings.

It is, as we might say, our soul's interest in the surrounding world which makes itself felt in this way. It belongs especially to the elemental world, and notably to our own etheric body. It is, above all, inherent in the forces of our etheric body, and it makes itself felt in this way. Sometimes we feel ourselves immediately 'caught' and interested. Such interest as is often woven from the very first moment between one human being and another is due to definite relationships which arise between the one – the one etheric human being – and the other, bringing about the play of imaginations hither and thither. We live with these imaginations and with our resulting sympathies, of whose effect and intensity we are often largely unaware, or aware only in the vaguest way. Indeed, when our everyday life is not wide-awake but runs along more or less obtusely, we often fail to observe them at all.

We belong with all this to the elemental world, for it is out of the elemental world that we have our own etheric body. Our etheric body is our instrument of communication with the elemental world. With it, however, we do not only spin out relationships to those other etheric bodies which belong to physical beings. We are also related with our etheric body to spiritual beings of an elemental character. The 'beings of an elemental character' are precisely those who are able to call forth in us imaginations – conscious or unconscious. We are perpetually related to a multitude of elemental beings. It is in this that one human being differs from another. They have their several relationships – one person to a given set of elemental beings, another to another set of elemental beings. Moreover, the relations of the one human being to certain elemental beings may sometimes coincide with the relations of the other to the same beings. One thing, however, must be observed in this connection. While we are always, in a manner of speaking, akin to a large number of elemental beings, we have relations of special intensity to one elemental being, who is in essence the counterpart of our own etheric body. Our own etheric body is intimately related to one particular etheric being. Just as our etheric body – what we call our etheric body from birth until death – develops its own relations to the physical world inasmuch as it is inserted in a physical body, so does this etheric entity, which is as it were the counterpart or counter-pole of our own etheric body, enable us to have relations to the whole of the elemental world – the whole of the surrounding, cosmic-elemental world.

We gaze upon an elemental world to which we ourselves belong by virtue of our etheric body, and with which we stand in manifold relations – specific relationships to such and such elemental beings. In the elemental world we make acquaintance with beings who are truly no less real than human beings or animals in the physical – beings, however, who never come to incarnation, but only to 'etherization', so to speak, for their densest corporeality is ethereal. Just as we go about among physical people in this world, so do we constantly go about among such elemental beings, while other elemental beings – more remote from ourselves – are related in their turn to other people. A certain number, however, are more nearly related to ourselves, and one among them – related to us most nearly of all – acts as our organ of communication with the entire cosmic-elemental world. Now in the time immediately following our passage through the Gate of Death, when for a few days we still bear our etheric body with us, we ourselves become precisely such a being as these elemental beings are. In a manner of speaking, we ourselves become an elemental being. We have often described this process of the passage through the Gate of Death, but the more exactly we study it, the clearer the imaginations it provides. For the impressions we receive immediately after the passage of a human being through the Gate of Death always consist in imaginations – make themselves felt as imaginations.

Observing the process more exactly, we find that there is a certain mutual interplay, immediately after death, between our own etheric body and its etheric counterpart. The fact that our etheric body is taken from us a few days after death is mainly due to its being attracted – drawn in, as it were – by this etheric counterpart. Henceforth it becomes one with the etheric counterpart. A few days after death we do in fact lay aside our etheric body, we hand it over, so to speak; but it is to our own etheric counterpart that we hand it over. Our etheric body is taken from us by our own cosmic prototype or image and, as a result, special relations now emerge between what is thus taken from us and the other elemental beings with whom we have been related in any way during our life. We might describe it thus: a kind of mutual relation now arises between what our own etheric body has become – united as it now is with its counterpart or counter-image – and the other elemental beings who accompanied us from birth till death. It might be compared to the relation of a sun to its associated planetary system. Our etheric body with its cosmic counterpart is like a kind of sun, surrounded – as a kind of planetary system – by the other elemental beings. This mutual interplay gives rise to the forces which instil into the elemental world – in the right manner and in slow evolution – what our etheric body is able to take into that world. That which we commonly refer to in abstract terms – 'the dissolution of the etheric body' – is essentially a play of forces, engendered by this sun-planetary system which we have left behind. Gradually, what we acquired and assimilated to our etheric body in the course of life becomes a part of the spiritual world. It weaves itself into the forces of the spiritual world. We must be very clear on this. Every thought, every idea, every feeling we develop – however hidden it remains – is of significance for the spiritual world. For when the coherence is broken by our passage through the Gate of Death, all our thoughts and feelings pass with our etheric body into the spiritual world and become part and parcel of it. We do not live for nothing. Even as we receive them into the thoughts we make our own, into the feelings we experience, so are the fruits of our life embodied in the cosmos. This is a truth we must receive into our whole mood and outlook; otherwise we do not rightly conduct ourselves in the spiritual-scientific movement. You are not a spiritual scientist merely by knowing about certain things. You are so only if you feel yourself, by virtue of this knowledge, within the spiritual world; if you know yourself quite definitely as a member in the spiritual world. Then you will say to yourself: the thought you are now harbouring is of significance for the entire universe, for at your death it will be handed over to the universe in such or such a form.

Now after a human being's death we may have to do, in one form or another, with what is thus handed over to the universe. Many of the ways in which the dead are present to those whom they have left behind are due to the fact that the etheric human being – which has, of course, been laid aside by the real individuality – sends back his imaginations to the living. And if the living person is sensitive enough, or if he is in some abnormal state or has normally prepared himself by proper spiritual training, the influences of what is thus given over to the spiritual world by the dead – the influences, that is to say, of imaginative natures – can emerge in him in a conscious form.

But there still remains a connection after death between the true human individuality and this etheric entity which has separated from him. There is a mutual interplay between them. We can observe it most clearly when by spiritual training we come into actual intercourse with this or that dead individual. A certain kind of intercourse can then take place, as follows: to begin with, the dead human being conveys to his etheric body what he himself wishes to transmit to us who are still in the physical world. For only by his transmitting it to his etheric body – as it were, making inscriptions in his etheric body – only by this means can we, who are here in the physical, have perceptions of the dead in terms of what we call 'imaginations'. The moment we have imaginations of him, the etheric body of the dead – if you will pardon my use of the trivial and all too realistic term – is acting as a 'switch' or 'commutator'. Do not imagine that our relations to the dead need be any the less deeply felt because such an instrument is needed. A person who meets us in the outer world also conveys his form to us by the picture which he calls forth in us through our own eyes. So it is with this transmission through the etheric body. We perceive what the dead wishes to convey to us by 'getting' it, so to speak, via his etheric body. This body is outside him, but he is so intimately related to it that he can inscribe in it what lives within himself, and thus enable us to read it in imaginations. There is, however, this condition. If a person who is spiritually trained wishes to come into connection with a dead human being through the etheric body in this way, he must have entered into some relation to the dead – either in his last life between birth and death, or out of former incarnations. Moreover, these relationships must have affected his soul – the soul of the one who is still living here – deeply enough for the imaginations to make an impression on him. For this can only be if in his heart and mind he had a definite and living interest in the dead person. Interests of heart and feeling must always be the mediator between the living and the dead, if any intercourse at all is to take place – conscious or unconscious. (Of the latter we shall speak presently.) Some interest of heart and feeling must be there, so that we really carry something of the dead within us. In a certain respect at any rate the dead person must have constituted a portion of our own soul's experience. Only one who is spiritually trained can make himself a certain substitute. For instance – (it may seem external at first sight, but spiritual training turns it into something far more inward) – one can give oneself up to the impression of the handwriting, or of something else in which the individuality of the dead is living. However, one can only do so if one has acquired a certain practice in making contact with an individuality through the fact that he lives in the writing. Or again, one may establish this possibility by entering with sympathy into the feelings of the physical survivors, partaking in their grief and in all the emotional interest they have in the dead person. By entering with sympathy into these real and living feelings, which flow from the dead into the dear ones whom he has left on Earth – or which remain in their inner life – a person of spiritual training can prepare his soul to read in the aforesaid imaginations.

But we must also realize the following. Though to perceive the imaginations which play over from the etheric body depends on spiritual training or other special conditions, yet at the same time what passes unperceived by people is there none the less. And we may truly say, those who are living in the physical world are not only woven around by the elemental forces, as imaginations, which proceed from other human beings living with them in the physical body. Whether we know it or not, our etheric body is constantly played-through by all the imaginations which we absorb from those who stood in any kind of relation to us and who passed before us through the Gate of Death. As in our physical life, in the physical body, we are related to the air around

us, so are we related to the whole of the elemental world –
including all that is there of the dead.

We shall never learn to know our human life unless we gain
knowledge of these relationships, albeit they are so intimate
and fine that they remain unnoticed by most people. After all,
who can deny that we do not always remain the same between
birth and death? Let us look back upon our lives. However
consistent we may think the course of life has been, we will
soon notice that we have often gone hither and thither in life,
or that this or that has occurred. Even if this does not
immediately change the direction of our lives, which it can of
course do, it nonetheless has the effect of enriching our lives
in one way or another – in a happy direction or in a painful
one. It brings us into different conditions – just as when you
go into another district your general feeling of health may be
changed by the different composition of the air.

These moods of soul, into which we enter in our life's
course, are due to the influences of the elemental world, and
in no small measure to the influences that come from the dead
who were formerly related to us. Many a human being in
earthly life meets with a friend or with some person with
whom he becomes connected in one way or another – to
whom, perhaps, he finds himself obliged to do this or that by
way of kindness or of criticism or rebuke. The fact that they
were brought together required the influence of certain
forces. He who recognizes the occult connections in the world
knows that when two human beings are brought together to
this end or that, sometimes one and sometimes several of
those who have gone before them through the Gate of Death
are instrumental. Our life does not become any the less free
thereby. We do not lose our freedom because we starve if we
do not eat. No one who is not deliberately foolish will say: how
can a person be free, seeing that he is obliged to eat? It would
be just as invalid to say that we become unfree because our
soul constantly receives influences from the elemental world
as here described. Indeed, just as we are connected with

warmth and cold, with all the things that become our food, and with the air around us, so are we connected with that which comes to us from those who have died before us. We are equally connected with the rest of the elemental world, but above all with that which comes to us from them, and we can truly say: man's working for his fellow human beings does not cease with his passage through the Gate of Death. Through his etheric body, with which he himself remains connected, he sends his imaginations into those with whom he was connected in his life. Indeed, the world to which we are here referring is far more real than that we commonly call real – even if, in our every-day life, for very good reasons, it remains unperceived. So much, for today, about the *elemental world.*

A further realm which is ever present in our environment, and to which we ourselves belong no less than to the elemental world, is the *soul world* – for so we may call it. (It is not the name that matters.) With the elemental world we are always connected in our waking life, and in sleep, too, indirectly, when with our ego and astral body we are outside the physical and the etheric; when our body that lies there in the bed, and our etheric body, are still connected with the elemental world. But with the higher world to which I now refer, we are connected most directly – only that this too cannot rise into our consciousness in ordinary life. We are connected with it in sleep when we have our astral body freely around us, and also in waking life – albeit then the connection, mediated as it is by forces which the physical body has drawn into itself, is no longer so direct.

Now in this world-of-soul (let us call it the soul world for the present; medieval philosophers referred to it as the heavenly world or the celestial) in this world, once more, we find beings who are just as real as we are during our life between birth and death, nay, more so. They are, however, beings who do not need to come to embodiment in a physical, or even in an etheric, body. They live – as in their lowest corporeality – in that which we are wont to call the astral body. Constantly, during our life and after our death, we are connected intimately with a large number of these purely astral beings. Here, too, human beings differ from one another inasmuch as they are related to different astral beings – albeit, here again, two people may have their relationships to one or more astral beings in common, while at the same time each of them has his several relations to other astral beings.

It is to this world, in which these astral beings are, that we ourselves belong from the time when, after passing through the Gate of Death, we have laid aside our etheric body. We with our own individuality are then among the beings of the soul world. We are such beings at that time, and beings of the soul world are our immediate environment. True, we are also related to the content of the elemental world, inasmuch as we can kindle in it that which calls forth imaginations as aforesaid. We have, however, the elemental world in a certain sense outside us – or, as one might also say, beneath us. It is a portion of which we rather make use for purposes of communication with the remainder of the world, while we ourselves belong directly to what I have now called the world-of-soul. It is with the beings of the soul world that we have our intercourse, including other human beings who have also passed through the Gate of Death and, after a few days, laid aside their etheric bodies.

Now just as we constantly get influences from the elemental world, although we do not notice it, so too we constantly receive influences – straight into our astral body – out of this world-of-soul which I am now describing. It is only the immediate, straightforward influences which we thus receive that can appear as inspirations. (Of the indirect influences via the etheric body we have already spoken.) You will understand the character of such an influence from the soul world if I describe once more in a few words how it appears to one who is spiritually trained – one who is able to receive conscious inspirations out of the spiritual world. It appears to him as follows. He can only bring these inspirations to his consciousness if he is able, so to speak, to take into himself some portion of the being who wants to inspire him – some portion of the qualities, of the inherent tendency in life, of such a being.

One who is spiritually trained to develop conscious relations with a dead person, not only via the etheric body but in this direct way through inspiration, must bear in his soul even more than mere interest or sympathy is able to call forth. For a short while, at least, he must be so able to transform himself as to receive into his own being something of the habits, the character, the very human nature of the one with whom he wishes to communicate. He must be able to enter into him till he can truly say to himself, 'I am taking on his habits to such an extent that I could do what he could, and in his way; that I could feel as he could, and will as he could, also.' It is the 'could' that matters – the possibility. We must, therefore, be able to live together with the dead even more intimately. For a person of spiritual training there are many ways of coming thus near to the dead, provided the dead person himself allows it. We should, however, realize that the beings who belong to what we are now calling the world-of-soul are quite differently related to the world than we are in our physical body. Hence there are certain conditions, quite definite conditions, of intercourse with such beings – and, among others, with the dead, so long as they are living still as astral beings in their astral bodies. We may draw attention especially to certain points.

You see, all that we develop for our life in the physical body – our many and varied relationships to other people (I mean precisely those relationships which arise through earthly life) – all this acquires quite another kind of interest for the dead. Here on the earth we develop sympathies and antipathies. Let us be fully clear on this. Such sympathies and antipathies as we develop while we are living in the physical body are subject to the influences of this our present form of life, which we owe to the physical body and to its conditions. They are subject to the influences of our own vanity and of our egoism. Let us not fail to realize how many relationships we develop to this or that human being as a result of vanity or egoism – or other things that depend on our physical and earthly life in this world. We love other people or we hate them. Verily, as a rule, we take little notice of the true grounds of our loving and our hating – our sympathies and antipathies. Nay, often enough we flee from taking conscious notice of our sympathies and antipathies, for the simple reason that, if we did so, highly unpleasant truths would as a rule emerge. If, for instance, we followed up the real facts which find expression in our not loving this or that human being, we should often have to ascribe to ourselves so much of prejudice or vanity or other qualities that we are afraid to do so. Therefore we do not bring to full clarity in consciousness why it is that we hate this person or that. And with love, too, the case is often similar. Interests, sympathies and antipathies evolve in this way, which only have significance for our everyday life. Yet it is out of all this that we act. We arrange our life according to these interests and sympathies and antipathies.

Now it would be quite wrong to imagine that the dead can possibly have the same interest as we earthly people have in all the ephemeral sympathies and antipathies which thus arise under the influence of our physical and earthly life. That would be utterly wrong. Truly, the dead are obliged to look at these things from quite another point of view. Moreover, we may ask ourselves, are we not largely influenced in our estimate of our fellow human beings by these subjective feelings – by all that lies inherent in our subjective interest, our vanity and egoism and the like? Let us not think for a moment that a dead person can have any interest in such relationships between ourselves and other human beings, or in our actions which proceed out of such interests. But we must also not imagine that the dead person does not see what is living in our souls. For it is really living there, and the dead one sees it well enough. He shares in it, too, but he sees something else as well. One who is dead has quite another way of judging people. He sees them quite differently. As to the way in which the dead person sees the human beings who are here on earth, there is one thing of outstanding importance. Let us not imagine that the dead has not a keen and living interest in the world of human beings. He has, indeed, for the world of human beings belongs to the whole cosmos. Our own life belongs to the cosmos. And just as we, even in the physical world, interest ourselves in the subordinate kingdoms, so do the dead interest themselves intensely in the human world, and send their active impulses into the human world. For the dead work through the living into this world. We have only just given an example of the way in which they go on working soon after their passage through the Gate of Death.

But the dead sees one thing above all, and that most clearly. Suppose, for example, that he sees a human being here following impulses of hatred – hating this person or that, and with a merely personal intensity or purpose. This the dead sees. At the same time, however, according to the whole manner of his vision and all that he is then able to know, he will observe quite clearly, in such a case, the part which Ahriman is playing. He sees how Ahriman impels the person to hatred. The dead actually sees Ahriman working upon the human being. On the other hand, if a person on earth is vain, he sees Lucifer working at him. That is the essential point. It is in connection with the world of Ahriman and Lucifer that the dead human being sees the human beings who are here on earth. Consequently, what generally colours our judgement of people is quite eliminated for the dead. We see this or that human being, whom in one sense or another we must condemn. Whatever we find blameworthy in him, we put it down to him. The dead does not put it down directly to the human being. He sees how the person is misled by Lucifer or Ahriman. This brings about a toning-down, so to speak, of the sharply differentiated feelings which in our physical and earthly life we generally have towards this or that human being. To a far greater extent, a kind of universal human love arises in the dead. This does not mean that he cannot criticize – that is to say, cannot rightly see what is evil in evil. He sees it well enough, but he is able to refer it to its origin – to its real inner connections.

What I have here described is not without its results, for it means that an occultly-trained person cannot consciously come near to one who is dead unless he truly frees himself from feelings of personal sympathy or antipathy to individuals. He must not allow himself to be dependent, in his soul, on personal feelings of sympathy or antipathy. You need only imagine it for a moment. Suppose that an occultly-trained, clairvoyant person were about to approach a dead human being – whoever he might be – so that the inspirations which the dead was sending in towards him might find their way into his consciousness. Suppose, moreover, that the one here living were pursuing another human being with a quite special hatred – hatred having its origin only in personal relationships. Then, of a truth, as fire is avoided by our hand, so would the dead avoid such a person who was capable of hatred for personal reasons. He cannot approach him, for hatred works on the dead like fire. To come into conscious relation with the dead we must be able to make ourselves like them – independent, in a sense, of personal sympathies and antipathies.

Hence you will understand what I now have to say. Bear in mind this whole relation of the dead to the living, in so far as it rests on Inspirations. Remember that the inspirations are always there, even if they pass unnoticed. They are perpetually living in the human astral body, so that the human being upon earth has his relations to the dead in this direct way, too. Now, after all that we have said, you will well understand that these relationships depend on our whole mood and spirit here in our life on earth. If our attitude to other people is hostile, if we are without interest or sympathy for our contemporaries – above all, if we have not an unprejudiced interest in our fellow human beings – then are the dead unable to approach us in the way they long to do. They cannot properly transplant themselves into our souls, or, if they must do so, in one way or another it is made difficult for them and they can only do it with great suffering and pain. All in all, the living-together of the dead with the living is complicated.

Thus man goes on working beyond the time when he passes through the Gate of Death, even directly, inasmuch as after death he inspires those who are living on the physical plane. And this is absolutely true. Notably as to their inner habits and qualities – the way they think and feel and develop inclinations – those who are living at any given time on earth are largely dependent on those who died and passed from the earth before them, who were related to them during their life, or to whom they themselves established a relation even after death – which may sometimes happen, though it is not so easy.

A certain portion of the world-ordering and of the whole progress of mankind is altogether dependent on this working of the dead into the life of earthly human beings, inspiring them. Nay, more, in their instinctive life people are not without an inkling that it is so and that it must be so. We can observe it if we consider ways of life, formerly very wide-spread, which are now dying out because humanity in the course of evolution goes ever onward to new forms of life. In bygone times when, generally speaking, they divined far more of the reality of spiritual worlds, people were more deeply aware of what is necessary for life as a whole. They knew that the living need the dead – need to receive into their habits and customs the impulses from the dead. What, then, did they do? You need only think of former times, when in wide circles it was customary for a father to take care that his son should inherit and carry on his business, so that the son went on working on the same lines. Then when the father was long dead, inasmuch as the son remained in the same channels of life, a bond of communication was created through the physical world itself. The son's activity and life-work being akin to his father's, the father was able to work on in him.

Many things in life were based on this principle. And if whole classes of society attached great value to the inheritance of this or that property within the class or within its several families, it was due to their divining this necessity. Into the life-habits of those who live later, the life-habits of those who lived earlier must enter, but only when these life-habits are so far ripened that they come from them after they have passed through the Gate of Death – for it is only then that they become mature.

These things are ceasing, as you know – for such is the progress of the human race. We can already see a time approaching when these inheritances, these conservative conditions, will no longer play a part. The physical bonds will no longer be there in the same way. But all the more, to compensate for this, people must receive such detailed spiritual-scientific knowledge as will lift the whole matter into their consciousness. For then they will be able consciously to connect their life with the life-habits of former times – with which we have to reckon in order that life may go forward with continuity. Since the beginning of the fifth post-Atlantean period we are living in a transition time. During this time a more or less chaotic state has intervened. But the conditions will arise again when in a far more conscious way – by recognition of the spiritual-scientific truths – people will connect their life and work with that which has gone before them. Unconsciously, merely instinctively, they used to do so – of that there can be no doubt. But even that which is still instinctive to this day must be transmuted into consciousness. Instinctively, for instance, people still teach in this way – only we do not observe it. One who studies history on spiritual lines will soon observe it, if only he pays attention to the facts and not to the dreadful abstractions which prevail nowadays in the so-called humanistic branches of scholarship. If we look at the facts we can well observe it: what is taught in a given epoch bears a certain character only because people attach themselves unconsciously, instinctively, to what the dead are pouring down into the present. If once you learn to study in a real way the educational ideas which are propounded in any given age by the leading spirits in education – I mean not the charlatans but the true educationists – you will soon see how these ideas have their origins in the habitual natures of those who have recently died.

This is a far more intimate living-together; for that which plays into the human being's astral body enters far more into his inner life than that which plays into his etheric body. The communion which the dead themselves, as individualities, can have with people on earth, is far more intimate than that which the etheric bodies have – or, for that matter, any other elemental beings. Hence you will see how the succeeding epoch in the life of humanity is always conditioned by the preceding one. The preceding time always goes on living in the time that follows. For in reality, strange though it may sound, it is only after our death that we become truly ripe to influence other people – I mean to influence them directly, working right into their inner being. To impress our own habits on any man who is 'of age' (I mean now, spiritually speaking, not in the legal sense) is the very thing we should not do. Yet it is right and according to the conditions of the progressive evolution of mankind for us to do so after we ourselves have passed through the Gate of Death. Beside all the things that are contained in the progress of karma and in the general laws of incarnation, these things take place. If you ask for the occult reasons why, let us say, the people of this year are doing this or that, then – not for all things but certainly for many – you will find that they are doing it because certain impulses are flowing down to them from those who died twenty or thirty years ago, or even longer. These are the hidden connections – the real concrete connections – between the physical and the spiritual world. It is not only for ourselves that something ripens and matures in what we carry with us through the Gate of Death. It is not only for ourselves, but for the world at large. And it is only from a given moment that it becomes truly ripe to work upon others. Then, however, it does become ever riper and riper.

I beg you here to observe that I am not speaking of externals, but of inner, spiritual workings. A person may remember the habits of his dead father or grandfather and repeat them out of memory on the physical plane. That is not what I mean; that is a different matter. I really mean the inspired influences – imperceptible, therefore, to ordinary consciousness – the influences which make themselves felt in our habits, in our most intimate character. Much in our life depends on our finding ourselves obliged, here or there, to free ourselves from the influences – even the well-meant influences – coming to us from the dead. Indeed, we gain much of our inner freedom by having to free ourselves in this way, in one direction or another. Inner conflicts of soul, which a person often does not know, will grow intelligible to him when he views them in this light or that, taking his light from spiritual knowledge of this kind. To use a trite expression, we may say: the past is rumbling on – the souls of the past go rumbling on – in our own inner life.

These things are facts – truths into which we look by spiritual vision. But alas, especially in the life of today, men have a peculiar relation to these truths. It was not always so. Anyone who can study history in a spiritual way will know this. Today people are afraid of these truths – they are afraid of facing them. They have a nameless fear – not indeed conscious, but unconscious. Unconsciously they are afraid of recognizing the mysterious connections between soul and soul, not only in this world, but between here and the other world. It is this unconscious fear which holds back the people in the outer world. This is a part of that which holds them back, instinctively, from spiritual science. They are afraid of knowing the reality. They are all unaware of how they are disturbing – by their unwillingness to know reality – disturbing and confusing the whole course of world-evolution, and with it, needless to say, the life that will have to be lived through between death and a new birth, when these conditions must be seen.

Still more mature – for everything that evolves, becomes ever riper and more mature – still more mature becomes that which lives in us when it no longer has to stop short at Inspiration but can become Intuition (in the true sense in which I used the word in *Knowledge of the Higher Worlds and its Attainment*). Now Intuition can only be a being that has none other than a Spirit-body (to use this paradoxical expression). To work intuitively upon other beings – and, among others, upon those who are still incarnated here in the physical life – a human being must first have laid aside his astral body; that is to say, he must first belong entirely to the spiritual world. That will be decades after his death, as we know. Then he can also work down on other people through intuition – no longer merely through Inspiration as I described it just now. Not until then does he as ego – now in the spiritual world – work in a purely spiritual way into other egos. Formerly he worked by Inspiration into the astral body – or, via his etheric body, into the etheric body of man. But one who has been dead for decades past can also work directly as an ego – albeit at the same time he can still work through the other vehicles, as described above. It is at this stage that the human individuality grows ripe to enter no longer merely into the habits of people but even into their views and ideas of life. To modern feeling, full of prejudice as it is, this may be an unpleasant truth – very unpleasant, I doubt not. None the less it is true. Our views and ideas, originating as they do in our ego, are under constant influences from those long dead. In our views and conceptions of life, those who are long dead are living. By this very means, the continuity of evolution is preserved – out of the spiritual world. It is a necessity, for otherwise the thread of people's ideas would constantly be broken.

Forgive me if I insert a personal matter at this point. I do so, if I may say so, for thoroughly objective reasons. For such a truth as this can only be made intelligible by concrete examples.

No one ought really to bring forward, as views or ideas, his own personal opinions – however sincerely gained. Therefore, no one who stands with full sincerity on the true ground of occultism – no one who is experienced in the conditions of spiritual science – will impose his own opinions on the world. On the contrary, he will do all he can to avoid imposing his own opinions directly. For the opinions, the outlook he acquires under the influence of his own personal tendency of feeling, should not begin to work until thirty or forty years after his death. Then it will work in this way: it will come into the souls of people along the same paths as the impulses of the Time-Spirits or Archai. Only then has it become so mature that its working is in harmony with the objective course of things. Hence it is necessary for everyone who stands on the true ground of occultism to avoid making personal proselytes – setting out to gain followers for his own personal views. That is the general custom nowadays. No sooner has anyone got an opinion of his own, he cannot hasten enough to make propaganda for it. That is what a real and practising spiritual scientist cannot possibly desire to do. Now I may bring in the personal matter to which I referred just now. It is no chance, but something essential to my life, that I began by writing – communicating to the world – not my own views, but Goethe's world-conception. That was the first thing I wrote. I wrote entirely in the spirit and in the sense of Goethe's world-conception, thus taking my start not from any living person. For even if that living person were oneself, it could not possibly justify one in teaching spiritual science in the comprehensive way I try to do. It was a necessary link in the chain, when I thus placed my work into the objective course of world-evolution. Therefore I did not write my theory of knowledge, but Goethe's – *A Theory of Knowledge Implicit in Goethe's World Conception* – and in this way I continued.

Thus you will see how the development of man goes on. What he attained on earth ripens not only for the sake of his own life as he advances on the paths of karma. It ripens also for the world. So we continue to work for the world. After a certain time we become ripe to send imaginations; then – after a further time – inspirations into the habits of human beings. And only after a longer time has elapsed do we grow ready and mature enough to send intuitions into the most intimate part of man's life – into the views and conceptions of people.

Let us not imagine that our views and conceptions of life grow out of nothing – or that they arise anew in every age. They grow from the soil in which our own soul is rooted, which soil is in truth identical with the sphere of activity of human beings who died long ago.

By knowledge of such facts, I do believe human life must receive that enrichment which it needs, according to the character and sense of our age and of the immediate future. Many an old custom has grown rotten to the core. The new must be developed, as I have often said; but man cannot enter the new life without those impulses which grow in him through spiritual science. It is the feelings that matter – the feelings towards the world in its entirety, and all the other beings of the world, which we acquire through spiritual science. Our mood of life grows different through spiritual science. The supersensible, in which we always are, becomes alive for us through spiritual science. We are and always have been living in it; but human beings will be called to know it, more and more consciously, the farther they evolve through the fifth, sixth and seventh post-Atlantean epochs and for the rest of earthly time.

These things I wanted to communicate to you today. They are indeed essential to the enrichment, the quickening of man's whole feeling for the world, and to the deepening of all his life. These things I wanted to kindle in your hearts, now that we have been able to be together once more after a lapse of time. May we be able to be together often again to speak of similar matters, so that our souls may partake in achieving that evolution of mankind which is the aim and endeavour of spiritual science.

XII. Concerning the Affinity of the Living and the Dead

Berlin, 5 February 1918

WE HAVE often remarked from various points of view that the alternation of waking and sleeping has a deeper significance than is apparent to ordinary observation. This fact needs to be kept well in mind when we are considering the world at large and – in an ideal but quite practical sense – where we as human beings stand in it. The apparent fact is simply that human consciousness is either awake or asleep, but we know this is only an appearance. As we have often said, the so-called sleep-condition does not last only from falling asleep until waking; in a certain part of our being it continues during the waking hours. We must realize that we are never completely, thoroughly, awake with our whole being; with part of ourselves we are always asleep. Hence we may ask: with what part of our being are we genuinely awake in the time between waking up and going to sleep?

We are awake as regards our perceptions – as regards all that we perceive through our senses. The mark of ordinary perception is precisely that on waking a state of detachment from the external sense-world gives way to one of association with it. The activity of our senses soon wrests us from the dull condition that in ordinary life we know as 'sleep'. With regard to our life of ideas we are less awake, as anyone can learn from accurate self-observation (you will find this treated more exactly in my book *Riddles of the Soul*); but we can still call it being awake. Thus we must distinguish the life of perception from the life of thoughts and ideas. When – withdrawn from sense-perception and therefore not outwardly active – we meditate, we are then awake both in the ordinary sense of the

word and in the higher. Even this state of being awake purely
in the realm of ideas always has a shade of dreaming about it
– more so with some people, less with others. Nevertheless,
although with many people a dreamlike element plays quite
strongly into the life of ideas, we can broadly say that, when
we are forming concepts, we are awake.

In the realm of feeling we are not awake. Certainly, feelings
well up from an undefined, undifferentiated soul-life, and
because we are conscious of them, and because a waking
activity of ideas is mingled with them, we suppose that we are
awake in our feelings; yet this is not really so. In fact, the
activity of the soul in feeling is exactly the same as in ordinary
dreaming. There is a profound relation between the dream-
condition and the actual condition of feeling. If we were
always able to illumine with ideas what we dream (the greater
part of our dream-life is lost to us), we should be as well
acquainted with the dream-life as with the life of feeling; for
the feelings present in the soul are no different from dreams.
No one can tell from his waking life what actually takes place
when he feels, or in that which he feels. Feeling surges up, as
I said, from the undefined, undifferentiated life of the soul
and is illumined by the light of concepts, but it is a dream-life.
This relationship of emotion and feeling to dreaming is well
known even to those who are not occultists; for example, the
distinguished aesthetician, Frederick Theodor Vischer, has
often emphasized the profound relationship between dreaming and feeling in the soul-life of man.[14]

Still 'deeper down' in the soul-life is the real life of will. What
does man know of all that takes place in his inner being when he
says, 'I will pick up a book', and his arm stretches out and picks
up the book? Of all that takes place between muscle and nerve,
of what goes on in the organism and even in the soul through
which an impulse of will passes into movement, into action, a
person is no more conscious than he is of events in deep,
dreamless sleep. It is true that our life of will is, in its turn,
illumined by the life of ideas, and thus it appears to us as though

we were conscious of it; but the real nature of the will remains, even from waking to falling asleep, in a condition of profound slumber.

Thus we see that, in the true sense of the word, we are really 'awake' only in our sense-perceptions and our life of ideas; in the life of feeling we are so near to sleeping as to be dreaming; and in the life of will we are always fast asleep. Thus the sleep-condition extends into that of waking. Let us picture to ourselves how we pass through the world. What we experience with our waking consciousness is only the sense-world and our world of ideas. Embedded in this experience is a world where our impulses of feeling and of will float; a world which surrounds us like the air, but does not enter ordinary consciousness. Anyone who thus approaches the matter will in truth not be very far from recognizing a so-called supersensible world around him.

Now all this has still more pregnant consequences. Behind what I have told you there are significant facts of life as a whole. Anyone who has come to know the life of the human soul between death and rebirth (described in a more abstract form in the lectures on *The Inner Nature of Man and Our Life between Death and Rebirth* given in Vienna in the spring of 1914) will see that in this world, through which we wander in a sleeping condition, we are living together with the so-called dead.[15] The dead are always present. They move and have their being in a supersensible world. We are not separated from them by our real being but only by our condition of consciousness. We are separated from them only as in sleep we are separated from the things around us; we sleep in a room and do not see the chairs and other objects. Although we do not describe it thus, yet as regards our feeling and our will we 'sleep' among the dead even while we are awake, just as we do not perceive the physical objects around us when we sleep. Thus we do not live separated from the world where the forces of the dead prevail; we are together with the dead in one common world. We are separated from them only by our ordinary state of consciousness.

This knowledge of our common life with the dead will be one of the most important elements which spiritual science has to implant in the general outlook and civilization of humanity in the future; for those who believe that what takes place around them occurs only through the forces perceived by the senses know nothing of the reality; they do not know that the forces of the dead are always at work, always present. If you remember that in this material age man has a quite false view of historical life because the real impulses of history are dreamt or slept through, you will be able to conceive the idea that the forces of the dead may live in what we dream or sleep through of historical life. In a future time history will be studied in a way which takes account of the forces of those who have passed through the Gate of Death, whose souls live in the world between death and rebirth. A consciousness of the unity of all mankind, including the so-called 'dead', will have to give human civilization a quite new colouring.

The method of observation employed by the spiritual investigator, who can make practical application of what has been said, discloses many concrete details of this joint life of the living and the so-called dead. If by his thoughts a person could throw light upon the nature of his feeling and impulses of will, he would have a continuously living awareness of the existence of the dead. This he does not have at present. His ordinary consciousness does not possess it because these things are remarkably distributed within our conscious life. We might say that for conceiving a higher, cosmic relationship there is a third consciousness, much more important than the waking condition or the sleep condition. What is this?

It is something lying between these other two, and for a person of today it is only momentary and passes him by. It occurs at the moments of waking and falling asleep. Today people do not pay attention to waking and falling asleep, yet these moments are extremely important. How important they are is disclosed when the unconscious experiences underlying ordinary consciousness are illumined by the experiences of clairvoyant consciousness. When we have prepared ourselves for such studies through many years, we can quite impartially illumine these things with supersensible facts.

It is quite possible for clairvoyant consciousness not only to become acquainted with general facts about the supersensible world where we dwell between death and a new birth, but also – though this is more difficult – to enter into contact, into communication, with individual souls among the dead. This we know. I will add only that the latter task is more difficult because there are many more obstacles to overcome. Although few persons today succeed in obtaining general scientific results concerning the supersensible world, this is not extraordinarily difficult; it is not very far beyond the ordinary capacities of the human soul. It is more difficult to enter into individual relations with the souls of the dead for the simple reason that anyone who strives for it and finds it within reach can to a certain degree live in the purely spiritual without realizing that in this realm the lower impulses of man can very easily be stimulated.

I have often explained why this is so. The higher faculties of supersensible beings are connected with the lower human impulses (not with the higher impulses of incarnate beings), while the lower impulses of supersensible beings are related to the higher spiritual qualities of man. This I have called an important secret in the intercourse with the spiritual world; a secret of such a nature that a person may easily be ship-wrecked by it, but if he can steer safely past this rock, if he is able to have intercourse with the supersensible without being diverted from the realm of spiritual experiences, such inter-course is quite possible. It proves, however, to be very, very different from what is usually regarded as 'intercourse' here in the world of sense.

I will put this in a quite concrete way: if we talk to one another here in the world of sense, we speak and the other person answers. We produce the words through our vocal organs; the words come from our thoughts. We feel that we are the creators of our words; we know that we hear ourselves speaking, and when someone answers we hear him; we listen and we hear him. We are profoundly accustomed to this because we are conscious only of having intercourse in the physical world with other human beings. Intercourse with discarnate souls is not like that. Strange as it may sound, intercourse with discarnate souls is exactly reversed. If we impart our own thoughts to a discarnate soul, *we* do not speak, but *he* speaks. It is exactly as though you were going to talk to someone, but you do not yourself say what you want to communicate; the other person says it. The reply of the so-called dead does not come to us from outside, but arises from our inner being; we experience it as inner life. Clairvoyant consciousness has to get used to the idea that we ourselves are in the other as questioner, and the one who replies is in us. This complete reversal of entities is necessary.

Anyone acquainted with such things knows that this reversal is not easy; it contradicts everything to which habit has accustomed us in the course of life. Not only that – it contradicts all our inborn tendencies, for it is inborn in us to believe that we ourselves speak when we ask a question, and that the other is silent when we answer him. Yet what I have said is true of intercourse with supersensible beings. From this reversal we can gather that one main reason why the dead are not perceived is because they have intercourse with the living in a way which appears to the living as not only quite unfamiliar, but actually impossible. The living simply do not hear what the dead say to them from the depths of their own beings; and they do not pay attention when another being says what they themselves are thinking, or what they want to ask.

Now it is a fact that of the two conditions of consciousness which slip so quickly past people today – those of waking and falling asleep – one is adapted for questions and the other for replies. The moment of falling asleep is specially favourable for putting a question to a dead person – that is, for hearing from him the question we put to him. We are specially disposed for this while we are falling asleep. Immediately afterwards we fall asleep, as far as our ordinary consciousness is concerned; the consequence is that we ask the dead hundreds of questions and talk with them about hundreds of things, but we know nothing of it, because we have already fallen asleep. This fleeting moment of falling asleep is of tremendous consequence for our intercourse with the dead. So, too, the moment of waking especially disposes us to receive the answers of the dead. If we did not immediately pass over to sense-perception, but were able to linger through the moment of waking, we should be very well adapted to receive their messages. These would appear as though arising from our own inner being.

You see, there are two reasons why the ordinary consciousness does not pay attention to intercourse with the dead. The first is that immediately on waking or falling asleep we meet a condition which is calculated to obliterate what we have experienced; the second is that when we fall asleep, unusual, really 'impossible' things occur. The hundred questions we can put to the dead – and do put – vanish in sleep-life because we are quite unaccustomed to 'hear' what we ask instead of 'uttering' it. Again, we do not judge what the dead say to us on waking as coming from them, because we do not recognize it; we take it as something arising within ourselves. That is the second reason why intercourse with the dead is so unfamiliar.

These general phenomena, however, are sometimes broken through in the following way. What a person experiences on falling asleep as putting a question to the dead from himself, continues in a certain sense during sleep. During sleep we look back unconsciously to the moment of falling asleep, and this can be reflected in our dreams. Such dreams can really be a reproduction of the questions we put to the dead. Far closer than we suppose do we approach the dead in our dreams, although what is experienced in the dream was said at the moment of falling asleep. The dream draws it up from the undifferentiated depths of the soul. A person may,

however, easily misconstrue this; he does not take the dreams
– if later he recollects them as dreams – for what they really
are. Dreams are really always a previous companionship with
the dead that rises up from our life of feeling. We have moved
towards the dead and the dream often gives us the questions
we have put to them. True, it gives us our subjective experience, but as though coming from outside. The dead speak to
us, but we have really said it ourselves. It only appears as
though they spoke. As a rule, it is not messages from the dead
that come to us in our dreams, but the expression of our need
to be with them, of our need to come near them at the moment
of falling asleep.

The moment of waking conveys to us messages from the
dead. This moment is quickly extinguished by a surge of
sense-impressions; but it is a fact that in waking we have
something rising up, as it were, from the inner depth of the
soul and we could be well aware of it if our self-observation
were more accurate. It does not come from our ordinary ego
and often it is a message from the dead.

You will gain a proper understanding of these ideas if you
can grasp deeply a relationship I will now mention. You will
say: the moment of falling asleep is adapted for putting
questions, that of waking for receiving answers from the dead
– yet these moments lie far apart! We can judge this rightly
only if we keep in view the relations of time in the supersensible
world. There the saying is true, spoken with remarkable
intuition by Richard Wagner: 'Time becomes space.'[16] In the
supersensible world, time really does become space – one
point of space here, another there. Time is not past, but only
a point of space, near or far; time actually becomes
supersensible space. The dead person gives his answers only
when he stands somewhat further from us. That again is an
unaccustomed thought; but the past is not 'past' in the
supersensible world. It is there; it remains, and to encounter
it one needs only to relate oneself to another place. In the
supersensible world the past is just as little done away with as

the house we have left to come here to-night. The house is in
its place; so, too, in the supersensible world, the past is not
gone but is in its place. It depends upon ourselves and upon
how far we have gone from them, how near or far we are from
the dead. We can be very far, or very near.

Thus, because we not only sleep and wake, but wake up
and fall asleep, we are in continuous correspondence and
contact with the dead. They are always among us, and we do
not act under the influence only of those living around us as
physical human beings, but under the influence also of those
connected with us who have passed through the Gate of
Death. Today I should like to bring forward some facts which
will lead us more and more deeply, from a certain point of
view, into the spiritual world.

We can distinguish between various souls who have passed
through the Gate of Death, once we have grasped that there
is continuous contact with them. Since we always pass
through the field of the dead, either on falling asleep, when we
ask them questions, or on waking, when we receive answers
from them, our connection with them must also be affected
by whether they died in youth or old age. (The facts underlying the following are evident only to clairvoyant
consciousness. That, however, is only the 'knowledge' of it;
the reality always takes place.) When the young – children or
young people – pass through the Gate of Death, it is seen that
a particular connection exists between the dead and the
living; a connection of a different kind from that which arises
in the case of older people who have gone through the Gate
of Death in the evening of their days. There is a decisive
difference. When we lose children, when the young are
apparently taken from us, they do not really leave us at all;
they remain with us. To clairvoyant consciousness this is
evident from the fact that the messages we receive from them
on awakening are so lively and vivid. The connection of the
dead with those remaining behind is then such that we can
describe it only by saying that a child or young person are not

lost at all; they are still there. This is above all because after death they feel a strong need to influence our waking-up time and to send us messages. It is very remarkable, but true, that those who die young have a great deal to do with this waking-up time. For clairvoyant consciousness it is specially interesting to find that we have to thank the youthful dead when living people feel a certain impulse towards religious devotion. A very great deal in respect of this devotional feeling is brought about by those who have died young.

It is different – clairvoyant consciousness shows us – with the souls of the old. We may say that they do not lose us; our souls remain with them. Observe the contrast. The souls of the young we do not lose, they remain with us; the souls of the old do not lose us, they take something of our souls with them, as it were – if I may use such a comparison. The souls of the old draw us more to themselves, whereas the souls of the young draw near to us. Therefore at the moment of falling asleep we have much to say to the souls of those who died old, and we can weave a bond with the spiritual world especially by adapting ourselves to address the souls of the old. We can really accomplish something in this way.

Thus we see that we stand in continuous relation to the dead; we have a sort of 'question and answer', a two-way intercourse with them. To qualify ourselves for questioning and approaching the dead, the following is the right course. Ordinary abstract thoughts, those taken from materialistic life, do little to bring us into relation with the dead. If the dead belong to us in any way, they even suffer through our preoccupation with purely material life. If we stand firm against this and cultivate ways of life which will bring us into relation with the dead through our feeling and our will, we are preparing ourselves very well to enter into relation with them at the time of going to sleep and to put appropriate questions to them.

This is more readily accomplished, of course, if the dead were closely related to us in life. The relationship in life forms and establishes the relationship after death. Naturally it makes a difference whether I talk to someone apathetically or with sympathy, whether I speak as one who feels affection for another, or as one who does not care. It makes a great difference whether I talk with someone as at a five o'clock tea, or whether I am quite specially interested in what I can come to know of him. When intimate relations are formed between soul and soul, founded on impulses of feeling and will, and if, after one soul has passed through the Gate of Death, the one left behind can retain his interest in the other person and is eager to receive answers from him, or if he has the impulse to be something to him and can live in his memories of him – not conceptual memories but those bound up with the relationship of soul to soul – then he will be particularly well adapted to put questions to him at the moment of falling asleep.

On the other hand, we are specially adapted for the reception of answers, messages, at the moment of waking if we were able and inclined to enter consciously into the being of the dead person during his life. Let us reflect how, especially at the present time, one person passes another by without really learning to know him. What do people really know of one another? There are striking examples of marriages lasting for ten years without either person knowing the other. This does happen. Yet it is possible (depending not on talent but on love) to enter into the being of another with understanding, and then to carry within one a real world of ideas drawn from the other. This is a specially good preparation for receiving answers from the dead at the moment of waking. That is why we are sooner able to receive answers from a child or young person, because we come to know a young person sooner than those who have deepened and grown old.

Thus we can do something towards establishing a right relation between the living and the dead. Our whole life is, in reality, permeated with this relation. We, as souls, are embedded in the same sphere where the dead are. The degree to which we are religious is very strongly connected, as I have said, with the influence of those who have died young; and were it not for this influence, there would probably be, in general, no religious feeling. The best way of relating ourselves to the souls of those who die young is to think of them in a collective way. Funeral services for children or young people should have a ritual, universal character. The Roman Catholic Church, which tones everything down to a child-like level and would really like to have to do only with children, with the guidance of child-souls, seldom gives an individual address when a child has died. That is particularly good. Our mourning for children is different from our mourning for older people. Our grief for a child I should prefer to call a sympathetic sorrow, for the sorrow we feel is in many respects a reflection of the attitude of our own soul towards the being of the child, who remains near us. We share in the life of the child and the child shares in our sorrow. It is a sympathetic mourning.

Our grief for an older person cannot be called a sympathetic mourning. It is 'egoistic', and is best borne by the reflection that an older dead person really 'takes us with him'; he does not lose us if we try to prepare ourselves to come near him. Hence we can form more 'individualized' memories of our older dead; we carry them in our thoughts and can remain united with them in the thoughts we shared with them, if we try not to behave as an uncomfortable companion. When we have thoughts which a dead friend cannot accept, he holds to us, but in a peculiar way. We remain with him, but we can be a burden to him if he has to drag us along while we fail to entertain any thoughts in which he can be united with us, or can perceive spiritually.

Let us reflect how concrete our relations to the dead appear, if we are able to see them in the light of spiritual science and to grasp the whole relationship of the living to the dead. This will become very important for the humanity of the future. Trivial as it may sound – for one can say that every epoch is a 'time of transition' – yet our own time really is a time of transition. It must pass into a more spiritual age. It must come to know what comes from the kingdom of the dead; it must learn that we are surrounded by the dead as by the air. In times to come there will be a real perception that when an older person dies we must not become an incubus to him, as we shall be if we have thoughts which he cannot entertain. Just think how much richer life can become if we accept this living-together with the dead as something real.

I have often said that spiritual science does not wish to found a new religion, or to introduce anything sectarian into the world; that would be to misconstrue it completely. On the other hand, I have often emphasized that religious life can be deepened by it, because for this it provides real foundations. Certainly, remembrance of the dead, services for the dead, have a religious side. Here a foundation for religious life will be created, if this is illuminated by spiritual science. If rightly done, these things will be lifted out of the abstract. For instance, it is not a matter of indifference for human existence whether a funeral service held is the right one for a young person, or is more suited to an old one. Whether right or wrong funeral services are held is of far greater importance for social life than all the regulations of town councils or parliaments – strange as that may sound. For the impulses working into life will come from the human individuals themselves when they are in a right relation to the dead.

Today, people want to have everything regulated by the abstract structure of a social order. They are pleased when they do not need to think much about what they ought to do. Many are even glad if they are not obliged to reflect upon what they ought to think. It is quite different when one has a living consciousness, not merely of a vaguely pantheistic connection, but of a quite definite one, with the spiritual world. One can foresee a permeation of religious life with concrete ideas when it is deepened by spiritual science.

As I have often related, 'spirit' was eliminated from western humanity in the year 869 at the Eighth Ecumenical Council in Constantinople. The dogma was then drawn up that Christians must not regard man as consisting of body, soul and spirit, but of body and soul only, though certain spiritual qualities were to be ascribed to the soul. This abolition of the spirit is of tremendous significance. In the year 869, in Constantinople, it was decided that man must not be regarded as endowed with *anima* and *spiritus*, but as possessing only *unam animam rationalem et intellectualem*. The dogma that 'the soul has spiritual qualities' was spread over the spiritual life of the West in the twilight of the ninth century.

This must be overcome. Spirit must again be recognized. A trichotomy of body, soul and spirit – regarded as heresy in the Middle Ages – must again be recognized as the true and exact view of man's nature. Several things will be required of those who today naturally challenge all 'authority', yet swear that man consists of body and soul alone. They are to be found not only in particular religious persuasions, but also among the ranks of those who listen to professors, philosophers, and so on. Philosophers, as you can read everywhere, distinguish only body and soul, omitting the spirit. That is their 'unprejudiced' philosophy of life; but it rests upon that fact that in the year 869 a Church Council decided not to recognize spirit. That, however, is overlooked. A well-known philosopher, William Wundt – a great philosopher by favour of his publisher, but at the same time renowned – of course divides man into body and soul, because he regards it as 'unprejudiced' science to do so; he does not know that he is simply following the decision of the Council of 869.[17] We must look into the actual facts if we wish to see what is really going on in the world. If a person looks at the actual facts in the realm that has particularly concerned us today, his consciousness will be opened concerning a connection with that world which in history is only dreamt and slept through. History, historical life, will be seen in the right light only when a true consciousness can be developed of the connection of the so-called living with the so-called dead.

XIII. Death as Transformation

Nuremberg, 10 February 1918

IN OUR study of spiritual science there is a great deal that we cannot, perhaps, directly apply in everyday life, and we may at times feel that it is all rather remote. But only the remoteness is apparent. What we receive into the sphere of our knowledge concerning the secrets of the spiritual world is at every hour, at every moment, of vital and profound significance for our souls; what seems to be remote from us personally is often what the soul inwardly needs. In order to know the physical world we must make ourselves acquainted with it. But to know the spiritual world it is essential that we ourselves shall think through and master the thoughts and conceptions imparted by that world. These thoughts then often work quite unconsciously within the soul. Many things may seem to be remote, whereas in reality they are very near indeed to the higher realms of the soul's life.

And so again today we will think of the life that takes its course between death and a new birth – the life that seems so far removed from the human being in the physical world. I will begin by simply narrating what is found by spiritual investigation. These things can be understood if sufficient thought is applied to them; through their own power they make themselves comprehensible to the soul. Anyone who does not understand them should realize that he has not thought about them deeply enough. They must be *investigated* by means of spiritual science, but they can be *understood* through constant study. They will then be confirmed by the facts with which life itself confronts us, provided life is rightly observed.

You will have realized from many of the lecture-courses that study of the life between death and rebirth is fraught with difficulty, because its conditions are so entirely different from those of the life that can be pictured by the organs of the physical body here in the physical world. We have to become acquainted with utterly different conceptions.

When we enter into relationship with the things in our physical environment we know that only a small proportion of the beings around us in the physical world react to our deeds, to the manifestations of our will, in such a way that *pleasure* or *pain* is caused by these deeds of ours. Reaction of this kind takes place in the case of the animal kingdom and the human kingdom; but we are justified in the conviction that the mineral world (including what is contained in air and water), and also, in essentials, the world of plants, are insensitive to what we call pleasure or pain as the result of deeds performed by us. (Spiritually considered, of course, the matter is a little different, but that need not concern us at this point.) In the environment of the dead all this is changed. Conditions in the environment of the so-called dead are such that everything – including what is done by the dead themselves – causes either pleasure or pain. The dead can do no single thing, they cannot – if I may speak pictorially – move a single limb without pleasure or pain being caused by what is done. We must try to think our way into these conditions of existence. We must assimilate the thought that life between death and a new birth is so constituted that everything we do awakens an echo in the environment. Through the whole period between death and a new birth we can do nothing, we cannot even move, metaphorically speaking, without causing pleasure or pain in our environment. The mineral kingdom as we have it around us on the physical plane does not exist for the dead, neither does the world of plants. As you can gather from my book *Theosophy*,[18] these kingdoms are present in an entirely different form. They are not present in the spiritual world in the form in which we know them here, namely, as realms devoid of feeling.

The first kingdom of those familiar to us on the physical

plane which has significance for the dead, because it is comparable with what the dead has in his environment, is the animal kingdom. I do not, of course, mean individual animals as we know them on the physical plane, but the whole environment is such that its effects and influences are as if animals were there. The reaction of the environment is such that pleasure or pain proceeds from what is done. On the physical plane we stand upon mineral soil: the dead stands upon a 'soil', lives in an environment, which may be compared with the animal nature in this sense. The dead, therefore, starts his life two kingdoms higher. On the earth we know the animal kingdom only from outside. The most external activity of the life between death and a new birth consists in acquiring a more and more intimate and exact knowledge [of the animal world].[18] For in this life between death and a new birth we must prepare all those forces which, working in from the cosmos, organize our own body. In the physical world we know nothing of these forces. Between death and a new birth we know that our body, down to its smallest particles, is formed out of the cosmos. For we ourselves prepare this physical body, bringing together in it the whole of animal nature; we ourselves build it.

To make the picture more exact, we must acquaint ourselves with an idea that is rather remote from present-day mentality. Modern man knows quite well that when a magnetic needle lies with one end pointing towards the North and the other towards the South, this is not caused by the needle itself; the earth as a whole is a cosmic magnet of which one end points towards the North and the other towards the South. It would be considered sheer nonsense to say that the direction is determined by forces contained in the magnetic needle itself. In the case of a seed or germinating entity which develops in an animal or in a human being, all the sciences and schools of thought deny the factor of cosmic influence. What would be described as nonsense in the case of the magnetic needle is accepted without further thought in the case of an egg forming inside the hen. But when the egg is forming inside the hen, the whole cosmos is, in fact, participating; what happens on earth merely provides the stimulus for the operation of cosmic forces. Everything that takes shape in the egg is an imprint of cosmic forces and the hen herself is only a place, an abode, in which the cosmos, the whole world-system, is working in this way. And it is the same in the case of the human being. This is a thought with which we must become familiar.

Between death and a new birth, in communion with Beings of the higher Hierarchies, a person is working at this whole system of forces permeating the Cosmos. For between death and a new birth he is not inactive; he is perpetually at work – in the spiritual. The animal kingdom is the first realm with which he makes acquaintance, and in the following way: if he commits some error he immediately becomes aware of pain, of suffering, in the environment; if he does something right, he becomes aware of pleasure, of joy, in the environment. He works on and on, calling forth pleasure or pain, until finally the soul-nature is such that it can descend and unite with what will live on earth as a physical body. The being of soul could never descend if it had not itself worked at the physical form.

It is the animal kingdom, then, with which acquaintance is made in the first place. The next is the human kingdom. Mineral nature and the plant kingdom are absent. The dead's acquaintance with the human kingdom is limited – to use a familiar phrase. Between death and a new birth – and this begins immediately or soon after death – the dead has contact and can make links only with those human souls, whether still living on earth or in yonder world, with whom he has already been karmically connected on earth in the last or in an earlier incarnation. Other souls pass him by; they do not come within his ken. He becomes aware of the animal realm as a totality; only those human souls come within his ken with whom he has had some karmic connection here on earth, and with these he becomes more and more closely acquainted. You must not imagine that their number is small, for individual human beings have already passed through many lives on the earth. In every life numbers of karmic connections have been formed and of these is spun the web which then, in the spiritual world, extends over all the souls whom the dead has known in life; only those with whom no acquaintance has been made remain outside the circle.

This indicates a truth which must be emphasized, namely, the supreme importance of earthly life for the individual human being. If there had been no earthly life we should be unable to form links with human souls in the spiritual world. The links are formed karmically on the earth and then continue between death and a new birth. Those who are able to see into the spiritual world perceive how the dead gradually makes more and more links – all of which are the outcome of karmic connections formed on earth.

Just as concerning the first kingdom with which the dead comes into contact – the animal kingdom – we can say that everything the dead does, even when he simply moves, causes either pleasure or pain in his environment, so we can say about everything experienced in the human realm in yonder world that it is much more intimately connected with the life of soul. When the dead becomes acquainted with a soul, he gets to know this soul as if he himself were within it. After death, knowledge of another soul is as intimate as knowledge here on earth of our own finger, head or ear – we feel ourselves within the other soul. The connection is much more intimate than it can ever be on earth.

There are two basic experiences in the community among human souls between death and a new birth; we are either within the other souls or outside them. Even in the case of souls with whom we are already acquainted, we are sometimes within and sometimes outside them. Meeting with them consists in feeling at one with them, being within them; to be outside them means that we do not notice them, do not become aware of them. If we look at some object here on earth, we perceive it; if we look away from it, we no longer perceive it. In yonder world we are actually within human souls when we are able to turn our attention to them; and we are outside them when we are not in a position to do so.

What I have now said is an indication of the fundamental form of the soul's communion with other souls during the period between death and a new birth. Similarly, the human being is also within or outside the Beings of the Hierarchies, the Angeloi, Archangeloi, and so on. The higher the kingdoms, the more intensely does man feel bound to them after death; he feels as though they were bearing him, sustaining him, with great power. The Archangeloi are a mightier support than the Angeloi, the Archai again mightier than the Archangeloi, and so on.

People today still find difficulties in acquiring knowledge of the spiritual world. The difficulties would soon solve themselves if a little more trouble were taken to become acquainted with its secrets. There are two ways of approach. One way leads to complete certainty of the eternal in one's own being. This knowledge, that in human nature there is an eternal core of being which passes through birth and death – this knowledge, remote as it is to the modern mind, is comparatively easy to attain; and it will certainly be attained by those who have enough perseverance, along the path described in the book *Knowledge of the Higher Worlds,* and in other writings. It is attained by treading the path there described. That is one form of knowledge of the spiritual world. The other is what may be called direct intercourse with beings of the spiritual world, and we will now speak of the intercourse that is possible between those still living on earth and the so-called dead.

Such intercourse is most certainly possible but it presents greater difficulties than the first form of knowledge, which is easy to attain. Actual intercourse with an individual who has died is possible, but difficult, because it demands scrupulous vigilance on the part of the one who seeks to establish it. Control and discipline are necessary for this kind of inter-

course with the spiritual world, because it is connected with
a very significant law. Impulses recognized as lower impulses
in people on earth are, from the spiritual side, higher life; and
it may therefore easily happen that when the human being
has not achieved true control of himself, he experiences the
rising of lower impulses as the result of direct intercourse
with the dead. When we make contact with the spiritual
world in the general sense, when we acquire knowledge
about our own immortality as beings of soul and spirit, there
can be no question of the ingress of anything impure. But
when it is a matter of contact with individuals who have
died, the relation with the individual dead – strange as it
seems – is always a relation with the blood and nervous
system. The dead enters into those impulses which live
themselves out in the system of blood and nerves, and
in this way lower impulses may be aroused. Naturally, there
is only danger for those who have not purified their natures
through discipline and control. This must be said, for it is the
reason why in the Old Testament it is forbidden to have
communication with the dead.[19] Such intercourse is not
sinful when it happens in the right way. The methods of
modern spiritualism must, of course, be avoided. When the
intercourse is of a spiritual nature it is not sinful, but when it
is not accompanied by pure thoughts it can easily lead to the
stimulation of lower passions. It is not the dead who arouse
these passions but the element in which the dead live. For
consider this: what we feel here as 'animal' in quality and
nature is the basic element in which the dead live. The
kingdom in which the dead live can easily be changed when
it enters into us; what is higher life in yonder world can
become lower impulses when it is within us on earth. It
is very important to remember this, and it must be emphasized when we are speaking of intercourse between the living
and the so-called dead, for it is an occult fact. We shall find
that precisely when we are speaking about this intercourse,
the spiritual world can be described as it really is, for such

experiences reveal that the spiritual world is completely different from the physical world.

To begin with, I will tell you something that may seem to have no meaning for man as long as he has not developed faculties of clairvoyance; but when we think it over we shall realize that it concerns us closely. Those who are able to commune with the dead as the result of developed clairvoyance realize why it is so difficult for human beings to know anything about the dead through direct perception. Strange as it may seem, the whole form of intercourse to which we are accustomed in the physical world has to be reversed when intercourse is established between the earth and the dead. In the physical world, when we speak to a human being from physical body to physical body, we know that the words come from ourselves; when the other person speaks to us, we know that the words come from him. The whole relationship is reversed when we are speaking with one who has died. The expression 'when we are speaking' can truthfully be used, but the relationship is reversed. When we put a question to the dead, or say something to him, what we say comes from *him*, comes to us from him. He inspires into our soul what we ask him, what we say to him. And when he answers us or says something to us, this comes out of our own soul. It is a process with which a human being in the physical world is quite unfamiliar. He feels that what he says comes out of his own being. In order to establish intercourse with those who have died, we must adapt ourselves to hear from them what we ourselves say, and to receive from our own soul what they answer.

Thus abstractly described, the nature of the process is easy to grasp; but to become accustomed to the total reversal of the familiar form of intercourse is exceedingly difficult. The dead are always there, always among us and around us, and the fact that they are not perceived is largely due to lack of understanding of this reversed form of intercourse. On the physical plane we think that when anything comes out of our soul, it comes from us. And we are far from being able to pay intimate enough attention to whether it is not, after all, being inspired into us from the spiritual environment. We prefer to connect it with experiences familiar on the physical plane, where, if something comes to us from the environment, we ascribe it at once to the other person. This is the greatest error when it is a matter of intercourse with the dead.

I have here been telling you of one of the fundamental principles of intercourse between the so-called living and the so-called dead. If this example helps you to realize one thing only, namely, that conditions are entirely reversed in the spiritual world, then you will have grasped a very significant concept and one that is constantly needed by those who aspire to become conscious of the spiritual world. The concept is extremely difficult to apply in an actual, individual case. For instance, in order to understand even the physical world, permeated as it is with the spiritual, it is essential to grasp this idea of complete reversal. And because modern science fails to grasp it and it is altogether unknown to the general consciousness, for this reason there is today no spiritual understanding of the physical world. One experiences this even with people who try very hard indeed to comprehend the world and one is often obliged simply to accept the situation and leave it as it is. Some years ago I was speaking to a large number of friends at a meeting in Berlin about the physical organism of man, with special reference to certain ideas of Goethe. I tried to explain how the head, in respect of its physical structure, can only be rightly understood when it is conceived as a complete transformation of the other part of the organism.[20] No one was able to understand at all that a bone in the arm would have to be turned inside out like a glove, in order that a head-bone might be produced from it. It is a difficult concept, but one cannot really understand anatomy without such pictures. I mention this in parenthesis only. What I have said today about intercourse with the dead is easier to understand.

The happenings I have described to you are going on all the time. All of you sitting here now are in constant intercourse with the dead, only the ordinary consciousness knows nothing of it because it lies in the subconscious. Clairvoyant consciousness does not evoke anything new into being; it merely brings up into consciousness what is present all the time in the spiritual world. All of you are in constant intercourse with the dead.

And now we will consider how this intercourse takes place in individual cases. When someone has died and we are left behind, we may ask: how do I approach the one who has died, so that he is aware of me? How does he come near me again so that I can live in him? These questions may well be asked but they cannot be answered if we have recourse only to concepts familiar on the physical plane. On the physical plane, ordinary consciousness functions only from the time of waking until the time of falling asleep; but the other part of consciousness which remains dim in ordinary life between falling asleep and waking is just as important. The human being is not, properly speaking, unconscious when he is asleep; his consciousness is merely so dim that he experiences nothing. But the whole man – in waking and sleeping life – must be held in mind when we are studying the connections of the human being with the spiritual world. Think of your own biography. You reflect upon the course of your life always with interruptions; you describe only what has happened in your waking hours. Life is broken: waking-sleeping; waking-sleeping. But you are also present while you sleep; and in studying the whole human being, both waking life and sleeping life must be taken into consideration.

A third thing must also be held in mind in connection with man's intercourse with the spiritual world. For besides waking life and sleeping life there is a third state, even more important for intercourse with the spiritual world than waking and sleeping life as such. I mean the state connected with the act of waking and the act of going to sleep, which lasts only for brief seconds, for we immediately pass on into other conditions. If we develop a delicate sensitivity for these moments of waking and going to sleep we shall find that they shed great light on the spiritual world. In remote country places – although such customs are gradually disappearing – when we who are older were still young, people were wont to say: when you wake from sleep it is not good immediately to go to the window through which light is streaming; you should stay a little while in the dark. Country folk used to have some knowledge about intercourse with the spiritual world and at this moment of waking they preferred not to come at once into the bright daylight but to remain inwardly collected, in order to preserve something of what sweeps with such power through the human soul at the moment of waking. The sudden brightness of daylight is disturbing. In the cities, of course, this is hardly to be avoided; there we are disturbed not only by the daylight but also even before waking by the noise from the streets, the clanging of tramcar bells and so forth. The whole of civilized life seems to conspire to hinder man's intercourse with the spiritual world. This is not said in order to decry material civilization, but the facts must be remembered. Again, at the moment of going to sleep, the spiritual world approaches us with power, but we immediately fall asleep, losing consciousness of what has passed through the soul. Exceptions do, of course, occur. These moments of waking and of going to sleep are of the utmost significance for intercourse with the so-called dead – and with other spiritual Beings of the higher worlds. But in order to understand what I have to say about this you must familiarize yourselves with an idea which it is not easy to apply on the physical plane and which is therefore practically unknown. It is this:

In the spiritual sense, what is 'past' has not really vanished but is still there. In physical life people have this conception in regard to space only. If you stand in front of a tree, then go away and look back at it later on, the tree has not disappeared;

it is still there. In the spiritual world the same is true in regard to time. If you experience something at one moment, it has passed away the next as far as physical consciousness is concerned; spiritually conceived, it has not passed away. You can look back at it just as you looked back at the tree. Richard Wagner showed that he had knowledge of this by the remarkable words: 'Time here becomes space.'[21] It is an occult fact that in the spiritual world there are distances which do not come to expression on the physical plane. That an event is past simply means that it is farther away from us. I beg you to remember this. For man on earth in the physical body, the moment of going to sleep is 'past' when the moment of waking arrives. In the spiritual world, however, the moment of falling asleep has not gone; we are only, at the moment of waking, a little farther distant from it. We encounter our dead at the moment of going to sleep and again at the moment of waking. (As I said, this is perpetually happening, only it usually remains in the subconscious.) As far as physical consciousness is concerned, these are two quite different moments in time; for spiritual consciousness the one is only a little farther distant than the other. I want you to remember this in connection with what I am now going to say: otherwise you may find it difficult to understand.

As I told you, the moments of waking and going to sleep are particularly important for intercourse with those who have died. Through the whole of our life there are no such moments when we do not come into relation with the dead.

The moment of going to sleep is especially favourable for us to turn to the dead. Suppose we want to ask the dead something. We can carry it in our soul, holding it until the moment of going to sleep, for that is the time to bring our questions to the dead. Other opportunities exist, but this moment is the most favourable. When, for instance, we read to the dead we certainly draw near to them, but for direct intercourse it is best of all if we put our questions to them at the moment of going to sleep.

On the other hand, the moment of waking is the most favourable for what the dead have to communicate to us. And again there is no one – did people but know it – who at the moment of waking does not bring with him countless tidings from the dead. In the subconscious region of the soul we are speaking continually with the dead. At the moment of going to sleep we put our questions to them, we say to them what, in the depths of the soul, we have to say. At the moment of waking the dead speak with us, give us the answers. But we must realize that these are only two different points and that, in the higher sense, these things that happen after each other are really simultaneous, just as on the physical plane two places are there simultaneously.

Some factors in life are favourable for intercourse with the dead, others are less so. And we may ask: what can really help us to establish intercourse with the dead? The manner of our converse cannot be the same as it is with those who are alive, for the dead neither hears nor takes in this kind of speech. There is no question of being able to chatter with one who has died as we chatter with one another at tea or in cafés. What makes it possible to put questions to the dead or to communicate something to him is that we unite the life of *feeling* with our thoughts and ideas. Suppose a person has passed through the Gate of Death and you want your subconscious to communicate something to him in the evening. It need not be communicated consciously; you can prepare it at some time during the day. Then, if you go to bed at ten o'clock at night having prepared it, say, at noon, it passes over to the dead when you go to sleep. The question must, however, be put in a particular way; it must not merely be a thought or an idea, it must be imbued with feeling and with will. Your relationship with the dead must be one of the heart, of inner interest. You must remind yourself of your love for the person when he was alive and address yourself to him with real warmth of heart, not abstractly. This feeling can take such firm root in the soul that in the evening, at the moment of going to sleep, it becomes a question to the dead without your knowing it. Or you may try to realize vividly what was the nature of your particular interest in the one who has died. Think about your experiences with him; visualize actual moments when you were together with him, and then ask yourself: what was it about him that particularly interested me, that attracted me to him? When was it that I was so deeply impressed, liked what he said, found it helpful and valuable? If you remind yourself of moments when you were strongly connected with the dead and were deeply interested in him, and then turn this into a desire to speak to him, to say something to him – if you develop the feeling with purity of heart and let the question arise out of the interest you took in him, then the question of the communication remains in your soul, and when you go to sleep it passes over to him. Ordinary consciousness as a rule will know little of the happening, because sleep ensues immediately. But what has thus passed over often remains present in dreams.

In the case of most dreams – although in respect of actual content they are misleading – in the case of most dreams we have of the dead, all that happens is that we interpret them incorrectly. We interpret them as messages from the dead, whereas they are nothing but the echoing of the questions or communications we have ourselves directed to the dead. We should not think that the dead is saying something to us in our dream, but we should see in the dream something that goes out from our own soul to the dead. The dream is the echo of this. If we were sufficiently developed to be conscious of our question or communication to the dead at the moment of going to sleep, it would seem to us as though the dead himself were speaking – hence the echo in the dream seems as if it were a message from him. In reality it comes from ourselves. This becomes intelligible only when we understand the nature of clairvoyant connection with the dead. What the dead seems to say to us is really what we are saying to him.

The moment of waking is especially favourable for the dead

to approach us. At the moment of waking, very much comes from the dead to every human being. A great deal of what we undertake in life is really inspired into us by the dead or by Beings of the higher Hierarchies, although we attribute it to ourselves, imagining that it comes from our own soul. The life of day draws near, the moment of waking passes quickly by, and we seldom pay heed to the intimate indications that arise out of our soul. And when we do, we are vain enough to attribute them to ourselves. Yet in all this – and in much else that comes out of our own soul – there lives what the dead have to say to us. It is indeed so: what the dead say to us seems as if it arises out of our own soul. If people knew what life truly is, this knowledge would engender a feeling of reverence and piety towards the spiritual world in which we are always living, together with the dead with whom we are connected. We should realize that in much of what we do, the dead are working. The knowledge that around us, like the very air we breathe, there is a spiritual world, the knowledge that the dead are round about us only we are not able to perceive them – this knowledge must be unfolded in spiritual science not as theory but so that it permeates the soul as inner life. The dead speak to us inwardly but we interpret our own inner life incorrectly. If we were to understand it aright, we should know that in our inmost being we are united with the souls who are the so-called dead.

Now it is not at all the same when a soul passes through the Gate of Death in relatively early years or later in life. The death of young children who have loved us is a very different thing from the death of people older than ourselves. Experience of the spiritual world discovers that the secret of communion with children who have died can be expressed by saying that in the spiritual sense we do not lose them, they remain with us. When children die in early life they continue to be with us – spiritually with us. I should like to give it to you as a theme for meditation, that when little children die they are not lost to us; we do not lose them, they stay with us spiritually. Of older people who die, the opposite may be said. Those who are older do not lose us. We do not lose little children; elderly people do not lose us. When elderly people die they are strongly drawn to the spiritual world, but this also gives them the power so to work into the physical world that it is easier for them to approach us. True, they withdraw much farther from the physical world than do children who remain near us, but they are endowed with higher faculties of perception than children who die young. Knowledge of different souls in the spiritual world reveals that those who died in old age are able to enter easily into souls on earth; they do not lose the souls on earth. And we do not lose little children, for they remain more or less within the sphere of earthly man. The meaning of the difference can also be considered in another respect.

We have not always sufficiently deep insight into the experiences of the soul on the physical plane. When friends die, we mourn and feel pain. When good friends pass away, I have often said that it is not the task of Anthroposophy to offer people shallow consolation for their pain or try to talk them out of their sorrow. One should grow strong enough to bear sorrow; not allow oneself to be talked out of it. But people make no distinction as to whether the sorrow is caused by the death of a child or of one who is elderly. Spiritually perceived, there is a very great difference. When little children have died, the pain of those who have remained behind is really a kind of compassion – no matter whether such children were their own or other children whom they loved. Children remain with us and because we have been united with them they convey their pain to our souls; we feel their pain – that they would fain still be here! Their pain is eased when we bear it with them. The child feels in us, shares his feeling with us, and it is good that it should be so; his pain is thereby ameliorated.

On the other hand, the pain we feel at the death of elderly people – whether relatives or friends – can be called egotistical pain. An elderly person who has died does not lose us and the feeling he has is therefore different from the feeling present in a child. One who dies in later life does not lose us. We here in life feel that we have lost him – the pain is therefore *ours;* it is egotistical pain. We do not share his feeling as we do in the case of children; we feel the pain for ourselves.

A clear distinction can therefore be made between these two forms of pain: egotistical pain in connection with the elderly; pain fraught with compassion in connection with little children. The child lives on in us and we actually feel what he feels. In reality, our own soul mourns only for those who died in the later years of their life.

It is a matter such as this that can show us the immense significance of knowledge of the spiritual world. For you see, Divine Service for the dead can be adapted in accordance with these truths. In the case of a child who has died, it will not be altogether appropriate to emphasize the individual aspect. Because the child lives on in us and remains with us, the Service of Remembrance should take a more universal form, giving the child, who is still near us, something that is wide and universal. Therefore in the case of a child, a simple ceremony in the Service is preferable to a special funeral oration. The Catholic ritual is better here in one respect, the Protestant in the other. The Catholic Service includes no funeral oration but consists in ceremony, in ritual. It is general, universal, alike for all. And what can be alike for all is especially good for children. But in the case of one who has died in later years, the individual aspect is more important. The best funeral Service here will be one in which the life of the individual is remembered. The Protestant Service, with the oration referring to the life of the one who has died, will have great significance for the soul; the Catholic ritual will mean less in such a case.

The same distinction holds good for all our thought about those who have died. It is best for a child when we induce a mood of feeling connected with him; we try to turn our thoughts to him and these thoughts will draw near to him when we sleep. Such thoughts may be of a more general kind – such for example as may be directed to all those who have passed through the Gate of Death. In the case of an elderly person, we must direct our thoughts of remembrance to him as an individual, thinking about his life on earth and of experiences we shared with him. In order to establish the right intercourse with an older person it is very important to visualize him as he actually was, to make his being come to life in ourselves – not only by remembering things he said which meant a great deal to us but by thinking of what he was as an individual and what his value was for the world. If we make these things inwardly alive, they will enable us to come into connection with an older person who has died and to have the right thoughts of remembrance for him. So you see, for the unfolding of true piety it is important to know what attitude should be taken to those who have died in childhood and to those who have died in the later years of life.

Just think what it means at the present time, when so many human beings are dying in comparatively early years, to be able to say to oneself: they are really always present, they are not lost to the world. (I have spoken of this from other points of view, for such matters must always be considered from different angles.) If we succeed in becoming conscious of the spiritual world, one realization at least will light up in us out of the deep sorrow with which the present days are fraught. It is that because those who die young remain with us, a living spiritual life can arise through community with the dead. A living spiritual life can and will arise, if only materialism is not allowed to become so strong that Ahriman is able to stretch out his claws and gain the victory over all human powers.

Many people may say, speaking purely of conditions on the physical plane, that indications such as I have been giving seem very remote; they would prefer to be told definitely what they can do in the morning and evening in order to bring themselves into a right relation with the spiritual world. But this is not quite correct thinking. Where the spiritual world is concerned, the first essential is that we should develop thoughts about it. And even if it seems as though the dead are far away, while immediate life is close at hand, the very fact that we have such thoughts as have been described today and that we allow our minds to dwell on things seemingly remote from external life – this very fact uplifts the soul, imparts to it spiritual strength and spiritual nourishment. Do not, therefore, be afraid of thinking these thoughts through again and again, continually bringing them to new life within the soul. *There is nothing more important for life, even for material life, than the strong and sure realization of communion with the spiritual world.*

If modern people had not lost their relationship with spiritual things to such an extent, these grave times would not have come upon us. Only a very few today have insight into this connection, although it will certainly be recognized in the future. Today people think: when a human being has passed through the Gate of Death, his activity ceases as far as the physical world is concerned. But indeed it is not so! There is a living and perpetual intercourse between the so-called dead and the so-called living. Those who have passed through the Gate of Death have not ceased to be present; it is only that our eyes have ceased to see them. They are there in very truth.

Our thoughts, our feelings, our impulses of will, are all connected with the dead. The words of the Gospel hold good for the dead as well: 'The kingdom of the Spirit cometh not with observation' (that is to say, external observation); 'neither shall they say, Lo here, lo there, for, behold, the kingdom of the Spirit is within you.'[22] We should not seek for the dead through externalities but become conscious that they are always present. All historical life, all social life, all ethical life, proceed by virtue of co-operation between the so-called living and the so-called dead. The whole being of man can be infinitely strengthened when he is conscious not only of his firm stand here in the physical world but is filled with the inner realization of being able to say of the dead whom he has loved: they are with us, they are in our midst.

This, too, is part of a true knowledge and understanding of the spiritual world which have, as it were, to be woven together from many different threads. We cannot say that we *know* the spiritual world until the way in which we think and speak about it comes from that world itself.

The dead are in our midst – these words in themselves are an affirmation of the spiritual world; and only the spiritual world itself can awaken within us the consciousness that in very truth the dead are with us.

Sources of the lectures by Rudolf Steiner

'Life between Death and Rebirth', 19 March 1914, is the first English translation of this lecture, by M. Barton.

'Metamorphosis of the Memory in the Life after Death', 10 February 1924, is included in *Anthroposophy and the Inner Life*, published by Rudolf Steiner Press, 1961.

'Our Experiences during the Night and the Life after Death', 18 May 1923, and 'Life Between Death and a New Incarnation', 17 May 1923, are included in *Man's Being, His Destiny and World Evolution*, Anthroposophic Press, 1984.

'The Working of Karma in Life after Death', 15 December 1912, is included in *Life Between Death and Rebirth*, Anthroposophic Press, 1968.

'Inward Experiences after Death', 23 November 1915, and 'The Moment of Death and the Period Thereafter', 22 February 1916, are the first published English translations of these lectures, by M. Barton.

'The Lively Interchange between the Living and the Dead', 10 October 1913, is included in *Links Between the Living and the Dead*, Rudolf Steiner Press, 1973.

'The Human Being's Experiences Beyond the Gates of Death', 17 June 1915, 'From a Memorial Speech', 29 June 1923, and 'On the Connection of the Living and the Dead', 9 November 1916, have been translated into English for the first time, by M. Barton.

'Concerning the Affinity of the Living and the Dead', 5 February 1918, is included in *Earthly Death and Cosmic Life*, Rudolf Steiner Press, 1964.

'Death as Transformation', 10 February 1918, was previously published as 'The Dead Are With Us', Rudolf Steiner Press, 1964.

Many of these publications are available from
Rudolf Steiner Press (U.K.) and Anthroposophic Press (U.S.A.)

Notes

GA = *Gesamtausgabe*, the collected edition of Rudolf Steiner's works in the original German (published by Rudolf Steiner Verlag, Dornach, Switzerland).

1. This lecture was held before a public audience in the spring of 1914. It belongs to a series of lectures which Rudolf Steiner gave each winter season from 1903/04 onwards in the Architects' House in Berlin. Many of his listeners had attended these lectures for several years and were therefore already familiar with anthroposophy. This was the first time, though, in this series, that Rudolf Steiner had spoken at length about life after death.

2. *Gedanken über den Tod* by Artur Brausewetter, Stuttgart 1913, page 198.

3. See Johann Peter Eckermann's *Gespräche mit Goethe in den letzen Jahren seines Lebens.* This refers to the conversation of 25 February 1824.

4. This lecture is the last of a series which Rudolf Steiner held for members familiar with anthroposophy, in January and February 1924, after the re-founding of the General Anthroposophical Society.

5. See Rudolf Steiner, *Theosophy: An Introduction to the Supersensible Knowledge of the World and the Destination of Man* (GA9), and *Occult Science: An Outline* (GA13).

6. See Rudolf Steiner, *Knowledge of the Higher Worlds: How is it Achieved?* (GA10), also available as *How to Know Higher Worlds.*

7. See Rudolf Steiner, *Theosophy.*

8. The *Titanic* was the largest passenger ship of that time; on its first voyage to America it hit an iceberg south of Newfoundland and sank on 15 April 1912 with the loss of 1500 lives.

9. See the fifth and sixth scene of the fourth Mystery Drama, *The Soul's Awakening* from *The Four Mystery Plays* by Rudolf Steiner (GA14).

10. In *Faust* part 2, 2nd act, Homunculus says to Mephistopheles: 'You from the North, in the age of mists grown young.'

11. The relevant descriptions are to be found in the chapter 'Sleep and Death' in *Occult Science* and in the chapter 'The Soul in the Soul World after Death' in *Theosophy*.

12. See Rudolf Steiner, *Occult Science: An Outline*.

13. See Rudolf Steiner, *The Gospel of St John and its Relation to the Other Gospels* (GA112), Anthroposophic Press, 1982.

14. Friedrick Theodor Vischer: 1807–87.

15. *The Inner Nature of Man and Our Life Between Death and Rebirth*, six lectures given in Vienna from 9–14 April 1914; GA153, Rudolf Steiner Press, 1994.

16. This is in *Parsifal*, Scene 1:
    Parsifal: I hardly take one pace
                        and yet it seems I journey far.
    Gurnemanz: It is so my son, for you see
                        that time here becomes space.

17. Wilhelm Wundt, 1832–1920, philosopher and psychologist.

18. The square brackets have been added by the editor.

19. In the fifth Book of Moses, chapter 18, verse 10: 'There shall not be found among you any one ... that useth divination or ... a consulter with familiar spirits ... For all that do these things are an abomination unto the Lord...' See also the first Book of Samuel, chapter 28 (Samuel and the witch of Endor).

20. See *The Wisdom of Man, of the Soul and of the Spirit*, 12 lectures, Berlin 1909–11, GA115, Anthroposophic Press, 1971.

21. Richard Wagner, 1813–83. See note 16.

22. Luke 17: 20–21.

Rudolf Steiner
Nature Spirits
Selected Lectures

Based on knowledge attained through his highly-trained clairvoyance, Rudolf Steiner contends that folk traditions regarding nature spirits are based on spiritual reality. He describes how people possessed a natural spiritual vision in ancient times, enabling them to commune with nature spirits. These entities—which are also referred to as elemental beings—became immortalised as fairies and gnomes in myth, legend and children's stories.

Today, says Steiner, the instinctive understanding that humanity once had for these elemental beings should be transformed into clear scientific knowledge. He even asserts that humanity will not be able to reconnect with the spiritual world if it cannot develop a new relationship to the elementals. The nature spirits themselves want to be of great assistance to us, acting as 'emissaries of higher divine spiritual beings'.

ISBN 1 855840 18 9; 208pp; £11.95

Rudolf Steiner
Evil
Selected Lectures

Despite the fact that evil is an omnipresent theme of our age, it remains one of the most problematic. Public references to it are continually made, but to what extent has society truly begun to understand its riddle?

In this selection of insightful lectures Rudolf Steiner addresses the subject of evil from the results of his spiritual research, offering an original and complex picture. He describes evil as a phenomenon which arises when a thing appears outside its true context, enabling something which is initially 'good' to become harmful. He speaks of the effect of particular spiritual beings—principally Lucifer and Ahriman—who work as polar forces, laying hindrances in our path. Yet, paradoxically, confronting and coming to terms with such difficulties ultimately furthers our development. Thus Steiner speaks of evil as a necessary phenomenon in human evolution, allowing for the possibility of freedom.

ISBN 1 855840 46 4; 224pp; £11.95

Rudolf Steiner
Self-Transformation
Selected Lectures

At the heart of Rudolf Steiner's spiritual philosophy is the
path of inner development leading to personal
transformation. Steiner shows how, through specific
meditative exercises, it is possible to break out of the restricted
world of everyday consciousness. He gives advice on the
development of inner qualities such as clear thinking, inner
tranquillity and positivity, which lay a necessary foundation
for esoteric work.

In contrast to many of the New Age paths available today,
Steiner's methods are based on the Western tradition, the
Rosicrucian path of initiation, as opposed to older Eastern
teachings. This modern way, he suggests, is a metamorphosis
of the Eastern paths and is best suited to modern
consciousness. Speaking as an initiate, he describes the levels
of attainment on this spiritual journey, the first being
'imagination' where the spiritual world is revealed in pictures,
followed by 'inspiration' and finally 'intuition'.

ISBN 1 855840 19 7; 256pp; £12.95

Rudolf Steiner
Angels
Selected Lectures

Religious and spiritual writings have always made reference to
beings from the spiritual hierarchies, especially those known
in Christian tradition as Angels. These spirits are the closest
to human beings and act as our invisible guides and
companions. They influence the life of the individual as well
as the evolution of humanity and the cosmos.

From his own clairvoyant vision Rudolf Steiner confirmed the
existence of such spiritual beings, and showed how modern
minds could gain access to their world. As he explains in these
inspiring lectures, it is important for us to understand and
cooperate with the work of the Angels today as this is crucial
for the further development of humanity.

ISBN 1 855840 60 X; 192pp; £10.95